JEHOVAH'S WITNESSES' ERRORS EXPOSED

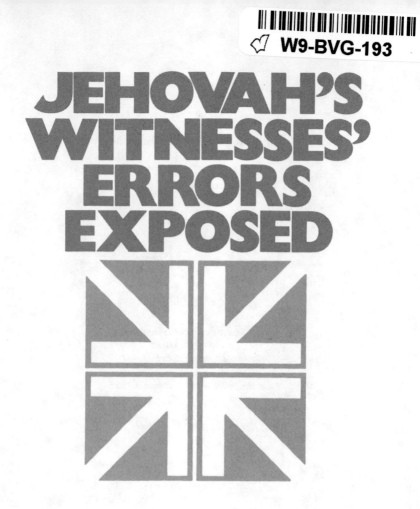

WILLIAM J. SCHNELL

BAKER BOOK HOUSE
Grand Rapids, Michigan

ISBN: 0-8010-8074-6

Formerly published
under the title:
Into the Light of Christianity

Twelfth printing, October 1980

PHOTOLITHOPRINTED BY CUSHING - MALLOY, INC.
ANN ARBOR, MICHIGAN, UNITED STATES OF AMERICA

JEHOVAH'S WITNESSES' ERRORS EXPOSED

Dedicated to Ethel, who, together with me, hand in hand, in
love for and faith in Jesus Christ,
our Saviour, walked out of error
and darkness into the light of
Christianity.

FOREWORD

From *Thirty Years a Watchtower Slave* to this book is a long journey. In the first book I could write only of my sad lot in the meshes of a cult. I could only report dolorously of a condition of heart and mind which made for frustration and defeat. Out of all of that error and darkness, however, there already shone one solid ray of light: I had found in Jesus Christ my Savior.

This book is as different from *Thirty Years a Watchtower Slave* as day is from night. Come with me, as I retrace the wondrous journey on which the Lord has taken me. Do not just see, but observe; do not just hear, but listen; do not just touch, but feel. For what I am writing about goes beyond the sense perception. It deals with the quickening of the spirit. All around me, as well as within my heart, was only death, error and darkness to report of my former life. But behold, this is a report of life, of truth and light, of a new birth, and a "sitting in heavenly places" within the precincts of historic Christianity.

Observe how the Lord took me by the hand and led me into situations where I had to confess what He had done for me. These confessions solidified the new life begun by the Lord. They also brought me into situations, where I had to prove and account for the faith which was within me. I had to dig into the Word of God and into the writings and confessions of other Christians. I began rightfully to divide the word of truth. In two short years the word of truth swept away all the errors of former years.

Techniques came to view, as one false doctrine after another fell before the excellency of the doctrines of historic Christianity. In astonishment I realized that at best I could travel only one mile with the seeming Scripture support of a Jehovah's Witness doctrine, but that I could walk more than two miles with full Scripture on the Christian doctrine. A great truth dawned on me: "If a man asks you to walk a mile with him, walk two." If the cultist comes to you with his so-called proof, do not argue, but listen to his proof. When he has exhausted it, as he will shortly, then you take up where he left off, and walk the second mile, "into the light of Christianity."

In this book I have used the writings and thoughts of many Christian writers. I have also used thoughts of Russellites, Jehovah's Witnesses, The Watchtower Society, The Bible Layman's

Movement, Back to the Bible Way papers. All of these are far too numerous to list singly. I acknowledge the great debt I owe to all of these sources.

I have come to the inevitable conclusion that a born again Christian can grow and mature only if he or she constantly confesses his or her salvation to other men. This is the New Testament way of preaching. The one who does this faithfully will be forced constantly to study God's Word, which in turn will become the living word of God in him (I Peter 1:23). In that way alone will the "image and likeness of God," our great Saviour Jesus Christ, come to full growth and development within our New Creation.

With great joy I realized that *this is* Christianity! Blessed is her lot, thrice blessed because she believes in her triune God. If you are still lost, if you are befuddled in error and darkness in a cult, if you are a "culture Christian" born into an association of your church, repent of the ways of flesh by acknowledging your sinfulness and accept Jesus Christ as your personal Saviour. If you do, you have the assurance that you are born again. That is the only birth that matters, for then you will grow and mature in "heavenly places" (John 1:12, 12).

W. J. Schnell

CONTENTS

Chapter 1

INTO THE LIGHT OF CHRISTIANITY

From Frustration to Assurance

The "light of the world," our Lord Jesus Christ, entered my heart, flooding it with grace as forgiveness came. With this grace came peace with God and men — a peace which goes beyond human understanding. Open Father arms received me back into His house, historic Christianity, that early morning of the night of April 18, 1952. What rich meaning Peter's words took on for me — "Grace unto you, and peace, be multiplied" (1 Peter 1:2).

How did this come about? In desperation, torn asunder by a troubled conscience, mindful of my sinfulness, and aware of my complete fiasco as a full-time servant of the Watchtower Society with its pensum of hours: works-religion and as a practicing Jehovah's Witness, I finally came to my senses.

All night long I had sought release and relief from the turmoil and frustration. What had made this quest so urgent?

Intensely active as a Jehovah's Witness from 1921 on, I had never come to a halt, or to a rest. Then a heart attack compelled me to halt, to rest. When my father became seriously ill and cancer was subsequently discovered, there came even a greater shock. An operation failing, father lingered on a forty-day death bed before he passed away. I visited him on numerous occasions during his ordeal. It was during these visits that father confessed to me that he had no assurance of salvation. He threw himself upon the mercy of the Lord and found forgiveness and grace and peace.

During my last visit with him, about a week before he died, he asked me to give his testimony for him over his grave. I can now gladly say, with his confession still ringing in my ears, that Father died a saved man. He had come free from Watchtower slavery.

I am ashamed to confess though, that I did not give his testimony for him at that time. My brother-in-law, to whom

11

I did not relate my father's wonderful conversion, as I still was much too shocked as a faithful Watchtower slave to accredit it, much less confess it, convinced me that it would be best to have a Bethelite come and give the funeral witness. I acquiesced. My father's confession would have to wait and would not be known to men until the Lord would free me.

No one will ever appreciate what a tremendous shock I sustained as a result of father's confession. It shook me to the core. It added fuel to the already large areas of doubt deeply working on me and expanding from within.

Seven Areas of Doubt

As I look back I can discover seven areas of doubt gnawing away at the Watchtower religion within me. What were they?

1. I knew enough of the Bible to realize that it teaches that our salvation was fought for and won by our Lord Jesus Christ almost 2,000 years ago, and that this was accomplished on the Cross at Calvary. Yet, as one of Jehovah's Witnesses I was constantly training people to look for salvation at some future date in Armageddon, convincing them to work hard for it as a Kingdom Publisher.

2. From many Scriptures I was aware that we are all lost in sin and death, and that we can be saved only by coming as sinners to our Lord Jesus, believing on Him, thus being born-again to a new life in the spirit.

As one of Jehovah's Witnesses I was looking for my salvation to be effected in Armageddon and that only, if I were "within the anti-typical city of refuge," which we believed to be the New World Society of Jehovah's Witnesses. Only by being in that Society could I be saved.

3. Having read Ps. 49:7, that no man, not even a perfect one, can redeem his brother, and in the 15th verse, that "God will redeem my soul from the power of the grave; for he shall receive me," I realized that I fell far short and was a sinner. Every effort on my part to become better before the Lord by works, created a horrible nightmare of self-atonement.

Yet, as one of Jehovah's Witnesses I taught others that the counting and reporting of hours of service to the Watchtower Society, the placing of their books, booklets and magazines with the people, meant their fulfilling of theocratic requirements which would assure all of us a place of safety in Armageddon. Salvation would come by works.

4. Our Lord Jesus Christ said if we come to Him we shall find peace and rest, no matter how heavy our burden.

For thirty years I had worked hard, been successful, and had led many into Watchtower service. I had come the Watchtower way unto the Lord — but I had found no peace and rest.

5. Ephesians 4, and other Scriptures, including 2 Tim. 1:13, show that a "form of sound words" has come down to us from our Lord Jesus, the apostles and prophets.

As a progressive light worshipper and a Jehovah's Witness in good standing, I had observed the Watchtower magazine change our doctrines between 1917 to 1928, no less than 148 times, and had witnessed this chimera take place many times later, and thereafter.

6. Having read of the events between the resurrection and ascension of our Lord Jesus Christ, I also read Acts 1:8, in which the Lord tells us to become "my witnesses," or Christ's witnesses.

Yet, here I was a "Jehovah's Witness"! Why? Because the Watchtower Society had given us that new name. Why did we get that new name? Because as partisans of Rutherford between 1925 to 1931, we had expelled and disfellowshipped some 40,000 Bible students from our midst. As partisans of Rutherford we needed a new name. We received it at the Columbus, Ohio, convention in 1931. Yet, Jesus said when the Holy Spirit would come, then we would become His Witnesses.

7. Assurance of salvation is prized amidst Jehovah's Witnesses. You work hard for it. But as you perform one task, other tasks loom ahead and you are never sure. For thirty years I sought assurance in this manner. I had not found it!

When I dropped my futile efforts to win such assurance as a Kingdom Publisher of Jehovah's Witnesses, and threw myself upon the mercy of the Lord, the Lord gave me grace and assurance in one night.

These areas of doubt had been enlarging and now with the added shock of my father's confession, I slowed down groggily; aimlessly I tried to "reason out," as my Jehovah's Witness training prompted me to do. Finally, hopelessly lost, I came to my senses. I went to the Lord in prayer.

Remembering the Days of My Youth

I remembered "the days of my youth," in which, during four blissful years, I had belonged to my Father's house — when I had been born again, a Christian, and had revelled in a personal relationship with our Lord Jesus Christ. I remembered those wonderful days, when every desire had become a prayer, every imagination had become a possibility of reality, as Christ dwelled within.

I had found Christ in those years — I recalled. I remembered that when I had found Him, I had found grace and peace. Peace had constantly been multiplied to me. God used the combination of my sore plight, and my remembrance of how it used to be with me in my Father's house, to bring me to my knees that April 18th night in 1952.

How meaningful became to me what once I had read in Eccl. 12:1, "Remember now thy Creator in the days of thy youth." What a blessing this was to become for me!

Coming Home Like a Prodigal

Like a Prodigal was I. At first, supplication came hard. There was pride left. Had I not been associated successfully with the Watchtower organization? Had I not done much work: four years in Bethel, twenty-one years in the full-time service; placed close to a quarter million books in my time; helped many into the organization? Had I not done this unto the Lord?

As long as I felt like that, prayer came hard. But as I continued, I was smitten by the Holy Spirit. I was smitten to the core. It dawned upon me, as the thought flitted for the first time across my brain, that I had not worked *for the Lord*. I had worked for rebels, heretics and apostates. I had worked for the "image" of Charles T. Russell, which is the Watchtower Society. I bore ·the "mark" of achievement on "my hand" and in "my forehead."

As my hands were stayed in prayer, my forehead became pierced by the Holy Spirit. I realized that I had sinned grievously against the Lord Jesus Christ, for salvation cannot come by achievement. Then, it struck me with awful force that what I had done was even worse! I had helped water down God's Word, the Bible. This I had done to the minds of many! Faces ... places ... circumstances, flooded back into my conscience. Horrible, horrible, torment and torture!

My thoughts, racing with frightful speed backwards into my life, unreeled a nightmare of sin, remorse, fear. Then, as

I kept praying, "Forgive, Forgive, Forgive," my thoughts jelled. I realized, suddenly, that I had smitten those who bore the name of Jesus by declaring them to be Satan's servants. I remembered I had helped gather evidence against Lutheran pastors, pastors of the very church of my ancestors and against which I had rebelled, long ago in the blasphemy trial at Magdeburg, Germany. I had attacked and had helped vilify the churches of Christianity. As I prayed, this array of misdeeds, once hidden behind the "mark in my forehead," were now brought to consciousness by the Holy Spirit. He pierced my conscience that night. This caused me to sink in abject fear and dejection into the deepest pit I had ever known. It was very close to Hell!

Hell was nigh to me that night. Not only was I a backslider; but in this night of prayer the Holy Spirit revealed to my heart and mind and soul the depravity into which I had sunk. I was eating for spiritual existence, the husks of the Watchtower field and feeding others therewith. It is then that I realized the nature of my plight.

Struck now with conviction as the worst of sinners, shock gave way to deep repentance. I laid all that I had been carrying around behind "the mark in my forehead," before the Cross. I laid it before the Lord with but one clear plea, a cry for forgiveness! As in the case of the Prodigal, it was essentially a cry for the kind of food I once had had in my Father's house — the pure word without Watchtower helps, or husks. I remembered that the right food, "eating our Lord Jesus, the bread from heaven," brought a new birth. The words of Peter came to my mind: "Being born again, not of corruptible seed, but of incorruptible, by the Word of God, which liveth and abideth forever" (1 Peter 1:23). The Holy Spirit then prompted me to pray for the right things, for release from the hypnotic trance of the Watchtower-Society-designed indoctrination. Its satanic implications became crystal clear to me.

Struggle for Freedom

Repentance and submission now entered my heart and prayer was the weapon on this battleground.

Event after event, I recited to the Lord in confession. Morning dawned. Forgiveness had not come. Never had I persisted in pleading like that in all my life! I realized, this was it, or never. Desperation overcame me. In that deep desperation I cried out, "Father, if it is thy will, I will write, publish and print what I have here confessed."

No sooner had that confession been put into words, then I felt some restraint vanish within my soul — a whole wall of self-will and pride tumbled. Why? I had just promised the Lord to put my whole life — my time of ill-practices — into print by confessing it publicly. Later I realized a person can make all the private confessions he wants to; they will be of no avail unless they are publicly repeated (Rom. 10:8-10).

I had committed great sins of error . . . . Merely leaving the Watchtower movement silently behind and entering into a new life which now beckoned, would never truly free me from Watchtower error and thinking. Looking about me at this stage, I recognize tens of thousands of former Jehovah's Witnesses who have left the Watchtower movement, or who have been disfellowshipped from it in purges, but who still are enslaved to it in at least eleven sects they have formed around it.

The words of the apostle John, found in I John 1:8-10, come to my mind: "If we say that we have no sin, we deceive ourselves, and the truth is not in us. If we confess our sins, he is faithful and just to forgive us our sins, and to cleanse us from all unrighteousness. If we say that we have not sinned, we make him a liar, and his word is not in us." Let's face it, all you who formerly were Jehovah's Witnesses and who still persist now in your doctrinal heresies, come all the way to the cross, and confess the sins of heresy and rebellion, which were our basic wrongs to start with.

Public Confession Brings True Freedom

Peace became multiplied to me in a strange and wonderful way. I could never have thought it up in a million years! It was the eventual appearance of my book *Thirty Years a Watchtower Slave,* in Oct. 1956, which started a chain of events, that brought me total deliverance from the Watchtower Society, and slavery.

This book actually became the public confession which not only led me to total freedom in Christ, but eventually became instrumental in helping more than two thousand Jehovah's Witnesses come free into the light of Christianity. These results in turn reveal clearly that I have not only found forgiveness, but that blessings have been added to me. My experience and confession has attracted many others to the Lord, and in that way peace has been multiplied unto me.

As a former Prodigal I have now a "feast in my Father's house," which I humbly confess, surpasses in blessings the lot of many "elder brothers." The thirty years of my life which the canker worm devoured have seemingly been restored by God and have become fruitful. I thought I had been useful in so-called service privileges in high places in the Watchtower organization, during which time I had been a servant. I now returned to my Father. I returned as a Son, and actually feasted on "so great a salvation" that had come to me. I shared it with my former brethren, Jehovah's Witnesses; and, wonder of wonders, many, many actually came free from the Watchtower field of service in "a far country."

With joy, therefore, I can say with the Psalmist, "The Lord is the portion of mine inheritance and of my cup; thou maintainest my lot. The lines are fallen unto me in pleasant places: yea, I have a goodly heritage" (Ps. 16:5,6).

Have You Ever Been in a Vacuum?

Things, however, were not very easy at first. I found myself in a complete vacuum.

I was not as yet totally free from the Watchtower movement. The Jehovah's Witnesses sensed it and kept working on that weakness on the local level. Pressures, ignited and intensified by fear of Armageddon, were brought on me in many insidious ways. This warped my thinking. Slowly bitterness took hold of my heart. This was a deep-rooted bitterness pertaining to everything about Jehovah's Witnesses, even including their persons.

On the other hand, I realized an even greater dilemma. I could not make any sense of many Bible doctrines. In fact, I confess to have been at that stage in a quasi-hypnotic condition, if there is such a thing. I now know I had reached the point many former Jehovah's Witnesses reached on their way out of Watchtower slavery. Upon coming free from Watchtower direction from Brooklyn, N. Y. USA, such usually gravitated into one of the eleven sects which in time had formed on the other periphery of the Watchtower movement. Such really are still in the Watchtower orbit, or course of action, even though now they are only satellites.

In my case that became even more aggravated. I had become fairly well known in Watchtower circles through my book business. A number of persons, themselves already on the fence in Watchtower thinking, were approaching me with the request to start Bible Studies and to arrange for Meetings. They wanted me to form, in fact, another sect.

The pressure brought upon me at this stage by Watchtower adherents was to keep me off balance. It resulted, however, in causing bitterness in my heart, and pushed me perilously close to the idea of forming a sect dedicated to "smashing" the Watchtower movement.

Unknown to me at the time, warped as I still was in my thinking, I was actually beginning to go the way of all "unreconstructed Russellites." I was throwing away "so great a salvation" in failing to center my life work in the blessed fact of what the Lord Jesus had done for me. Instead of singing to Jehovah's Witnesses the glorious new song of the Lamb, and of salvation through Him, I was about to embark on losing myself once again by "wreaking vengeance upon the Watchtower Society." How foolish!

First Manuscript Discarded

Under such circumstances, I wrote my first manuscript for *Thirty Years a Watchtower Slave*. Is it any wonder that this first manuscript was a clarion call to all opposers of the Watchtower movement to unite and to smash them! It took me three years to put it together!

Came the day when it was completed! I read it. At once I realized this was not what I had promised the Lord I would write. There came back to my mind the picture of my abject humility and contrition on the night I became free. Had I not confessed to the Lord my misspent life as a Jehovah's Witness, as a faithful adherent of the Watchtower movement, during which phase of my life I had spread hatred, vilification, and error about Christianity? Had I not helped conjure up the picture in the minds of the Jehovah's Witnesses that the Christian church with its clergy, its doctrines, and its practices, was an enemy? I thus helped make the Jehovah's Witnesses enemies of truth and organized Christianity. In this manuscript I was making a complete turnabout and was heaping this very same hatred and vilification upon Jehovah's Witnesses. Enemies of Christianity the Jehovah's Witnesses have become. Bitter enemies they are. But enemies must be loved, not hated. One destroys enemies of Christianity by winning them for Christ. In that way they eventually have to become friends.

This manuscript had been written, I realized at that reading, more in the spirit of my former life as a Watchtower adherent. As a practicing Jehovah's Witness before I had returned to the Lord, I had been a very belligerent man. I had fomented strife. I had led a cane swinging brigade in a head-smashing expedition at Madison Square Garden. I had caused legal troubles, forced arrests, helped pad records. I had eliminated from the congregations as opposers, brethren who would not abjectly go along with the Watchtower Society. When I read this manuscript which related my story in a spirit of acrimony, I realized that I could not release it. In fact, I no longer was the same man. I had found the Lord Jesus and He had come into my heart. I just could not put that manuscript out! I threw it into the wastepaper basket.

Why could I not publish this manuscript? It would have really hit the Watchtower Society a smashing blow!

But things had changed. In the place of belligerence, the Lord had put humility and meekness. He had placed on me a burden to *win* Jehovah's Witnesses, not to *hit* them. I realized that I had been in the pond of despair, slowly sinking into Hell. The Lord had rescued me! Now that I was free I could not turn around and hit others who were sinking in that pond, and who might be hopeful of coming free.

A great salvation and much forgiveness had come to me! I had been shown great mercy and now I could love much. Thus I felt that my attitude towards the Jehovah's Witnesses should become one of mercy and love, not bitterness and hatred.

The Lord Blesses the New Manuscript

I completely rewrote my manuscript for the book *Thirty Years a Watchtower Slave*. It now conforms to the promise made in April, 1952. It is a true facsimile of the gist of the confessions I made that night, in which I found forgiveness and freedom in Jesus Christ.

Oh, how glad I am that the Lord led me to do this! Why? Now it has become evident, so very evident, that this compilation has created a mirror. The pathos and shades of an actual life lived under Watchtower conditions as related in that book etch out in stark relief the pattern of a life under a false Gospel.

In my book, *Thirty Years a Watchtower Slave*, first of all there are depicted for all Jehovah's Witnesses to see, all the areas of doubt I know exist in their hearts. These are doubts which no Watchtower dinning into their ears can erase.

But more than that. By focusing attention on the fact that the Jehovah's Witnesses blindly and abjectly follow Watchtower organization instructions and thinking to the exclusion of their own thinking, this book for the first time affords Jehovah's Witnesses a look at what they are doing, and what was and is being done with them and to them by the Watchtower Society.

As many see themselves — and they are indeed many — for the first time in the reading of this book they are shocked. Their letters to me show that. They instantly see themselves in the book. One of many writes: "When I look back at it all I simply stand aghast at the fact that I could have been such a fool as to fall for such a cult. Oh, how I thank God that I am now not a walking, talking tool of Satan . . . ." Another writes: "I followed your account all the way through. First I was hurt, then enraged, then determined to really tell you off. I sat down to write, but, I never finished the letter. I knew for the first time, definitely, that there were among the things you described, two points I had actually done myself. That stopped me. I decided to wait before writing. Now, six months later, after looking at myself and the Watchtower Society with new eyes, I saw what had happened to me." Just today, at this writing, came another letter. (They come daily). In it a former Jehovah's Witness says in part, "I have come a long way since I wrote you some time ago. Time and good reading have erased some of the bitterness the Watchtower Society left in my heart, as I now know Christ as my personal Saviour . . . ." More than two thousand letters of this kind have come to me because of this book. You see, sharing "so great a salvation" which had come to me, truly multiplied peace to me.

I Sit Back to Enjoy a Rest

Once *Thirty Years a Watchtower Slave* had been completed and the Baker Book House had put it into print (October, 1956), I settled back, peacefully, content to sit at home. I did not know it then, but I was still in a stupor. I felt I had finished my promised task for the Lord and now could prepare for a pleasant life of mere church attendance and listening to sermons. Had I been allowed to follow my fleshly inclinations, I would never have fully come into the light of Christianity.

Again the Lord showed me His marked favor by leading the way. Of course I did not know this at first. No sooner had my book appeared in print when to my great surprise, and I assure you it was wholly unsuspected, I began to receive many invitations from pastors and churches to come and give my public testimony.

Have you ever been fully taught never to go into a certain place? That such a place is unclean? That it is to be shunned at all costs? I had. To me Christian churches were places in which were roosting all unclean things. I had been taught to think of the Christian churches as Babylon the Great. Having believed that so long of the churches of organized Christianity, it had become second nature to me.

Can you imagine the quandary into which such an invitation put me? I had newly come from Watchtower slavery. But I was still brainwashed to their way of thinking. I instinctively shied away from Christianity. Much less was I prepared to go to their churches and talk to them! I did not want to go there. The Lord knew though that as a former rebel, I was a heretic and apostate from the faith. If I were ever to come into the light of Christianity, I would have to find a way back to associate in fellowship with His people.

Now I thank the Lord for *making* me go. It appears to me now, in the light of what transpired, that the Lord took my hand and led me into the light of Christianity.

I procrastinated. But invitations persisted. Finally, I accepted the first call — to St. Paul and Minneapolis, Minnesota. On my way, while changing stations in Chicago, I almost turned back. But the taxi drove on, bless its driver, and I caught the train and subsequently arrived in St. Paul. There was no one there to welcome me or meet me, and I felt deeply lost as I repaired to my reserved hotel room.

But these feelings were soon dispelled by the Lord in Minneapolis. Speaking in the Fourth Avenue Baptist Church, a servant of the Lord came to my aid. Dr. Richard Clearwaters, the pastor, watched me with compassion. He sensed my uncertainty about what I was doing. At the end of the meeting he encouraged me. The next night, at the Evangelical Free Church I had a completely overcrowded church, and the pastor, a child of God, gave me a wonderful brotherly fellowship.

Later, in a letter, Dr. Clearwaters drew my attention to the 1900 edition of the Goodspeed New Testament translation and asked me to read its foreword. In it, Dr. Goodspeed says one third of the whole text of the New Testament is taken up with the battle contra-heresy. This amazed me.

Dr. Clearwaters continued in his letter: "That is how

important the battle contra-heresy was in the first century. You, having come by the hand of the Lord out of the most modern and efficient of heresies of this twentieth century, have been raised up by the Lord as one voice to use your former experience and insight into these matters to help Christianity in her battle and to win Jehovah's Witnesses for Christ." My eyes were open now. I have since never failed to give public testimony in any and all churches, wherever and whenever the opportunity has presented itself. The Lord had shown me that what I foolishly had thought unclean, was clean. The Lord used one of his faithful servants to give me focus. Here, the Lord gave me a clear indication of His will. How thankful I am for His leading! It has truly led me into pleasant places.

Public Ministry Begins

As soon as it became clear to me that this was what the Lord wanted me to do, I began accepting invitations from all over the USA and from Canada. I made up my mind at the time that I would serve all denominations that needed me.

Lutheran Churches called me to Wisconsin in February, 1957. Then I received a call, my first one, from Canada. Dean W. Gordon Brown of the Baptist Seminary in Toronto, Ontario, Canada, invited me for an eight-day engagement. I gave my public testimony in many Fellowship Baptist Churches during that tour. Dean Brown, I was later appraised, is often called in Canada, Mr. Baptist. But to me, he became a friend and brother in Christ, giving me a real spiritual boost. The meetings there were a success. More than three hundred fifty copies of my book were placed at the end of the meetings. I was recalled for a fourteen-day period in April, 1957.

Included in this second appearance, was a one-day appearance at the large Peoples Church in Toronto. This church is a bulwark of Evangelism in Canada. Its love and passion for lost souls reaches out into the entire world. It was not surprising, therefore, for Dr. Oswald Smith to give me, at this stage, such a valuable boost. Dr. Oswald Smith presided at this meeting and later, in a torrid question and answer meeting, sparked by many Jehovah's Witnesses, did a wonderful MC job.

It appears to me that Canadian churchmen are keenly aware of the grave inroads the Jehovah's Witnesses are making in the thinking of the people. In the USA I have found more often an apathy and an ostrich-like unawareness of the seriousness of the implications the New World Society poses to Christianity.

Other men in Canada and in the USA invited me into their churches. Invitations came to me from Lutheran, Baptist and many other churches. Of the Evangelical denominations I had marvelous and special help from such groups as the Christian and Missionary Alliance, The Assemblies of God and the Christian Reformed Churches. Unstintingly, they afforded me all the assistance they could marshal, and created for my testimony a continent-wide platform which spanned from Tampa to Montreal, from New York City to Seattle, from Vancouver to Eugene, Oregon, and crisscross across the USA and Canada. Churches from the largest to the smallest were put at my disposal. Some of the ablest men in Christianity honored the platform with their presence. Audiences ranged from a mere ten, to two thousand in one night. Only the Lord could do that!

In the summer of 1957 I was invited to come to North Dakota by a Christian bookseller, Mr. Chris Losby. He had written me that he felt a real burden for Jehovah's Witnesses. His sincerity impelled me to accept his invitation. Upon arriving in Minot, North Dakota, I found a man totally crippled in his body, able only to move his neck and ankles, otherwise totally rigid. His body was rigid, but his soul and heart were flexible in the service of the Lord. This man, having a bed rigged horizontally in his station wagon, together with his wife and me, travelled over North and South Dakota and Montana, and appeared every night to give my witness. This brother has since gone home to the Lord, but I live on as a witness for what the Lord Jesus did for him and for me, because of his devotion in the face of such difficulties. The Lord blessed us.

In 1958, in January of that year, I was given one of my greatest boosts. I was called by a stalwart Christian pastor, W. H. Brooks, of Vancouver, B.C., Canada, pastor of the Alliance Tabernacle Church there. He invited me to speak to audiences of several large denominations in Vancouver. For fourteen days I spoke in Baptist, Foursquare, Assembly of God, Alliance, Lutheran churches, and at huge Youth for Christ and Mennonite rallies. I spoke in both the English and the German language, and had a total attendance of 12,500, and placed 979 copies of my book, *Thirty Years a Watchtower Slave.*

These hundreds of books were bought by Christians who are determined to use my book as a missionary and as a source for questions to be levelled at Jehovah's Witnesses to force them to defend their organization. By marking the numerous organizational changes revealed in the book and by putting bookmarks in such places to insure a ready reference, they now effectively confront the Jehovah's Witnesses who call at their doors.

A week later, under the auspices of the Lutheran Council of Seattle, Washington, and the Lutheran Bible Institute of Seattle, another 6,500 heard me give my public testimony in the foremost churches of Lutheranism.

Pastor Brooks truly became an instrument of the Lord, for it was his effort which caused my being called into churches all over Canada, from Vancouver to Montreal. He subsequently sponsored me on an eight-week tour, which provided me with a listening audience of thirty-one thousand and with thirty-eight radiocasts with unnumbered audiences.

Truly, the Lord was causing friends to come from everywhere, to assist in giving this testimony. Christian publishing houses followed in the train. The Baker Book House has done an unstinting job in putting my book before the public. Evangelical Publishers of Toronto, Canada, have pushed the book in Canada. Marshall, Morgan and Scott, London, England, in Empire editions, has spread the book across the whole English-speaking world. You can today find copies of it as easily in Kingston, B.W.I., or Singapore, as you can in Hongkong or Capetown. Jan Haan of Groningen, the Netherlands, put it into the Holland language. Fosterlands-Stiftelsen of Stockholm, put it into Swedish. Now comes forth an edition in Danish by the house of Credo, soon to be followed by an edition in Norwegian. The Christliche Verlagsanstalt of Kanstanz a Bodensee, Germany, is busily engaged in translating it into German, so that it is soon to appear in that language. A Spanish edition is available from Baker Book House. And so the testimony goes over the whole world; and I stand in utter speechless amazement!

Whence comes such unselfish co-operation? How different from the Watchtower Society did Christianity behave towards me! How wrong I had been about it in my warped Watchtower thinking! How blessed a fellowship is the communion of Christianity!

Chapter 2

MY LOT HAS FALLEN IN PLEASANT PLACES

Comes the Experience of My Mahanaim

The Bible abounds in incidents of men and women breaking away from selfishness to the service of the Lord. It appears that when such breakaways reached the stage of crisis, such men and women experienced unusual help from friends appearing from out of nowhere, as if sent by the Lord.

Take Jacob's breakaway. He had served Laban for years in a huckster-like way. Remembering the promise of Bethel, at God's command he finally broke with Laban and fled with his family to freedom in the promised land. Because of this breakaway he experienced a crisis.

Things were at their darkest, and it appeared as if Jacob might be overwhelmed. The day of crisis was about to dawn for him. He was about to face his brother Esau, whom he had cheated — and he feared greatly. Encamped at a place called Mahanaim, Jacob suddenly found himself surrounded by angels. They came as if to say: "Jacob, we protected you against Laban from the rear, and we will screen you against Esau ahead." We can hear them continue "Welcome to the land of thy fathers." That was Jacob's Mahanaim, when the help of God was proffered in unmistakable terms by angels who had expressly come to visit him. Needless to say, he made good his escape (Gen. 31-32).

On another occasion, at precisely the same spot, at Mahanaim, sat David. He was a fugitive from his son Absalom. He had been dethroned and had no comforts about him. His needs at the moment were different than had been those of Jacob who was loaded with foodstuffs and travel gear. At this hour of crisis in David's life, when it appeared that all friends had left him, when food and water was lacking, David's needs were physical.

Then when things were darkest, lo, here comes Shobi, the rich man; here comes Machir; here come many with all the things he needed. These men, not angels this time, brought things angels probably could not have brought him. They came just when they were most needed. Their appearance helped David make good his escape. This was David's Mahanaim (2 Sam. 19).

My Mahanaim came when it appeared, as some Jehovah's Witnesses boastfully said, "Schnell's story will soon die out and be forgotten, and he will be sorry and will return to the fold." As I stated, at this stage of crisis for me, invitations came from pastors and churches everywhere, giving me the finest nation-wide platform a man ever had for a public witness. The Lord had raised up the very kind of friends that were needed to help me, and others after me, to make good our escape. The Lord raised up help for my warfare from among the very ones I had wronged so often, and from whom I expected no help.

Oh, that all who have been proselyted by the cults into fleshly servitude would take this to heart!

The Christian church longs in love and compassion to help save you! Thirty-eight denominations called me into their midst and backed me up in my testimony for one sole reason — to help win those souls, lost in the cults, for Christ.

Being led by the Lord to give my testimony about the deliverance which came to me, with the generous backing of friends from everywhere, I soon began to realize that my lot had "fallen unto me in pleasant places." Two wonderful things began to emerge out of those meetings.

Doctrinal questions forced themselves almost at once upon my attention. They were most distressing at first. Though I had been thoroughly trained by the Watchtower Society to become a glib user of Scripture in the Watchtower way in arguing Jehovah's Witness tenets, I suddenly found that I knew nothing real about the Bible. Its treasures, its depths, its cleansing power as the "water of truth" and its facility to bring about a new birth, were unknown to me. All I knew was an acquired juggling dexterity with torn out Scripture texts used by Jehovah's Witnesses. It was a most disconcerting experience.

What was I to do? I was in a dilemma. Not only was I wrongly dividing the Word of God, but I was being pressed with questions about it in these public meetings. It was one thing to testify as to my experiences in Watchtower slavery and to expose it, but it was quite another matter to give an account of what I now believed.

When I came free from the Watchtower movement I was thrown into a complete spiritual vacuum. I now could see so clearly that I had been limited to a narrow organizational line of thinking. Perverted to human adaptation of spiritual truths, I had been hypnotized to Watchtower invented indirection. I was drawn inwardly to the core of the organization, the Watchtower Society and the Watchtower magazine. I could not soar outward beyond the orbital limitations set by an occult-like inversion. Complete inertia in spiritual matters had taken hold of me now and my mind remained blank, as the flesh attacked Watchtower practices from which I had been jarred.

I was free physically from Watchtower direction, but spiritually I was forced into a vacuum. Why? Because I continued to accept and believe in the errors of Russellism: no Hell; no immortal soul; denial of the Deity of Christ; disbelief in the Trinity and a denial of the Lord's bodily resurrection. At this point I had eddied and then become stagnant. Was my escape going to be good? This was my crisis!

It is then that I began to discern what had happened to tens of thousands of Jehovah's Witnesses and Russellites from 1912 on — those who were either cast out of the Watchtower organization, or who had rebelled against it and left. Though free from Watchtower direction in a physical way, they remained enslaved in orbital thinking of rebellion and heresy. The brainwashing they had undergone had completely bereft them of the ability to use God's word properly.

Many of my friends today find themselves in sects led by men who indulge in attacking the Watchtower organization in the most vociferous way. In addition these errorist leaders attack one another in their papers. But all keep on preaching the heresies of Russellism. As long as they do this, they cannot make good their escape from the Watchtower movement.

All those caught in the meshes of the eleven sects orbiting as satellites around the Watchtower subversion fail to realize their great dilemma of "double damnation." Jesus pointed up the deep-rooted plight of what I term "double damnation" when He told the Pharisees, who like present-day cultists, were expert proselyters, "Woe unto you, scribes and pharisees, hypocrites! for ye compass sea and land to make one proselyte, and when he is made, ye make him twofold more the child of Hell (Gehenna) than yourselves" (Matt. 23:15). That is the true dilemma of the sects of Russellism. In their effort to come free they fail to come all the way, and as a result double damnation enthralls them.

How grateful I am to the Lord for having forced me out of the condition of feeling sorry for myself — for extricating me from the usual lethargy in spiritual things which engulfs a cultist as he comes physically free from a cult.

The Lord led me out of it all in the hour of my crisis, when total escape hung in the balance, by sending me friends from everywhere — drawing me out in a positive way to be guided into a place of fellowship in historic Christianity. May I say to all Jehovah's Witnesses who have come out of the fire of direct Watchtower slavery into the frying pan of reflected inversion of the sects: On your trek to freedom do not stop at Haran too long. Come all the way to the promised land. Come fully into historic Christianity, even if you do not know where specifically you will eventually find a church home. That of course, is what you must long for and find.

If you stay a Russellite, you will never come home to your Father's house. The Watchtower Society will laugh at your ineffectuality. Can you not hear them smugly saying, "You see, once they leave us they can not be useful anywhere else. They lose all service privileges." How wrong they are, if you come free all the way!

These questions and discussions about "the faith once delivered to the saints" (Jude 3), which I increasingly encountered in the many meetings, challenged me. They impelled me to dig into the Scriptures day and night, as I had never done before. I read the Bible from cover to cover. As I read, just simply reading, and then thinking over what I had read, I noticed my brainwashed mind discard Watchtower errors. While reading a certain chapter I would suddenly remember a favorite Watchtower text, only it was being debunked by what the chapter as a whole taught. In this manner, step after step, Watchtower errors were washed out of my mind — washed out by the water of truth, the Word of God. It is just as simple as that.

You will read later in this book how the Holy Spirit step by step opened up the Word for me and led me quite rationally into the light of Christianity. The manner in which this was done, can become for you the most effective technique of refuting Watchtower and other cultist errors without the hardening effects of argument. It will just wash away the errors.

You will marvel at this fact, as you learn with me on my trek to freedom in Christ, that a Jehovah's Witness, in his doctrines, can go a mile with you with seeming Scripture support; then he reaches his *ultimo ratio*. Espousing the spiritual doctrines of historic Christianity you can surge on another mile, and then some. Side by side, thus, I placed Jehovah's Witnesses doctrines and their proofs, and then followed up with spiritual doctrines and their proofs. In every instance, without a single exception, I found that the proofs of the doctrines "once delivered to the saints" outdistance the doctrines of heresy. It became obvious to me, that the doctrines of historic Christianity were truths, while the teachings of the sects were unscriptural, or at best half-truths.

I learned fast, because I had to use this knowledge to "earnestly contend for the faith" almost immediately.

Flight From a Cult Must Quickly Be Followed By a Washing With the Word

Many Jehovah's Witnesses encouraged by coming to my public meetings, began to take hold of reading the Bible without Watchtower Society helps. They marvelled at what they found. Before me I have one of hundreds of letters received from Jehovah's Witnesses, who true to my own experience, were led farther than a mere breakaway from physical Watchtower control. Share this letter with me:

Dear Mr. Schnell:

"I have just read in the *Evangel Magazine* about the wonderful results you have had in the publishing of your book, *Thirty Years a Watchtower Slave*. I was overjoyed to read that 663 have come out of that sect as a result of reading your book. I too, because of it, came out two years ago and was converted. Then my mother who was also a Witness, read your book and came out. I had been in the organization about five years and Mama about the same.

"When I first left the organization I began studying the Bible like I never had before and to my amazement I discovered that the Watchtower sect had so very little Scripture truth and so much of what they falsified and wrested from their chapters and true meanings or contexts. I also went to the Library and got a Bible Dictionary and an Encyclopedia and Hitchcock's *Analysis of the Bible* and other books and I truly learned the real truth through studying WITHOUT Watchtower helps. And I know it was God that really opened my mind and blind eyes...."

Mrs. C. G. N.

Precisely in this manner, although a bit more forcefully, did I experience the power of God through His word to wash away the errors of heresy. That is the only way it can be done. And most sincerely, to all who still are caught in their flight in some of the eleven sects who now vegetate on the half-way route, like Lot's wife turned into a pillar of salt, outside of the Watchtower Organization, I say, Do not remain in these intermediate places on your flight. Flee fast, for these in-between places are still in the orbit of the Watchtower movement!

Let the God of truth lead you through His word. Break the spiritual shackles which rivet you to heresy. Get rid of the errors of Russellism in doctrines by allowing the water of truth to wash them away. Then you will fully return to "the faith of our fathers" and your long condition of rebellion will come to an end. Prodigal, you will come home. It can be done. The above cited sister had it happen. Twenty-one hundred others have had it happen. Above all, I can testify that it took the water of truth, rightly handled, but two years to wash all Watchtower errors away. Not a trace of them is left now.

Thus guided by the Lord's hand into sharing my testimony with others, rather than sitting comfortably at home and regretting my losses of thirty years and feeling sorry for myself, I experienced the work of *the truth* in me liberating me fully. I can testify to the veracity of the Lord's statement in John 8:32. "And ye shall know the truth, and the truth shall make you free."

But why? Here is the real reason: "Then said Jesus to those Jews which believed on him, If ye continue in my word, then are ye my disciples indeed" (John 8:31) ; and then, and only then does the 32nd verse above quoted come fully into play. It came to me that way. It came to Mrs. N. that way. It already has come to twenty-one hundred Jehovah's Witnesses that way. I confidently believe it can come to millions that way.

Christianity Has Held Fast "the form of sound words"

But I spoke of two wonderful things which happened to me as a result of my public testimony. The second one came to me as a startling surprise!

Truly the Lord was showing me His wonders. Dinned into my ears and jelled into my thinking from 1921 on, when I was but sixteen years old, was the Watchtower contention that all Christendom is doomed. Over and over, time and again, we were told that her churches were all rejected — that they had become Babylon the Great — that everything that was unclean was found in their midst — that they were divided right down the middle — that they differed in every way — that they even opposed one another. In short, we were told that they were absolutely hopeless.

It was as a result of that brainwashing that I was very reluctant to accept the invitations of pastors and churches to come to their places of worship and give my testimony. To me, in my brainwashed condition and hardened heretical thinking, the churches were like a "mess of unclean foods," and "out-of-bounds" even to a respectable ex-Watchtower slave. I could not imagine myself going there any more than could Peter persuade himself to sit down and eat the mess of food put before him in the dream.

Former Russellite friends upon hearing of my going to these churches, wrote me long letters telling me how improper and unclean it was to do so. Jehovah's Witnesses everywhere snickered and said, "Schnell has sold out all the way now." But letters also came from members of many sects other than Russellites and Jehovah's Witnesses warning me about going back to the "flesh-pots of Egypt" and of going down to "Egypt for help." It appeared that all the proponents of heresy frowned upon my course of action!

I am here to testify against this long backdrop of thinking and ill-practise. It was the goodness of the Lord which caused me to go to these churches; and in going I took the only way open to me to find true freedom. I am convinced that it is God's way.

What did I find in the churches? I made an amazing discovery. Let me share it with you.

Since I followed the Lord's leading and began testifying publicly in the various churches, I have served thirty-eight different denominations. I have found something truly amazing. I have found that in all of these thirty-eight denominations of historic Christianity which I have come to know, they have kept "the form of sound words," of which Paul speaks in 2 Tim. 1:13. They actually believe the same doctrines "once delivered to the saints": hell a place of eternal punishment; immortality of the soul; deity of Christ; trinity; bodily resurrection of Jesus Christ; and the gospel of Jesus Christ. I have found something even more startling. In all of them I found the apostolic set-up of pastors, teachers and evangelists, handling the Word of God to all the brethren. So far there is not one scintilla of difference. The differences lie in techniques resulting from the peculiar oddities of the human mind and human proclivity for adaptation. Not only did this amaze me; it strengthened me like nothing else ever could. It gave me a wonderful insight into historic Christianity. It has made me a staunch defender and lover of Christianity.

Denominations Are Gifts of Diversity

Having come from the monolithic top-down concept of an authoritarian set-up, I can appreciate the value of non-conformity in the realm of fellowshipping. In the New Testament way of preaching, which has every saved one going forth and confessing as to his or her salvation in order to win lost souls for Christ, however, there must be complete unanimity in practice. Unity in the churches and denominations is achieved not ecumenically, but in a healthy manner in the field of the world.

During question and answer portions of my meetings I always allow open questions, shot right from the shoulder. This permits me to come more quickly to grips with what is in the mind of my hearers. I am often queried by attending Jehovah's Witnesses, and often also by other exclusivists, "Now that you no longer belong to the Watchtower, how can you pick the right denomination?" Of course, this is often meant to be a leading question designed to entrap me. However, it does not bother me at all. Why? Because of my long experience in a forced top-down *gleichshcaltung* set-up, I have come to see the great wisdom of the Lord in having diversity of gifts crystalize into different denominations (1 Cor. 12:5).

I came to appreciate the Lord's letters to the "seven churches in Asia." The point to me was, there *were* seven different churches, and the Lord sanctioned these. Study them in Rev. 2 and 3. Notice how different they were from one another. Yet each was a golden "candlestick." Of the seven churches only one, that of Laodicea, was spewed out; and still, promise for salvation by way of repentance is made also to them. I asked myself, Why seven churches? Why such diversity in structure? and still, why is each described as a "candlestick"?

This is the very thing I have verified in my communion with modern denominations, at least the thirty-eight · in which I served. There is great diversity in practises, in techniques, even in interpretations — all caused by man's inherent proclivity for adaptation. But I have discovered complete unanimity in that every one confesses and believes in the Deity of Christ.

Thus such questions about denominations do not bother me at all. The Holy Spirit has shown me historic Christianity as a true "magnificat," useful across time and space, completely adaptable to all nations, kindreds and tongues: to all types of humanity, even the most unique individuals preferring the oddest kinds of garb. Christianity was not meant to become rigid with humanly devised authoritarianism. It was divinely ordained to be loosely structured on earth, designed to accommodate within its bounds of fellowship kindred souls, on their long, tedious, pilgrim journey toward the heavenly home.

I simply answer the question about denominations with the same insight another heretic, Augustine, found: When Solomon constructed his temple, it was built up without noise and sound of hammer, chisel, etc. Why? Because every stone had been chiseled to size in the quarries; every beam had been cut to fit on location in the forests of Lebanon. All the noise of hammering and chiseling, was done there. It is the same way with the church. When it is completed in heaven, where it becomes the heavenly Jerusalem, there will be no division, no strife, no testing. It will be cemented with love and in quietness. All the hammering and chiseling which is done here on earth, is done in the various denominations; and *there,* in heaven, it will have come to an end.

Thus, I conclude my reply to the questioning Jehovah's Witnesses: Let us have a vision of the completed church in heaven and as we come out of Watchtower slavery, let us seek in various churches or denominations such a church home which will make for our peculiar kind of uniqueness a happy place in this strange pilgrim land as we travel on to Zion, our mother which is above. Make sure though, that the church you select is a golden "candlestick," is based on the Rock, our Saviour-God Jesus Christ, that it is fundamental, and that it teaches the word of God and preaches the gospel of Jesus Christ.

Going from denomination to denomination I marvelled at the manner in which the Lord worked through many different churches His wonders to perform. My appreciation for historic Christianity deepened. Do I consider Christianity divisive? No, it is just blessed with such a superabundance of diversity of gifts, that no one group or segment can contain them all. How wonderful is historic Christianity which already on this earth contains so many different mansions, presaging our future home in our Father's house of many mansions! How wonderful that so many different fellowships for edification exist, that no one, not even the most unique of humans, can fail to find a place suitable to his peculiarity, to become in practise fitted for heaven, our future home!

What is Christianity? Is it a strait jacket? Is it a rigid, unyielding total entity of human form? No, Christianity is the expression of two great realities. She is the home of all in whom the Holy Spirit is fashioning the *image and likeness of our Lord Jesus Christ,* impressing upon our souls the new image in the place of the old one we had lost in sin and death after Adam. She consists of a brotherhood of saved ones on earth in their pilgrim journey towards the promised land, sharing their salvation with all the inhabitants of earth who are still lost, confessing to them what the Lord Jesus did for them, if haply they might lead such to salvation.

As I went from church to church, denomination to denomination, giving my testimony, exposing Watchtower tricks, I was soon led by the Lord to inject the gospel of Jesus Christ and His wondrous grace into my testimony. I observed that in almost all churches in which I appeared, people were being saved from perdition by being born again, by being led to repentance and receiving forgiveness, and coming into the communion of the saints.

As a matter of fact, I became so impressed with this, that I soon shared the good news of my salvation with the intent of drawing others to Jesus. I had found another great boon. I found that in confessing what the Lord had done for me, not only in saving me from sin and death but from the "dual damnation" of a heretic, I was continually being strengthened in the most holy faith. I found that lost ones responded, and soon found that upon invitation they would come to the altar to present themselves to the Lord. I had become a fisher of men.

It was in fellowship with Christians of thirty-eight different denominations that I found this great boon. Not only could I joyously confess what the Lord had done for me, but in Christianity's hallowed tabernacles I found hearing ears of seekers who were lost, who not only listened, but also were attracted! I had never witnessed such a thing in a Kingdom hall of Jehovah's Witnesses. *The Lord was using me to help save souls.* That, as I now know, *is* Christianity, and I found it in the churches of the various denominations! I did not find it in all my thirty years of book selling, time counting service of the Watchtower organization.

With that, however, came even a deeper insight into historic Christianity than already had been mine by emulating Augustine. Here, in thirty-eight different denominations I observed the same things happening which puzzled the disciples, when John said, "Master, we saw one casting out devils in thy name; and we forbade him, because he followeth not with us." It was then that the Lord gave me insight into Christianity, seemingly divided, with the same words that had cleared up the matter for John so long ago, when he said in Luke 9:50, "And Jesus said unto him, Forbid him not; for he that is not against us is for us." I will never forget that lesson.

In my wonderful journey to freedom, within the midst of these many different denominations, I have seen as wonderful works and as deep a love and as diverse gifts and as many faults, as were described for us by the Lord Jesus in Rev. 2 and 3, when He reviewed the "seven churches of Asia." I have seen Christianity drawing men into discipleship with Jesus Christ. Indubitably, *they are golden candlesticks!* I hope that the candid discussion of these many wonderful experiences will help Jehovah's Witnesses, and other cultists who look down their noses when speaking of historic Christianity — so they will be advised to walk softly, and to look circumspectly around them before they attack historic Christianity on the score of devisiveness.

I hope that Jehovah's Witnesses will become wise and be advised to refrain from sinning with their mouth, and refrain from denying Christianity its great works of love: for in denying these they unwittingly become the tools of exclusivists and top-down organizers, and of such like the Watchtower Society, who toss them to and fro, and carry them about "with every wind of doctrine, by the sleight of men, and cunning craftiness whereby they lie in wait to deceive" (Eph. 4:14).

Especially is this true now, when cults are coming in like a flood on one side, and super organizers on the other side are attempting to construct a world-wide strait jacket for historic Christianity. "Little children, it is the last time: and as ye have heard that antichrist shall come, even now are there many antichrists; whereby we know that it is the last time. They went out from us but they were not of us; for if they had been of us, they would no doubt have continued with us: but they went out, that they might be made manifest that they are not all of us" (I John 2:18, 19).

With so many cults appearing on the horizon, and with such

a formidable array of workers of iniquity straining to perfect a strait jacket for Christianity, how much wiser than condemning would it be to look at "the works" and the "fruits"; and in finding them, as I found them when I was led into thirty-eight different denominations, how blessed will you be! For in finding them, you find historic Christianity, loosely organized in many richly endowed spiritual fellowships. In Rev. 2 and 3 note how the Lord views the diversity of denominations or churches. Look at this diversity as a gift, as a blessing in disguise.

From the apostasy of the Watchtower system I came free in one night of prayer. But from heresy and rebellion I only came free by being washed with the Word of God and in fellowship with the churches of historic Christianity. And thus, led by the Lord's hand, I walked "into the light of Christianity." The Lord be praised!

Chapter 3

"REBELLION IS AS THE SIN OF WITCHCRAFT"

"For rebellion is as the sin of witchcraft, and stubbornness is as iniquity and idolatry" (1 Sam. 15:23).

A great truth dawns upon me as I look with knowing eyes upon the beginnings of the Watchtower Society. It becomes etched out in bold relief as its history of eighty years passes in review before my eyes. It cries out as I scan the fate of its adherents. How like Saul is the course of the Watchtower Society! How applicable to it, as they were to Saul, are the above quoted words of the prophet Samuel.

Saul then, as well as the Watchtower Society in its beginning, obviously had failed in some vital way. "Because thou hast rejected the word of the Lord, he hath rejected thee from being king."

The word of the Lord had laid out the way in which Saul was to behave. The Word of God has established the way which Christianity is to function. Saul rejected the word of the Lord and followed his own, so-called better way of sacrifice. The Watchtower Society rebelled against the way of Christianity and followed its own "better light." To both comes down the verdict: "Obedience is better than sacrifice."

Word of God Describes the Structure of Christianity

Historic Christianity was established by Jesus Christ who is its foundation stone. Because of this fact it has the truth and manifests all the evidences of solid continuity.

In Eph. 4:7-12 we read: "But unto every one of us is given grace according to the measure of the gift of Christ. Wherefore he saith, When he ascended on high, he led captivity [the way of the flesh] captive, and gave gifts unto men. (Now that he ascended, what is it but that he also descended first into the lower parts of the earth? He that descended is the same also that ascended up far above all heaven, that he might fill all things.) "

Historic Christianity, note, thus is built upon the solid foundation of Jesus Christ. It is He who fills all things — things below and above, on this earth below, and in heaven above. Therefore, Christ *is* the center. Therein lies Christianity's foundation.

All flesh must descend into the grave. All who on their way to the grave are drawn by Christianity into the new center Jesus Christ, experience a new birth in the spirit while in the flesh. As they become filled with Christ, they grow into the image and likeness of God, and now on the way to the grave have become captive in Christ. Descending now with the image of Christ growing within, the flesh dies; but automatically the soul ascends totally to its new center Christ Jesus. This ascending seemingly working at cross purposes to the descending, while it takes place already in this life in faith and spirit, becomes in heaven a reality.

Christianity, therefore, is that heavenly society which functions on earth to draw, and eventually to fill, all who come unto the Lord Jesus in faith. Christianity is thus the most unifying and compact entity ever envisioned and finds its completion in Christ Jesus in heaven, there becoming the "fullness of him that filleth all in all" (Eph. 1:23).

Only God can work such a work in us. The Holy Spirit was sent to perform this work in each and every individual so drawn into Christianity. This happened at the very beginning of Christianity and happens today. Each and every one born again, from flesh into spirit, grows to the extent that he confesses to lost ones what Christ has done to and for him. Only the measure of the individual's gift — or, in terms used by Scripture, the pound, or talent — sets the limit of growth or outreach.

But it pleased God to raise some who are gifted beyond the measure of the capability of most individuals to assimilate and confess before men the good news of salvation. They have this position not of merit, but by grace. God has endowed them in a special way in order that they may become an instructing, edifying and perfecting gift unto all within historic Christianity.

Why were the additional gifts added unto us, since we are already rich beyond compare and measure, each one of us in Christianity having Jesus Christ · as our central gift of life? In Eph. 4:11-13 we read: "And he gave some, apostles; and some, prophets; and some, evangelists; and some, pastors and teachers; for the perfecting of the saints, for the work of the ministry, for the edifying of the body of Christ: till we all come in the unity of the faith, and of the knowledge of the Son of God, unto a perfect man, unto the measure of the stature of the fulness of Christ."

Your pastors, teachers and evangelists then, are gifts. These gifts are given by the Lord Jesus to historic Christianity, given not to lord it over her, but to perfect, edify and minister unto her. There almost leaps into view one benefit which the Lord Jesus through grace worked through them for us. Perhaps, I, as a former heretic, can see it more quickly and more readily. If so, then I am obliged to draw your attention to it with the greater clarity. They, and their ministry, have been used throughout all these centuries to preserve the "good thing which was committed unto thee by the Holy Spirit which dwelleth in us." How? As Paul says in 2 Tim. 1:13, "Hold fast the form of sound words, which thou hast heard of me, in faith and love which is in Christ Jesus."

Continuity of Christianity Assured

From this we see that the continuity of Christianity is based in the main on two factors, which in interplay effect a change in different ways in different individuals on the one hand, and itself become unchangeable as a mode of operation across time and space on the other hand.

We will use the last aspect first in the framework of this discussion. Through the agency of pastors, teachers and evangelists, who were gifts given by the Lord to Christianity, would be preserved "the form of sound words" or "the faith once delivered to the saints." This would make, throughout the whole tenure of Christianity, for "sound doctrine" which in turn would form a solid foundation for the individual to ascend into the "image and likeness" of the Lord, and into heaven. Someone once said "Doctrines are the rungs of the ladder upon which we walk into heaven." That is precisely the thought here.

Paul clinches this by saying, that pastors, teachers and evangelists are given "for the perfecting of the saints, for the work of the ministry, for the edifying of the body of Christ."

Now we come to the first aspect. The ministry of pastors, teachers, and evangelists in preserving "sound doctrine" would dovetail into the work of the individual: enhancing, perfecting, polishing, making more effective "the good thing which was committed unto you by the Holy Spirit which dwelleth in us." But the ministry of these gifts, could not produce salvation, or a new birth. That alone could come to an individual in coming to the center of Christianity, Jesus Christ. Once that gift was within an individual, these other gifts: pastors, evangelists and teachers could perfect, minister unto, and edify in each.

Mode of Operation of the Two Aspects

This then would be the mode of operation in Christianity. The pastors, teachers and evangelists would work on earth to generate for Christianity an atmosphere and a backdrop of solid unchangeable truths which would be as solid in operation as is the actual foundations of Christianity, which is its center Christ Jesus in heaven.

Christ Jesus within us as the image and likeness of God, which results from the new birth, brought to perfection by the edifying, ministering and perfection of the saints by the work of pastors, teachers and evangelists, would bring about an effectiveness of Christianity's mission on earth which would result in bringing untold millions unto Christ from out of time and space.

Christianity's magna carta, therefore, is found in Matt. 28:19, 20. There the three-fold commission is "Go ye, therefore, and teach all nations, baptizing them in the name of the Father, and of the Son, and of the Holy Ghost: Teaching them to observe all things whatsoever I have commanded you . . . ."

Note the two aspects here? (1) All are to go out and draw all nations by telling them of what Christ has done for us. (2) After such are drawn into a personal relationship and have been baptized as outward evidence of their being born again, they must be taught to observe *all* things whatsoever I commanded you.

The work of the Holy Spirit is different in every way in every one of us, and is attuned to the measure of the gift in us. It becomes evident and fruitful not only if and when we become inwardly filled with it, but when outwardly in our relationship and fellowship with others "we all come in the unity of the faith, and of the knowledge of the Son of God, unto a perfect man, unto the measure of the stature of the fullness of Christ" (Eph. 4:13) .

"The measure of the stature of the fulness of Christ" is attained when the image and likeness of God become totally our center of life. Christianity thus in fellowship, edification, teaching and ministering, provides on earth the amenities of

a heavenly society in which Christ as the image and likeness
of God is the center. In a broad sweep, Christianity thus
unifies the many differences, but does not eliminate them.
It unites the many lives which were scattered by sin and death,
but not by putting all into one earthly mold of custom,
language or dress. Christianity, by the testimony of the saved
to the unsaved, seeks to draw others to Christ. It carefully
watches for the first sign that the Lord Jesus has brought
about a new birth, and immediately starts its intimate work
of perfecting, ministering and edifying so that such may
become totally absorbed by Christ Jesus within them.

Cults Are Counterfeit in Structure

I had just come out of the New World Society of Jehovah's
Witnesses. When I discovered the mode of operation of Christianity and its purpose of creating a spiritual society on earth
across time and space, on our pilgrim's trek towards heaven,
where the reality is, I marvelled at the depravity of the Watchtower subversion. This was indeed an amazing discovery to
me who had for thirty years denounced Christianity.

I now know that all cults, including the heresies of the
early Christian age, interpose an intermediary center for salvation. In this way they sidetrack the true purpose of Christianity, which is, to give the image and likeness of Jesus Christ
full play for growth in the individual. The cults eliminate
Christ as the center.

In order to create the position of becoming the intermediate center, they must destroy "the form of sound words"
and eliminate the gifts appointed to preserve these intact. They
must eliminate the positions of pastors, teachers and evangelists by setting themselves up, in their new center of things,
as promulgating *new* truths. These truths must be everchang-
ing to maintain a platform of something fresh and new
emanating from this new center. This must be so to cover up
the absence of Holy Spirit. Such have to be raised over their
converts so that they may rule top down, in contrast to pastors, teachers and evangelists, whom the Holy Spirit raised
out of Christianity to work for each one a perfecting, ministering and edifying work.

Thus gradually from this newly created center, which can
be just one man, or several, or a group, come top down all
instructions, revelations, teachings, evangelizing. This is not
done to dovetail with "the work the Holy Spirit which dwell-

eth in us," but to bring about adherence to the instructions of the cult, thus synchronizing the lives of all cultists into a fleshly unity, or a counterfeit unity in contrast with the perfect unity in the stature of the fullness of Christ. The cult thus frankly negates Christianity and is anti-Christ.

Notice the Change of Lot Upon Coming Into Christianity

The proof of this can be vividly demonstrated by my own experience, by what actually happened to me.

In contrast to this "top-down" activation to which I had been subjected for thirty years, I found that in one night I had been lifted up out of this milieu. How? By reading Watchtower books? No! By the grace shown and granted me by God that night I was lifted unto "heavenly places."

Looking back upon this remarkable demonstration of liberation from the rules of the flesh, and from the inverting force of the herd instinct of organized flesh centered in Brooklyn, New York, as The New World Society, I know what Paul meant when he said in Ephesians 2:5, 6 "Even when we were dead through our trespasses, made us alive together with Christ (by grace have ye been saved) and raised us up with him, and made us sit with him in heavenly places in Christ Jesus."

What a difference this is compared to my life as a Jehovah's Witness in the New World Society! As a faithful Kingdom Publisher and Jehovah's Witness for the long span of thirty years, I was pushed down, and the Faithful and Wise Servant Class of Brooklyn, New York, was raised up over me. I was under their thumb. They, perched high on the ladder of the hierarchy, taught me top-down.

Instead of preaching the gospel of Jesus Christ, in which there is power unto salvation, as a Jehovah's Witness I preached "The Gospel of the Kingdom," "another gospel." The gospel of Jesus Christ raises us up to "sit with him in heavenly places." The Watchtower "Gospel of the Kingdom" enslaves men to a herd-like routine of the flesh. I am now aspiring to the unity of faith which is the image and likeness of God, or Christ within me; then I was striving by way of achievement, to create a fleshly unity, with the evidence of the "mark on my hands" and the mark "on my forehead." In Christianity now, gradually the image of God is impressed on my soul; in the cult I was being branded with the mark of a "beast."

But when I came to the Lord in prayer that night and shed these marks of achievement as entrees for salvation, confessing my sins, I was humbled low. I died unto the fleshly works and its thinking. It is then that I was raised up, as a Christian, as an individual, to a place with Christ. I now can joyously confess that it turned out to be a "heavenly place." What a blessing that was!

I had turned from the Watchtower Society, and its works of witchcraft, from its "sleight of men, and cunning craftiness." I had come home to learn "that obedience is better than sacrifice."

Chapter 4

"HEARSAY" RESULTS IN CULTS

Heresy Begins Early

To the extent Christianity failed to "earnestly contend for the faith" and individual Christians failed to practice the New Testament way of preaching by "discipling" or "witnessing," to that extent heresies came in. Someone once said quite aptly "Heresies are the unpaid bills of Christianity."

As I looked back into early times of Christianity, as I eagerly did upon coming free, it appeared that when light shone its brightest, and true knowledge was diffused everywhere, certain shadows which could lead to darkness were already flitting across the scene. This process usually affected individuals who had failed to become synchronized and brought into unity of the faith, and who therefore looked with contempt upon the work of pastors, teachers and evangelists. The moment that happened, such were no longer guided by the Holy Spirit, but became addicted to false teachings, harkening unto such as dwelt in the shadow of Christianity. That is why in the final analysis, their behavior became like witchcraft, leading to rebellion to practice it.

In the very age and century, when the truths "once delivered to the saints" had just been given, in which the church had just been established upon the foundation or center of Jesus Christ, you would think that preaching by "hearsay" of men would be entirely impossible.

But, even while the apostles were still alive, divisiveness was in evidence in Corinth and in many other places. Could it be that the early emergence of false teaching believed on by "hearsay" from some man, caused the Lord to give Christianity its special gifts of pastors, teachers and evangelists?

What were these spirits against which John warned when he said, "Believe not every spirit..."? They were, no doubt, teachings distracting from Jesus Christ as the center of their salvation, or having looked upon Him as the brilliant light of the world for a moment caused them to turn away from Him. That moment of not walking towards the Lord and turning their backs upon Him was sufficient to cause them to walk in their own shadow away from Him. Fleetingly, no longer looking upon Christ as the center, they began to divide the word of God wrongly. It is in the wrong use of God's word that heresy is effected.

Paul commends the method of study practiced by the Bereans. He asked Christians to check in the Scriptures the statement made by men about them. While it is commendable to study all spirits, that is, read or listen to the teachings of those who claim to be born-again Christians, Paul warns the Thessalonians to "prove all things; hold fast that which is good ..." (Thess. 5:21). Already at that time the apostle John could say "Believe not every spirit, but prove the spirits, whether they are of God" (I John 4:1).

To what are we to "hold fast"? Paul admonished Timothy as follows: "Hold fast the form of sound words, which thou hast heard of me, in faith and love which is in Christ Jesus" (2 Tim. 1:13). The attack of the enemy early came against the Word of God, particularly against the doctrines "once delivered to the saints." It came by rebellion, or witchcraft, in teaching new and changing doctrines based on a man's interpretation.

Why were Christians already warned at that time to prove all things, or spirits? It was because many would-be teachers were no longer adhering to "the form of sound words." John says "because many false prophets are gone out into the world." Why "gone out into the world"? They had rebelled against the Lord's arrangement and had left the community of Christianity. These "false prophets" are men who claim to have to do with spiritual things when in reality they are not spiritually minded. They no longer hold fast or adhere to the "form of sound words."

Departure from the Faith

Such departure from the faith came very early. It came by way of rebellion. It came by way of individuals who manifested a perverse spirit and who promulgated false teachings. Each, in order to vie with others, had to have teachings just a shade different from those taught by others and completely different from the truths "once delivered to the saints." These individuals designed their teachings to draw followers after them. Such followers looked upon these teachers as new centers. They were, therefore, taught to accept teachings based upon the "hearsay" from the teacher. To the extent they fell for this, to that extent they departed from the word of God. They were trained to use the word of God deceitfully, tearing Scriptures out of their context in order to prove the statements of their leaders or teachers to be true. That is how heresy came in.

At first this departure from the faith was barely perceptible to them and in them. It came to expression in reasonings of men as these men evolved their own way of interpretations. But in their repetition such human interpretations soon became embellished, and gradually began to congeal and harden. Those who thus departed from the truth actually converted themselves to their own aberrations, and subsequently became hypnotized in their false teachings. Thus they convinced themselves of the correctness of their conclusions. They became hardened by practice, their conscience became sered by the constant repetition of error. That is precisely the process we as Jehovah's Witnesses hoped to accomplish when we devised the "seven step program" for proselyting as you read in my book *Thirty Years a Watchtower Slave.*

To the extent hearers of a false leader believed in the hearsay of his doctrines, to that extent did they cease to believe in Jesus Christ. Faith in what a man said, took the place of faith in what Jesus said. The instructions of Jesus as recorded in Matthew 28:20 "teaching them to observe all things whatsoever I have commanded you," were disregarded. Jesus Christ, with His teachings and commandments, no longer was the center of all things to them. They now had their own teacher, or teachers and teachings.

That is how heresy is born. It is born of disobedience. It is rebellion, and "is as the sin of witchcraft" (I Sam. 15:23). It is no longer based upon the revelation of God given in Jesus Christ, maintained by apostles, prophets, pastors, teachers, and evangelists and the form of sound words laid for us in God's word. It refuses to accept the ministry of pastors, teachers and evangelists. It dotes upon the reasonings and spirit of one man, or a group of men, who are actually outside of Christianity and in open rebellion to it.

Willfulness Forces Wrong Decision

Those who follow the teachings of a heresy, or of a man, do so willfully. They prefer to "heap to themselves teachers, having itching ears" (2 Tim. 4:3).They like something new all the time. Theirs is a sense religion. Because of that they depend upon the whims and caprices of men rather than upon the work of Holy Spirit within them. The worship they prefer is a worship based on the rules of adaptation, or the flesh. Such worship is in opposition to the spiritual worship practiced in historic Christianity, based on the spirit, with its center in heaven.

Willful men follow such a lead. Those taking the lead in such a system are anti-Christs. Most of such leaders originally sinned against better light. They did so deliberately, as John says in the above quoted passage. Seldom, therefore, will you be able to win these back to the grace of God.

But do not be discouraged. Rather be concerned that you may ever be "earnestly contending for the faith" against such, with the souls of lost men as your battleground. In fact heresies were able to rise and divert many souls to perdition because Christianity has often in its history failed to "defend the faith everywhere" by using the New Testament way of preaching, or witnessing.

A Study of How Error Is Organized

Another chapter will graphically show just how such errors came to counteract Christianity in the hearts of many. That happened already in early centuries. But here let me say briefly that the Scriptures teach us that by far the greatest dangers to spiritual worship are to arise in "the last days." We read Paul's warning to Timothy, "But the Spirit saith expressly, that in later times some shall fall away from the faith, giving heed to seducing spirits, and doctrines of demons, through the hypocrisy of men that speak lies, branded in their own consciences as with a hot iron" (1 Tim. 4:1).

In what way do such errors come in? Paul shows that they first come in by way of doctrines. Double-facedness, or hypocrisy, causes partisans to take up these doctrines and spread them. Then that sort of thing hardens and becomes fixed.

How does it harden? It becomes systematized into routine, or a "new system of things," as Jehovah's Witnesses designate their routine. Such systems emphasize the necessity of work and thought for the effectuating of salvation. Salvation as a gift of grace is thus forced into the background. That is how these systems prove that they are demon-inspired. And they lead to perdition which is the lot of the demons.

In what way do false teachings make their inroads into the realm of sound Christian doctrines? If you listen often enough to false doctrines and say nothing to counteract them in every instance, their very repetition may give them the sound of truth to you. That is why Paul admonishes early Christians and us later ones, too, to "prove all things; hold fast that which is good" (1 Thess. 5:21). In other words, he warns us to be discerning. How are we to do so? We are to counteract such "doctrines of demons" with "the form of sound words," and our minds will be renewed and strengthened with every onslaught. Defense of the faith is the best insurance against reception of error and a hardened conscience caused by repetitious hearing.

However, if one constantly listens to the repetition of error and does nothing to renew his knowledge of "sound words" by the daily reading of God's word, then there results almost surely a departure from the faith. In speaking of the work of false teachings in latter times, Paul shows that it results in a complete departure from the faith on the part of those who give heed. He describes the result of such departure from sound doctrine into a system of works as being a "defiled" or "seared" conscience.

It plainly means that their worship becomes routine and habitual. It is not daily renewed by the Holy Spirit. It is controlled by the flesh which creates instincts for religious behavior or a worship in a carnal way. Worship has become a mass system, from which all personal relationship to Jesus has been blotted out.

How far has he come at this stage from that in which, as Paul put it, we are led by "the Holy Spirit which dwelleth in you"? The promise of the Lord Jesus that the Holy Spirit "shall lead you into all truth" no longer applies here. Those who are addicted to heresy instead, are "led through the hypocrisy of men that speak lies."

The above are the last stages of heresy. No longer do such teachers, as at first they had done in the apostolic age, give expression to fine shades of views on doctrines, based on "the truth once delivered to the saints." No, here already these truths are totally subverted. Hypocritically mouthing faith in the Bible as a come-on, these false teachers use the Bible deceitfully, as I will graphically demonstrate later we did as Jehovah's Witnesses. They pervert and twist with lies of cunningness, Scripture passages torn out of context, which chimerically change again and again in the retelling. That is how it was done at the beginning of the Christian age, and that is how it works today.

Latter Times, Why Worse

Heresy and error are to become worse in the "latter days." Will it be in terms of numbers of adherents, or in degree and kind of deception, or what is even worse, in efficiency?

Nothing has aided the propagation of heresy more than the invention of movable type, or printing. This came in the 16th century. We have seen that the effectiveness of heresy against the "word of truth" lies in its repetition. False teachers soon sensed the possibilities. They saw that this retelling of lies could be immeasurably augmented by print. These lies could be printed in books and distributed in the place of the Bible. They could in time, take the place of God's word. This subversion could be repeated and repeated in millions of copies! It would be read by millions in the form of books, booklets, pamphlets and magazines. It works out that way too. Its repetition gradually causes a hardening of such statements into accepted facts in the minds of the readers. Slowly method is interwoven into the process of retelling, and a system is created. Insensibly these patterns are arranged to create an orbit around a center and then the center throws itself above the system and forms a cult below, which becomes a schism or a sect. This trend leads away from spiritual places. It is really the introduction of the herd-mentality of the beast into the realm of human behavior. Heavenly places fade from view.

Humanism, or Humanizing, Salvation

The proclivities of the flesh have always enabled man to adapt himself to his environment, as well as to mold the environment to suit him. This adaptability was created right into Adam. He was able to dress and keep the garden, to adapt himself to dominion over the beasts, etc. Depraved as all flesh now is, it invariably wars against the spirit. That is our great weakness in the flesh, in this body of death. Flesh, plus the devil, have tremendous power over us.

Flesh Enters Almost Always Into Every Move We Make

Let me take an example. The Pharisees were accused by the Lord of having done the same thing in relation to the Law. The Lord says to them, "for ye tithe mint and anise and cummin, and have left undone the weightier matters of the law" (Matt. 23:23).

What were the weightier matters of the law? They were justice and mercy and faith, and those the Pharisees had left behind. They substituted a system of routine. With two-faced hypocritical mien they replaced justice with fleshly banalities of time counting, weighing, reporting and outward rituals of performances. All of these, as you note, are human equations.

This tells us something very revealing. The cults and heresies of these latter times, even as the Pharisees which most effectively opposed Christianity, are therefore not in absolute opposition to everything Christian. This makes them the more dangerous. The Jehovah's Witnesses because of their almost perfect chimerical blend of Scripture, are the most dangerous in my judgment. I say this advisedly, as one having come out of this heresy. I know how it works. We must look for the quirks of the heretical mind. One of these is flesh, or rather the ability of the flesh slightly tinged with the spirit, to adapt the spiritual to the fleshly. This creates the appearance of rightness of worship based on the Bible. Heretics mouth many Scriptures. But note how they misuse the Scriptures. They use them to prove that they are right. That is of utmost and primary importance to them.

Above all they use terms similar to those used by Christianity. And never lose sight of this fact, they are following a hearsay interpretation of men. They subscribe to listening to a select group at some headquarters.

Such systems become even more dangerous when they have lasted more than two generations. By that time they have gone to seed. Misled first by false teachings, then by their own reasonings in the second generation, they become finally so hardened and set in error that they readily become martyrs for their tenets. In fact they are as willing to die for their error as if it were the truth. May I say, as my book *Thirty Years a Watchtower Slave* shows (therein lies its significance) that this has already happened to the Jehovah's Witnesses.

When such a system of things begins to produce martyrs, it

becomes "hardened." That is a tragic fact. But far more tragic is the fact that the Lord then sends them a strong delusion. Right after our court battles, all the way to the United States Supreme Court, during which thousands were jailed, there came the great delusion of *The Theocracy* of 1938.

How has this altered the behavior of the cult? Now the adherents believe that they are right, that their way alone is right. As proof, we have the fact that thousands have gone to jail for it and others have died for it. As you will read in my book *Thirty Years a Watchtower Slave,* and it is important that you do read it, I myself was happy and willing to go to jail sixteen times, to be stoned once and to be mobbed twice. I would gladly have died for the Watchtower way of error. The members of the sect or cult out of which the power of the gospel of Jesus Christ miraculously saved me, Jehovah's Witnesses, pride themselves "that their foreheads are become as hard as flint," adapting to their own use the Isaiah Scripture. Alas, it also shows though, that they have the "mark in the forehead" of the Watchtower heresy gone to seed.

Chapter 5

HOW RUSSELLISM STARTED

How Did They Get That Way?

Sharpened by what happened to me for thirty years, I have traced for you the inception, the formation, the spreading, and the hardening of heresy contra historic Christianity. I have also demonstrated for you its method of operation to be that which the Scripture describes as "rebellion and witchcraft." Now we move from the general to the specific. Let us examine the early beginnings of Jehovah's Witnesses.

Charles T. Russell became an agnostic in 1872. He rebelled against historic Christianity and left the spiritual worship of God. Being in the state of rebellion against God, which is the condition of all rebels, he looked around to find some handle by which he could justify his position of agnosticism. A few years later it came his way. How?

Cut Loose from Christianity, One Is Tossed To and Fro

In Christian circles to be sure such rebellion results in a "departure from the faith." This is normally followed by a smiting of one's former brethren followed by filthy dreams defiling the flesh, despising dominion and speaking evil of dignities (Jude 8).

Having freed himself from the benevolent gifts of Christianity — the pastors, teachers and evangelists — Russell came across the writings of Mrs. Ellen White. They fascinated Russell. He was particularly fascinated by the newly invented doctrines that Hell is the grave. This did for him, what Paul said unsound teaching generally does to those who rebel against God; it tickled his ears. It did that and more. It obliterated for him the true Bible doctrine that Hell is the place of eternal punishment of lost souls in torment.

Not only did Russell joyfully espouse this doctrine that Hell is the grave; he noticed the techniques Mrs. White used in argumentation, and which is pungently described by Paul as "deceitfully handling the word of God."

In this frame of mind he began to study the Bible with the thought of finding texts to support his rebellion. His spirit of inquiry was one of opposing "sound doctrine," and he needed the color of Scripture to make his teachings acceptable. He had to find all kinds of passages which would support his views even as Mrs. Ellen White had done. Soon because of his improper spirit of inquiry, he began to get what may be termed half-knowledge of things pertaining to God's word. He became the counterpart of an able minister of the New Testament. But he ministered to the letter of the word, not to the spirit as did and do the faithful pastors, teachers and evangelists of historic Christianity. The result was that his "letter ministry" killed off all spirituality (2 Cor. 3:6).

A closer knowledge of Russell's experience has led me to recognize the manner in which I was diverted from historic Christianity. Also I know now from wide experience how the Jehovah's Witnesses were severally and collectively diverted from historic Christianity. With this knowledge we can accurately determine how to work with them. This is very important! All who have turned away from the faith look for Scripture passages to disprove historic Christianity. You must never allow them to bandy God's word about in your presence in this manner. If you do, you are helping them to convert themselves to heresy right in front of you. They need your help to free themselves from this stunt of inversion for which they have been trained. Stop them every time by making them read in its context every Scripture they quote to you.

Being a methodical man, Russell began publishing FOOD FOR THINKING CHRISTIANS, and set up the banner line; HELL IS THE GRAVE. This then is the method of heresy. Gather all passages which seemingly contradict the Bible doctrine you wish to oppose, and tear them out of context. This was and is the age-old trick of heresy. Set your doctrine, then marshal all the passages of Scripture you can to buoy it up and to give it Bible color. In that way a barrier is erected against proper study of the Bible. In this manner one Bible doctrine after another topples and falls. It is done by misusing God's word, by using it deceitfully to prove oneself right. That is why you must never allow a Jehovah's Witness or any other cultist to bandy God's Word in front of you. Defend the honor of

God's Word! Protect the heretic against himself! (2 Tim. 2:24-26).

Russell's Heresy Could Only Be Effective Outside of Christianity

How could Russell get away with such doctrinal subversion? True, he would attract many who too were rebellious and who disliked the Bible doctrine of Hell as a place of eternal punishment in torment. Flesh and blood have always disliked that doctrine. It hurts! That is why it is played down and watered down in the thinking of many so-called Christians today. Show me one who denies the existence of Hell and I will show you one who is Christian in name only. But could Russell continue his subversion to the point where it would become a sustaining way of life?

Russell Engineers Layman's Revolt

Being a layman, Russell naturally led a layman's revolt from historic Christianity.

His problem was to find a way to establish himself as a center of a movement of men. In what garb should he appear? He hit upon it. He would don the garb of a teacher. How could he put himself across as a teacher? He would start a new way of Bible study. First he would set up a pattern of what he wanted to prove. He would make sure this pattern was in contradiction to some Bible doctrine of historic Christianity. Then he would proceed to do research, in order to find all sorts of Scripture passages to prove his postulate.

In this manner he raised a wall and a tower, a watch tower, which gave him the mien of a seer on higher ground than the rest. He began to formulate such findings in a publication which he called FOOD FOR THINKING CHRISTIANS. This pamphlet was printed and broadcast everywhere.

But more happened. In the process he became the sole arbiter of what was to be published, and what combination of Scriptures was to be used. That made him the dispenser of new knowledge, or as he called it, "food." Whence came this new food? It certainly did not come from God. It was not the bread "Jesus Christ" who came from heaven. No, this new food was expanded from the humanly devised FOOD FOR THINKING CHRISTIANS to a bi-monthly paper THE WATCHTOWER and was subsequently augmented by six volumes of SCRIPTURE STUDIES. These publications were put out by the millions of copies. They became "food for," as Russell put it,

"The Household of Faith." No longer was the Bible, God's Word, this food. His literature took its place. Cultism had come in. It centered first around his person, then around his Image. His Image was and is THE WATCHTOWER BIBLE AND TRACT SOCIETY, Inc.

Remember my former description of how heresy made its entry in former ages? Keep that in mind. Now let us evaluate Russellism at this stage in that light. What was Russell's primary aim? It was to usurp the task of the Holy Spirit and thus thwart the interplay of the two aspects of Christianity. In this manner there emerged a new center, albeit an intermediary one, which deflected the eyes from Jesus Christ and focused the attention on the Watchtower Society. The drawing-power of Russell and his collaborators was no longer an expression and confessing of what the Lord had done for them, but a humanly devised system of subtle arguments. Thus no one was drawn to Jesus Christ. All were drawn into a new way of thinking and then into the Watchtower Society. This subversion rapidly became complete. It could be termed occult, or witchcraft in nature.

Forming a Gospel as Spearhead for Heresy

The gospel, or the good news of salvation in Jesus Christ, is the tremendous winning force of evangelization. With it Christianity has effectively drawn millions to Christ. Evangelization is therefore a publishing work of great magnitude. It is not only or first to be proclaimed by the printed page, for each Christian is a letter written by the Holy Spirit. However, he is not a minister of the letter (2 Cor. 3:6, and also 2 Cor. 3:2,3), but of the spirit.

In contrast to the decay and death of flesh of every generation everywhere, the Christian confession and witness carries with it the demonstration of a tremendous change of life and presages a coming life in the spirit in heaven as no book or pamphlet could ever convey. It is a certificate of a new birth and indisputably draws millions of lost souls to salvation. This is THE NEW TESTAMENT WAY OF WITNESSING.

Russell cleverly counter-poised this genuine gospel with a spurious Harvest Gospel. Condemning historic Christianity, he declared that the harvest of the world had begun and now that all wheat would be gathered in out of historic Christianity and be brought into a new bin. Those brought out of historic Christianity would enter a new arena of worship.

This was very clever. This kind of message was plausible and effective only because we are living in what appear to be the last days. Its very plausibility points it up as a serious danger to Christians and historic Christianity. Let us face it, therefore. Let us not hide ostrich-like from it.

This sort of thing, however, is not new. Cults usually preach a form of gospel, or cry "another gospel" (Gal. 1:6-9). The cry goes out "Christ is with us" (Matt. 24:23,24). "He is here."

Russell was a very shrewd student of human nature. He had some knowledge of Christianity. He knew that in her midst was a devoted class of men who were pastors, teachers, and evangelists; and he knew why they were there. Because of that it was obvious to him that his heresies could never flourish within historic Christianity. So, already evincing the nature and talent of a false teacher, or anti-Christ as described in 1 John 2:18,19, he came to his departure from the faith.

In order to destroy the confidence of his adherents in the benevolent services of the pastors, teachers and evangelists of historic Christianity, Russell attacked them. He declared that the clergy had become a condemned class. He alluded that in the place of the clergy the Lord had set him and his Image, the Watchtower Society. As "later servants," they would now fructify the Bible, or bring forth "new light" or "present truth," as he coined it. Who would be the preacher of this "present truth"? It would be a new mouthpiece, or paper, entitled ZION'S WATCHTOWER AND HERALD OF CHRIST'S PRESENCE. This was in the year 1879.

Solid Ground Gives Way to Constant Change

That the Jehovah's Witnesses are addicted to heresy is proved by what happened to their predecessors once they left historic Christianity behind. There began to obtain an unhealthy condition of flux, with light ever changing, and with revelation by revolution.

FOOD FOR THINKING CHRISTIANS and ZION'S WATCHTOWER AND HERALD OF CHRIST'S PRESENCE, became the stage upon which was performed a continuing act of ventriloquism. Many poorly informed laymen became fascinated by the performance. Many who had rebellious thoughts against historic Christianity in common, rallied around Russell and his act. The mouthpiece was performing effectively.

But the mouthpiece had to have a body. Six other men were prevailed upon in 1884 to come in with Russell and appear before a court of minor jurisdiction in Allegheny County, Pa., and ask for a corporate charter. Russell was laying the basis for a legal stability which could protect his writings, and which would insure continuation of his heresies. He was here creating his Image, to be revived again should he die before his organization was taken to heaven. This was to become an unusual organization which *was* (while he was alive it was his dummy), and which *was not* (a year and a half after his death it was dissolved legally by a Federal District Court for the alleged treason of its leaders), and *was again* (when Rutherford revived the Image in 1919).

Under its aegis as a dummy corporation, or as the Watchtower once called it, "a beast of Burden," THE WATCHTOWER BIBLE AND TRACT SOCIETY for a time served as a "front" for Russell. It gave the appearance of many for one man. It allowed him to assume leadership and gave time for his position to jell into an exclusive position amidst his adherents. Laymen were deliberately led to lose sight of the "form of sound words." Hell as the place of eternal punishment or torment, the Scriptural teachings of the immortal soul, the Deity of Christ, the Trinity, the bodily resurrection of Jesus Christ, and the gospel of Jesus Christ, were subverted and systematically overthrown in their thinking.

This new system of things, like BABYLON THE GREAT, gradually became filled like a cage full of unclean things. This was done by constantly repeating in different combinations, passages of Scripture to ventriloquize doctrines of demons. These are and were that Hell is the grave, that man is on a par with the beast, that Jesus Christ is not God but God's first creation, and that the Trinity is false. These heresies Russell did not invent. He borrowed them from former heretics: Arians, Gnostics, Manicheans and Montanists.

Adaptation of Spiritual Truths to a System of Flesh

Russell now held the fleshly means for gradually welding his "hearsay" gospel into a new system of things to counteract Christianity.

The WATCHTOWER magazine thus became the mouthpiece of both Russell and his dummy, the Watchtower Society. Once its readers lost sight of the true doctrines of historic

Christianity and the benefit of the ministry of pastors, teachers and evangelists with which Christianity was gifted, they fell easy prey to the *cunning craftiness* of this WATCHTOWER magazine.

In its pages doctrines were discussed in a new way. They were not presented positively as solid, sound forms of words. No, doctrines were tossed to and fro, kicked around. Words of God, torn out of their proper setting, emerged in many gyrations as the new doctrines of the cult. These new doctrines were never based on the solid ground handed down by the Lord Jesus, the apostles and prophets. They were the product of the winds of imagination. All solidity ceased. A nightmare began. This was eventually to become the Watchtower Society designed nightmare.

Russell and his collaborators consistently worked through his dummy, the Watchtower Society. This was a work of fleshly amalgamation. In the place of Holy Spirit, who works differently in each heart, the Watchtower began to create "reasonings" to work within the minds of its adherents. This was not an establishing work. It essentially resulted in a complete dissociation of these adherents for all time from Christianity.

No longer did Holy Spirit work in these soul-washed followers of Russell, nor was "He dwelling within them." In fact, they had been led to deny the person of the Holy Spirit. In their thinking they had demoted the Holy Spirit to be but the active influence of God, or the "wind." And, *ipso facto,* since God's wind or influence now solely worked through the WATCHTOWER, using it as a mouthpiece, instead of working in the heart of each adherent, they claimed to get their new doctrines out of the air. They were quite candid, for every "wind of doctrine" created in each subsequent WATCHTOWER issue by the "sleight of man," actually did begin to "toss them to and fro," from issue to issue (Eph. 4:9-14). A kaleidoscopic change thus worked on them to eliminate all semblance of personality and individuality in thinking, until they all thought alike.

How did they do it? They invented the scheme of presenting gradations of truth in layers of time. That proved effective. The WATCHTOWER magazine began the system of presenting to its readers so-called "present truth." The expression "present truth" is, of course, a paradox. But, because their teaching was presented piecemeal, in a revelation by revolution patterned way, it constantly changed in essence, but it remained "present" in aspect because it was "presently," for that particular issue at least, what WATCHTOWER leaders proclaimed to be truth. "Present truth" became present by continuous change.

To make this cult become a living thing it was necessary to give it an ideal and also a modicum of Good News in order that it might generate "another gospel." It had to have a sensational aspect about it. It had to cause a change of position in its adherents.

What expectation amidst Christians has the greatest pull on the imagination of man? Ever when men leave historic Christianity behind, they begin to speculate about the Second Coming of Christ. Even in early Christianity that happened again and again. Take the case of the Thessalonians. The entire Chapter 2 of 2 Thessalonians shows that the Thessalonians too speculated about the Lord's coming again, and needed correction. The apostles kept them in line.

In this layman's movement of the WATCHTOWER SOCIETY though, God's gift to Christianity — pastors, teachers and evangelists — no longer wielded any influence. Russell had astutely discredited and discarded them. Thus the Russellites were fully at the mercy of Russell and his imagination. What was one of their great delusions? They declared our Lord Jesus had returned in His Second Coming unobserved to human eyes. Rather amazingly, they did not recognize this return until 1876, two years after it actually happened. It was supposed to have transpired in 1874.

Like the Thessalonians, they had speculated and reached their conclusions. It took them, however, all of two years to recognize the Lord's return. Yet, as Paul says, in 1 Thessalonians, when the Lord comes, it will not take two years to recognize his return, for he shall descend with a SHOUT...!

Thus the departure from the faith was signaled in a unique and novel way. The WATCHTOWER magazine for the first time in the history of the last 2,000 years, promulgated something quite new, which no other heresy had ever proclaimed. They declared the Lord's return to be invisible. They made much of the new term they had coined "the second presence of Christ." This was indeed a departure!

It was sensational! It drew thousands into the WATCHTOWER orbit. It really tickled the ears of the old heretics! Jesus had promised, though invisibly, He would always be present to his disciples throughout the age by saying, "and lo, I am with you alway, even unto the end of the world" (Matt. 28:20). Russell now inferred that Jesus had not been right, that in fact he had been absent all the age. Now, only since 1874, was He really beginning to be "present." Overcasting the true meaning of the Lord's return in glory and power, Russell reasoned down through three Greek words: *Parousia, Epiphania* and *Apocalypse.* These so-called three stages of the Lord's return, all invisible, even including the Apocalypse which means revelation, were successively revealed in the columns of THE WATCHTOWER AND HERALD OF CHRIST'S PRESENCE.

We see the creation of an occult media with Machiavellian cunning. This media is also the channel through which enlightenment and instruction are to flow which accompany the Lord's Second Presence in order to bring about the setting up of a new world, THE NEW WORLD SOCIETY on earth.

The *parousia* of Christ, which literally means "coming near," was interpreted to mean "presence," and this "presence" was said to be an invisible one. Once this interpretation was accepted, it became very easy for Russell to set himself up as a teacher. He now had a field all of his own choosing.

But more, this gave Russell a mission to this world. Christ had revealed Himself to him alone and could only be discerned by the watchmen standing upon the ramparts of his WATCH-TOWER SOCIETY. Christ's *epiphania* or appearance could only come into view through the interpretations given in the columns of THE WATCHTOWER. These excathedra statements and reports would form the new GOSPEL OF THE KINGDOM, for which they misused Matt. 24:14. In other words, the second stage of Christ's return, of His *epiphania,* or His appearing to view, could only materialize to Watchtower enlightened eyes. Witchcraft was at work!

Apocalypse, or Revelation

Armageddon will bring in the Apocalypse! The WATCH-TOWER indeed is a revelation! In connection with this coming revelation of Jesus Christ from the heavens, and the false interpretation of it, is revealed the attitude of the coming anti-Christ.

When shall this wicked one be revealed? Paul says "and then shall the wicked be revealed, whom the Lord shall consume with the spirit of his mouth, and shall destroy with the brightness of his coming: even him, whose coming is after the working of Satan with all power and signs and lying wonders, and with all deceivableness of unrighteousness in them that perish: because they received not the love of truth, that they might be saved [but deceived it to argue their religion by misusing it], and for this cause shall God send them a strong delusion, that they should believe a lie" (2 Thess. 2:8-11). We see this prophecy fulfilled in the Jehovah's Witnesses.

Delusions

The greatest delusion which the Jehovah's Witnesses have accepted is the doctrine of THE THEOCRACY OF 1938. I penned from a lifetime of experience in THIRTY YEARS A WATCHTOWER SLAVE the steps leading to its unveiling, and also painted with a true-to-life brush the effects this THEOCRACY HAD upon the Jehovah's Witnesses up to 1952. Space here will not permit to discuss thoroughly the implications, and to unearth the sinister aspects of it, as it bids fair to become the greatest delusion of all time. In a coming book, The NEW WORLD SOCIETY OF JEHOVAH'S WITNESSES, this will be completely exposed to view.

But what are these strong delusions in the lesser sense? Let us trace a few of them.

From the moment the WATCHTOWER was published, it was designed to give voice to a great delusion, namely, as its subheading proclaimed for all to see, to be ZION'S WATCHTOWER AND HERALD OF CHRIST'S SECOND PRESENCE.

On its pages, subsequently, we see fulfilled everything predicted in 2 Thess. 2. Step by step the reader's conscience became hardened and a new world view altogether foreign to historic Christianity was fashioned. By means of speculation, changes, new light, new dates, new doctrines, its adherents were tossed to and fro, and kept employed in a gasping chase. To all this were added breathtaking expectations!

The panoramic view used by Satan in his third temptation, was used with great effect in the columns of the WATCHTOWER. It brought forth things old and new. Long before the invention of the moving picture, the WATCHTOWER effectively applied its principle to hold fast the attention of its viewers. It began in the 1880's with the conjuring up of prophetic predictions which made for great expectations. The term "times of the Gentiles" was given a bizarre connotation, to give credence to the predictions for 1914. Then the "seven times" of Leviticus 26 came into use, and was harnessed to put the accent on 1914.

Slowly 1914 jelled in their thinking. Everything and everybody in the organization strained towards that date when all expectations were to be fulfilled. The faithful would be translated to heaven; the unfaithful would be destroyed in Armageddon which would then be fought; the world would come to an end.

In the Place of Pastors of Christianity, a Pastor

Charles T. Russell became the sole arbiter of "present truth." Insensibly his adherents began to accept him as "Pastor" everywhere. His WATCHTOWER became the "Teacher." His dummy, The Watchtower Society, became his evangelist. Really, he became all three in one. In time he was elected as Pastor of more than one thousand congregations. Truly, now he fulfilled 2 Tim. 4:1-4. But he did it only in a minor, bagatelle way, as it turned out later. The real subversion on that score was several shades lower when it came in some twenty years later.

By 1912 Russell was generally hailed and accepted to be that "Faithful and Wise servant" mentioned in Matt. 24:45-46. Note how far the subversion from historic Christianity had come from the date of the laymen's rebellion, which had begun in 1876.

In the place of Christ Jesus as the center of salvation, the laymen's rebellion of 1876 had placed the WATCHTOWER SOCIETY, which was to become the IMAGE of a man.

In the place of the gifts of Christianity: pastors, teachers and evangelists, it placed ONE man.

In the place of the "form of sound words" and of a ministry "for the perfecting of the saints" so that they might come "to the measure of the fulness of Christ" they had put the idea of revelation by revolution, truth changing as new light.

In the place of the "faith which was once delivered to the saints," had now come the thesis of ever changing doctrines.

In the place of growth towards a filling with the image and likeness of God, our Lord Jesus Christ, had come a straining towards a date, 1914.

In the place of salvation from sin and death for *all,* had come the "salvation" of a mere 144,000 to go to heaven to sit on thrones and a Great Multitude getting a second chance to stand before the throne as servants.

In the place of the present Jesus Christ, who promised to be with His church always, had now come a mouthpiece whose reports alone materialized Christ's presence for them in its columns.

A Way That Seemeth Right

This way of error was now flourishing like the grass. It had been devised cunningly to establish a new system of things to take the place of historic Christianity. Fellow Christian, make no mistake about this. The WATCHTOWER SOCIETY then established, poses now as "God's organization," and has eliminated contemptuously and with malice aforethought, Christianity, by putting it as SATAN'S ORGANIZATION. As such, the Watchtower Society now campaigns for the full destruction of Christianity in an Armageddon to come.

According to this concept the harvest, or gathering of all the faithful to the Watchtower nucleus began. This nucleus now became the Remnant of the whole age. Thus they established successive limitations for Christianity.

Automatically another limitation was placed, namely, a limit of 144,000 members was decreed for the Church in heaven. These were daubed "the Little Flock." This remnant, gathered around the WATCHTOWER, was to be saved during the third stage of the Lord's Second Presence, the Apocalypse. This was to be the battle of Armageddon to be fought in 1914, when this world would end.

So little did they, by that time, think of Christianity, that they averred that only a small number of the 144,000 were saved during the whole gospel age, and that the overwhelming number were being saved through the WATCHTOWER organization between 1874 to 1914. To their way of thinking Christianity had been a total failure.

Way of Error Comes to Naught

A house had been built. This house was not built upon the foundation which is Jesus Christ. Nor did it have apostles and prophets as pillars. It lacked pastors, teachers and evangelists as adorners.

Long ago, historic Christianity was built upon Jesus Christ. It grew throughout two millennia in its two aspects: the earthly drawing, and the heavenly place. Soon will come its fulness in heaven when the Lord of Glory appears in the clouds.

The house Charles T. Russell built and which he laboriously erected between 1874 and 1914 was completed according to contract in 1914. There was only one thing wrong with it. It had been built upon the shifting sands of human interpretations. The movement it housed was born in rebellion and nurtured in witchcraft and was full of unclean things and heresies. When 1914 came and the predictions made for it did not transpire, there came a big storm as all the winds of false doctrines eddied around its center and inventor. Charles T. Russell died two years later, in 1916. His house crumbled with him in utter ruin to the dust. It was a terrible fall. But such is human stubbornness that it could be put back together again.

How? Charles T. Russell had left behind his dummy — the corporate charter of THE WATCHTOWER SOCIETY — as his IMAGE. It is truly to become a system that was — then was not. Would it be again?

Chapter 6

HISTORIC CHRISTIAN DOCTRINE: HELL IS A PLACE OF ETERNAL PUNISHMENT

Bequeaths Heresy

In this IMAGE, the corporate charter of THE WATCH-TOWER BIBLE AND TRACT SOCIETY, Russell left behind more than a vehicle of rebellion and a vista of a NEW WORLD SOCIETY. With it, he willed a heresy accomplished. So potent was this organized "departure from the faith," that it has held under its thrall not only the Jehovah's Witnesses, but àlso all the eleven sects which have revolted against the IMAGE. These latter rebelled against the manner in which the IMAGE was revived in the form of the NEW WORLD SOCIETY. On their trek out of it, they could not go back farther than the accomplished heresy of Charles T. Russell.

Herein lies the danger of Watchtower supervised soul and brainwashing. This is not only a danger for Jehovah's Witnesses, Russellites, or other lost souls; it is a present danger to all Christians. Present-day Jehovah's Witnesses know the value of attacking Christian thinking with their heretical doctrine: Hell is the grave. They already do this unconsciously. It was the original pattern of their departure from the faith. They follow in Russell's pathway, who had rebelled against historic Christianity and denied the Bible doctrine that Hell is a place of eternal punishment in torment.

Once the fatal step to deny this Bible doctrine is taken, then insensibly the need for salvation from sin and death, ceases. Only the enormity of a conscious fate in hell, will bring many unsaved ones to a conviction of sin and to a realization of their hopeless plight. No works, no system of things devised by humans, can exert benevolent strictures upon this fate in the hereafter. Only salvation in Jesus Christ can save to the uttermost, because only the Lord Jesus is Lord over the living and the dead. So much so, and so all-comprehensively, that Paul could say, in Philippians 2:11: "That every tongue should confess that Jesus Christ is Lord, to the glory of God the Father."

In the 10th verse Paul says, "That at the name of Jesus every knee should bow, of things in heaven, and things in earth, and things under the earth." The tongue and knees are organs and parts which only bend and speak while there is life. If those in and under the earth (and the sea for that matter too) are annihilated and unconscious, how can they speak or how can they bend their knees?

Only a true recognition of what our fate in Hell can be, brings us to a conviction of sin and unto Jesus Christ our Lord and Saviour. Lose sight of that, deny this doctrine, and you can from this viewpoint of the flesh be converted to a salvation in the flesh by some system where pride of achievement can be employed. That would not lead to salvation. It would result in perdition.

Only Way Into the Light of Christianity

When once I came free from the thrall of the Watchtower system, I found myself in a vacuum as far as doctrines is concerned. But the Lord took me by His hand, and led me step by step to discard the heresies of Russell. False doctrine after false doctrine fell before the word of God when once I learned to "rightly divide it."

The manner of describing what happened is a living one. It is nothing more than a faithful eye-witness report of what happened, to my thinking, step by step as the Lord led me out of heresy into the light of Christianity. This book is as much an eye-witness account of coming all the way free, as THIRTY YEARS A WATCHTOWER SLAVE was an eye-witness account of how the IMAGE of Russell was revived and brought to life again. Both books together can be an inestimable boon to those entrapped in heresies, as well as a great help to *stay* free to those who might be in danger. Both books can be used effectively as *missionaries*. May the Lord bless what now follows in a special way, as it is truly the result of amazing grace that a report such as this can be written. It is a finding of life.

The Fate of the Wicked

Up to the time of my coming free, in my thinking "the wicked" were all those of this generation between 1914 and Armageddon who failed to become Jehovah's Witnesses. But that has now been debunked, as I reported in the beginning chapters of this book. The Lord has shown me that this view was a warped one. It has now become clear to me that at the core of this error is a wrong understanding of what the fate of the wicked really is.

Studying God's word without Watchtower helps, I found that from ancient times comes Jehovah's positive statement, "There is no peace to the wicked" (Isa. 57:21). Presaging the coming of peace to those souls whose spirits failed before the Lord, "whose souls I have made" (Isa. 57:16), it is shown that the Lord's wrath was upon all the souls He had created (Isa. 43:7).

Reading from the 16th to the 19th verses of Isaiah 57, I began to see the Lord's procedure of enlivening the spirit, or God-consciousness, of the Israelites. Of course, this concerns souls other than Israelites, too. All this has an emphatic conclusion. The fate of those souls which are lost is described, "But the wicked are like the troubled sea, whose waters cast up mire and dirt. There is no peace, saith my God, to the wicked" (Isa. 57:20,21).

Echoing, as coming from out of the depths of ages of dying ones on sea, in the earth, in Hell and Heaven, I found this positive statement in Rev. 14:9-11: "And the third angel followed them, saying with a loud voice, If any man worship the beast and his image, and receive his mark in his forehead, or in his hand, the same shall drink of the wine of the wrath of God, which is poured out without mixture [of mercy] into the cup of indignation; and he shall be tormented with fire and brimstone [Gehenna-Hell] in the presence of the holy angels, and in the presence of the Lamb: and the smoke of their torment ascendeth up for ever and ever: and *they have no rest day and night,* who worship the beast and his image, and whosoever receiveth the mark of his name." Note, "there is no peace for the wicked." That is the ever-recurring refrain.

Flesh Denies Hell, Because It Wants to Escape Punishment

Men who are only born of blood, and of the will of flesh, and of the will of a man, but are not born of God and deny that they possess an immortal soul (John 1:13 in reverse application), I realize from my own background, will willfully deny that they are created in the image and likeness of God (Gen. 1:26,27). We, of Jehovah's Witnesses in order to erase the implications of an eternal punishment in torment, conditioned our thinking by willfully painting our lot to be the same as that of a beast. In this way we adapted our human fate to that of a beast, by the art of reasoning. Herein, I suddenly realized, lies the tremendous appeal to flesh of the heresy THAT HELL IS THE GRAVE. This immediately reveals the true flaw in the Jehovah's Witnesses reasoning. For the startling fact is, that the beast is made in the image of its own, or species, and is perpetuated by the process of procreation and birth.

Russell had ventriloquized his denial of Hell as the place of punishment in torment, by using the above phenomena in giving his wrong conclusions weight. He misused Eccl. 3:18,19, "I said in mine heart concerning the estate of the sons of men, that God might manifest them, and that they might see that they themselves are beasts, for that which befalleth the sons of men befalleth beasts; even one thing befalleth them: as the one dieth so dieth the other; yea, they have all one breath; so that a man hath no pre-eminence above a beast: for all is vanity."

We lost sight, however, in the misuse of this Scripture, of the fact that man had lost "the image and likeness of God" which had become marred by sin and death. Pointing up this present-day estate of the flesh in sin, degradation and death, so different from what man was created to be, Solomon adds this significant statement, "Who knoweth the spirit of man that goeth upward, and the spirit of the beast that goeth downward to the earth?" That which is of God ascendeth, that which is not of God, but of the earth, descendeth.

Seeing the text in its context suddenly opened my eyes. I saw that Eccl. 3:18,19 in context points up quite succinctly, that the fate of a beast is quite different from that of a man. When man loses his body by dying, something else in him, which the beast hath not, man's soul, returns to God and that, upward! Rather than teaching that the end of man and beast are the same it teaches quite the opposite.

But my mind insisted on formulating Solomon's query "Who knoweth?" In Ezek. 18:4 I got the answer. It says there, "Behold all souls are mine." Later, in another chapter, we shall thoroughly discuss this entire context and not just this one verse. God thus is not only the Creator, but far more important He is pictured here to be the owner of all souls. They are to all intents and purposes, His vessels. They are His to do with as is His will. Whether dead (not living unto God, or separated from Him), or alive (living unto God) not separated from Him, such souls are His.

Two Kinds of Vessels

The distinction of two kinds of vessels is evident only in existence. The distinction of the fate of two kinds of vessels of God can only be made if we think of both kinds as consciously alive.

This point is raised by Paul, in Rom. 9:21: "Hath not the potter power over the clay, of the same lump to make one vessel unto honor, and another unto dishonor?"

This Scripture opened my mind to see how foolish was my thinking as a Jehovah's Witness. Men who arrogantly claim to die like beasts are accused by Isaiah, "Surely your turning of things upside down shall be esteemed as potter's clay: for shall the work say of him that made it, He made me not [in his image]? Or shall the thing framed say of him that framed it, He had not understanding?" (Isa. 29:16). This made me realize that it was high time for me to remain quiet, to stop the foolish process of "reasonings" or contending with the Lord about my fate and nature. It dawned upon me I better "shut up" or I would be talking myself into potter's clay to be molded into a "vessel of dishonor" before I went into the grave.

I concluded right then and there, it is far better for me to say, "But now, O Lord, thou art our Father: we are the clay, and thou our potter; and we all are the work of thy hand" (Isa. 64:8). Wisdom was slowly coming into my foolish heart as true knowledge of God dawned.

Why is the above a better attitude for us? Isaiah says, Woe unto him that striveth with His Maker! Let the potsherd strive with the potsherds of the earth [the cultists among themselves — arguing Hell to be the grave, denying it to be the place of eternal punishment in torment]. Shall the clay say to him that fashioned it, What makest thou? or thy work, he hath no hands? (Isa. 45:9). The full force of this question came home to me when I read the whole context, particularly the verses that follow it. Will you read them?

Pride of the Flesh Does Not Allow You to Think Rationally About Hell

Proud men in times past, and now in present times, have denied the ancient Christian doctrine of Hell as the place of eternal punishment in torment. Why?

They desire not to repent of their evil and hate to come humbly in repentance to the Lord. To cover up this willful wickedness, they behave like the ostrich, burying their heads into the earth (claiming that Hell is the Grave) so that they can live in the flesh as they please.

Why had I accepted Russell's heresy? I too liked to sugar-coat my obstinacy by misusing God's word to give authority to my foolish views. Because the Watchtower kept me busy fabricating such foolish views, I fell for them. Upon my conversion I had to face this fact. I was much more to blame for what happened to me, than were they. They had merely given me a means of accommodating my flesh, so that I could have a "form of godliness" while denying "the power thereof." I had, ever thereafter, helped raise the cry: "Hell is the Grave," and had become an interested party to it.

Reading more of God's word by itself without Watchtower helps, I began to realize that we Jehovah's Witnesses were not the only foolish ones. We had lots of company. Israel had often been like that too. To them the prophet Jeremiah had to say, "O house of Israel, cannot I do with you as this potter? saith the Lord. Behold, as the clay is in the potter's hand, so are ye in my hand, O house of Israel. . . . If it do evil in my sight, that it obey not my voice, then I will repent of the good, wherewith I said I would benefit them" (Jer. 18:6,10).

It is almost as if these admonitions are spoken to the Jehovah's Witnesses: "And they said, There is no hope: but we will walk after our own devices, and we will every one do the imagination of his evil heart" (Jer. 18:12). Thus, rather than to seek to be vessels of hope, when they died and were buried they went to Hell forever, from whence their spirit will be called on the day of Judgment (Rev. 20) and united with a horrible body of their own wickedness, because they are objects of eternal wrath.

How the above opened my eyes! Hope is possible only to one who is in danger of becoming a vessel of wrath in a condition and place of punishment in which such could consciously feel wrath. It is then that Rom. 9:22 became clear to me: "What if God, willing to show His wrath, and to make His power known, endured with much long-suffering the vessels of wrath fitted for destruction."

Why, all this long time has God endured such, without sealing their fate? "That He might make known the riches of his glory on the vessels of mercy, which he had afore prepared unto glory" (Rom. 9:23).

Do the Kinds of Vessels Have Something in Common?

To understand the fate of the vessels of wrath and that of the vessels of mercy, I had to understand what they had in common, if anything. I found it in Rom. 9:23 in this statement, "Which He had afore prepared unto glory."

What was that? God made man in "His image and likeness" an immortal soul in a body of flesh. He, afore made him thus constituted, for His glory! That is why Ezekiel speaks of Jehovah saying, "I have no pleasure in the death [cease to function as a vessel of glory for which I originally fashioned him] of the wicked; but that the wicked turn from his way and live" (Ezek. 33:11).

Obviously all, whether good or evil, experience physical death. If the wicked repents while in his flesh and returns from his ways, what is his destiny? Does he still die physically, as if he had not repented at all? That was the question which now agitated my thinking.

Peter helped me out of that sordid way of reasoning. He says, "Blessed be the God and Father of our Lord Jesus Christ, which according to his abundant mercy hath begotten us again unto a lively hope by the resurrection of Jesus Christ from the dead" (1 Peter 1:3).

I was quick to note that the vessels of mercy spoken of by Paul in Rom. 9:23, appear here again. This puzzled me. Why are they called vessels of mercy? Why not vessels of glory if they are saved? It dawned upon me. They had sinned and had become vessels of wrath, fitted for destruction only. But now, they had been born again or begotten anew to a lively hope.

Hopeless indeed was the fate of man. Look at the type of sentence that would be levelled against him if he sinned, "But of the tree of the knowledge of good and evil, thou shalt not eat of it: for in the day thou eatest thereof thou shalt surely die." If the death, as threatened here, would be an unconscious state, then why does the Hebrew in this text say, "dying thou shalt die"? This is not the death of a beast. When a beast dies it ceases to exist and is forgotten. It is true, its kind is carried on by procreation and birth. This, of course, makes no difference because the beast has no soul, is not God-conscious. It is self-conscious only to the degree that it feels body pain, satisfaction, contentedness, etc. All that comes to an end when the animal dies. But Adam was differently constituted.

Adam was not only sense-conscious as was the beast, able to use five senses. Adam had a soul within him. Therefore he was actually self-conscious and God-conscious. Not only like the beast is mankind carried on by procreation and birth. Adam was immortally conscious of the fact that he was Adam and not his sons.

As man's body slowly dies daily, and that amidst torture and torment of pain, worries and troubles, and then this body is in utter decay, it would seem outwardly as if man were actually dying like a beast. But this similarity is only up to the grave. Here the similarity ends, as Solomon in Ecclesiastes so forcefully shows, man's spirit "goeth upward" to God and the spirit of the beast "goeth downward to the earth." As man's spirit, which was given him by God, turns upward, he remains *he,* self-conscious, continuing in the soul, which is separated from the body.

What sort of destiny is to be theirs who are vessels of mercy? Peter continues, "To an inheritance incorruptible and undefiled, and that fadeth not away, reserved in heaven for you."

This inheritance of all such vessels of mercy, then, is in heaven. It is no more on earth, as would have been Adam's if he had not sinned. The inheritance of such is — as is their soul in separation from the body which has decayed — immortal, or incorruptible. But what in the vessels of mercy is saved? The body? The spirit? The soul?

Reading on in 1 Peter 1:9, I got a startling answer: "Receiving the end of your faith, even the salvation of *your souls.*" If then the "vessels of mercy" experience salvation of their souls with Jesus Christ, what about the "vessels of wrath," fit only for destruction? Especially so since both the just and the unjust will receive resurrection bodies in the Day of Judgment (John 5:28,29) .

Hell Is a Place

Slowly I began to realize that what Peter is saying here is, that these "vessels of mercy" have a soul which, while they are dead physically, lives on. For why else, if they did not live on, would it matter if they were saved? If the end of their salvation of the soul is an inheritance in heaven, then they are in a *place?* If the souls of those who are "vessels of mercy" are in a place called heaven, then those who are "vessels of wrath," whose souls are not saved, must be somewhere else. If not, then all of this makes no sense whatever.

I was really getting into something here that was quite damaging to my smug Jehovah's Witnesses reasoning. At once I had to ask myself, If it is the souls of the "vessels of mercy" which are saved, and that in heaven, what happens to the souls of the "vessels of wrath"? With a soul-piercing shock, I realized how foolish I had been glibly to use Eccl. 3:18,19 as depicting soul annihilation, especially when I read in the 21st verse, "Who knoweth the spirit of man that goeth upward?" Nobody knows that by himself, nor by reason of other humans and their teachings. God alone knows that.

God knows — for He knows "what is in man." What God already knows about my destiny, alas, will become common knowledge in the Day of Judgment when all will be revealed. If that is so, then I will be there: either as a "vessel of mercy" or a "vessel of wrath." It will be I, either in a body of evil in which a perverted soul will recognize itself, and I will therefore know it; or in a new and glorious body saved by grace with all deformity and sins eradicated by the blood of Jesus Christ.

Daniel writes of that Day of Judgment when all this will be revealed: "And many of them that sleep in the dust of the earth shall awake, some to everlasting life, and some to shame and everlasting contempt" (Dan. 12:2). Shame and contempt are vivid feelings which are possible only because the soul, or self-consciousness of the creature, is alive! If these feelings are everlasting, then what is the fate of the soul? It is either eternal life or eternal death!

Could this really be, I mused? The chain reference of Daniel 12 led me to our Lord's words where He says, "Marvel not at this; for the hour is coming in which all that are in the graves [the Greek here means "remembrance"] shall hear his voice, and shall come forth: they that have done good [built up their God-consciousness in the spirit] unto the resurrection of life; and they that have done evil [lived only to gratify a sense-consciousness of their depraved flesh] unto the resurrection of damnation" (John 5:28,29).

This text says *all* that are in the graves, *all* without exception will hear that call! This is a call not only for the body, but is a call for the soul to reunite with the body! That is what *resurrection* means. If that is so, then the grave must have been the point of separation of body from soul. If this were not so the term resurrection would make no sense whatever.

This text speaks of the resurrection of all — to be united again, body and soul. Bodies may be in the sea or in the earth; both are their graves. When that call for resurrection goes forth, and new bodies are received, or old ones brought together from the fragments of the earth, then even the appearance of these will already indicate their eternal destiny. The soul of the wicked will be reunited with its erstwhile body, reflecting the evil he practiced on earth before he died, to live in everlasting shame and contempt. On the other hand, the soul that was saved by the blood of Jesus Christ and cleansed white, will receive a new wonderful glorified body that will instantly respond to every command of its soul for good. Such a body will shine like a star in heaven. That will *be life* as it was meant for the "vessel of glory." Then, Paul says He will "change our vile body, that it may be fashioned like unto His glorious body."

Those having lost the *image and likeness of God* shall never find it in the resurrection, unless it has once again become impressed upon them in a new birth in the spirit. Then they will receive a body fashioned after His glorious body. Otherwise they will appear in the image of the earthly Adam to "everlasting shame and contempt."

The end almost always reveals more about the beginning than does the beginning. With great interest I read of this sad fact as displayed in Eccl. 8:6, "For to every purpose there is a time and judgment, therefore the misery of man *is* great upon him [here and hereafter]." Why? Because he is conscious, "For he knoweth not that which shall be; for who can tell him when it shall be? There is no man that hath power over the spirit to retain the spirit; neither hath he power in the day of death."

My utter foolishness to believe the grave to be the end of the soul was brought forcibly home to me as I continued to read this Scripture to which I had been led. In the second portion of verse 8 of chapter 8 "and *there is no discharge in that war*: neither shall wickedness deliver those that are given unto it." Oh Lord, what an escape! Where had I been traveling? I had been telling so many that the wicked are annihilated! That the grave is the end!

But still not knowing the full measure of this truth, I kept on reading the 8th chapter of Ecclesiastes to the tenth verse:

"And so I saw the wicked buried, who had come and gone from the place of the holy, and they were forgotten in the city where they had done so: ... because sentence against an evil work is not executed speedily, therefore the heart of the sons of men is fully set in them to do evil."

What was I reading here? All of this turned out to be a description of what happens to the wicked after he dies and has been buried, as shown in verse 8. With full force came the implication of all this into my mind as I continued reading the 12th and 13th verses, "Though a sinner do evil a hundred times, and his days be prolonged, yet surely I know that it shall be well with them that fear God, which fear before him; but it shall not be well with the wicked, neither shall he prolong his days, which are as a shadow; because he feareth not God."

Search as I will, I cannot find out the destiny of each and every soul individually, and thus Eccl. 8:17 concludes, "Then I beheld all the work of God, that a man cannot find out the work that is done under the sun: because though a man labor to seek it out, yet he shall not find it: yea further: though a wise man may think to know it, yet shall he not be able to find it." The answer to man's destiny cannot be found on earth under the sun, as that of a beast can be determined, because man was created "in the image and likeness of God" who is in heaven.

I now know it, because I have learned to appreciate what our Lord Jesus said in John 5:28,29. There will be a day of Judgment of the "vessels of mercy" and "the vessels of wrath," and I, and we all will be there and *we will know it.* It may be the most shameful and contemptuous experience of our existence, setting an eternal pattern of immortality; or the most glorious and joyous experience of our existence, in such heavenly places as eye hath not seen, nor ear has heard of.

Human Terms Seek to Describe the Fate of the Soul

"Dust" and "grave," "sleep" and "death" are vivid human terms used to describe man's departure from physical life on earth. Where does man go when he leaves the earth? Has the war come to an end for him? Death and grave seem to be the gates by which man leaves the earthly scene. Is death and the grave, Hell? If they are, do the good and the evil both go there? If they do, why is a distinction made between "vessels of mercy" and "vessels of wrath"? This was tantalizing me. It agitated my innermost soul.

This much I know. When men began to die, they learned how to dig a grave. As they described what they had dug, those who spoke Hebrew called it *Queber* or sometimes *geburah*. Here is where my Bible dictionary came in handy.

Thoughtfully, since they really did not know what truly happened to man in the grave, other than that the worms ate up his body, they were unsure what happened to his identity or person, or his soul. Then divine revelation led them to another term, *sheol*. Sheol to them quite often embraced more than the grave. It meant to them the "place of the unseen dead." In many places in the Hebrew Bible we see the context limit the meaning of this remarkable word Sheol just to the grave. But in far more places the context gives its full meaning much broader play as the place of the unseen dead. This was a vague foreshadowing of a future life.

While *Queber* can always be translated "grave," it is so translated, I seem to find, thirty-seven times in the Old Testament. Sheol should never have been translated at all. Its true meaning is always determined by the context in which it is found. The King James Version translated this remarkable word Sheol: thirty-one times "grave"; thirty-one times "hell"; three times "pit."

As for *Queber* or grave, it may belong to a person and thus be located in a definite locale and can be dug, or hewn out of a rock (Gen. 50:5). There are many graves in the land (Ezek. 14:11), and people when dead, are laid into a grave (1 Kings 13:30). In cemeteries graves are located alongside each other (2 Sam. 19:37). Often men sprinkle dust over a grave (2 Kings 23:6).

This was certainly revealing to me, as we of the Watchtower did not use the term *Queber* very much. We preferred to insist on Sheol. But Sheol, I began to find out as I continued studies in the Bible without Watchtower helps, in most instances, is not apposite to the body. It is apposite, or fitting only to be used in connection with the soul.

Now wait, said my conscience: certainly a body has been known to go to Sheol. Often the context makes Sheol out to be the grave. But, such Scriptures which we Jehovah's Witnesses used, as "the dead know not anything," or "that they cannot work in the grave, nor have they any more a reward," etc., with what did they deal? Let me check. Context after context was read. Every context on these various Scriptures used by the Jehovah's Witnesses shows that they speak of the sense-perceptions of the body, and not about the soul.

Because these Scriptures show this, the cults love to tear them out of context, ostensibly to fling them at historic Christianity, but more subtly to deceive. Our Jehovah's Witness technique was to rivet a Christian's attention on these torn out verses so that the context would escape him.

As to what these Scriptures, so lovingly used by the Jehovah's Witnesses, actually mean if left in their context, I will demonstrate to you in a coming chapter by full use of the context. With great surprise you will then see that such texts were deliberately torn out, to blind the eyes of the unwary to precious truths embodied in them. You will then appreciate why the apostle describes the doctrines of heresy as doctrines of demons. It is Satan's work, and diabolically clever.

Sheol, unlike *Queber,* does not always mean "grave." We read of "the sorrows of Sheol" in 2 Sam. 22:6. Surely there is no sorrow of any kind, or any kind of feeling in the grave, where the body with its sense perceptions destroyed, is buried (Eccl. 9:5,10).

In Deut. 32:22, the word Sheol is wrongly translated "Hell." Man's anger already reaches to the grave or Sheol. But that the fire of God's wrath goes beyond the grave, is really what Deut. 32:22 postulates. This, in fact, is one of the clear projections of Hell beyond the grave. The grave, as is death, is but one of the gateways to Hell (Luke 16:22,23).

Pursuing this fascinating subject further, I noticed that revelations given to prophets brought to the fore the first contrasting statements regarding the destiny of souls. This left the destiny of the body in the grave. Job, under inspiration, could already in his day say, "Canst thou by searching, find out God? Canst thou find out the Almighty unto perfection?" (Job 11:7).

For that matter, What is the range of God's love, or the depth of His wrath? That is what Job is driving at. That is what is definitely in his mind, for he continues, "It is as high as heaven; what canst thou do? deeper than Sheol; what canst thou know?" (Job 11:8).

As my study continued, and much later in the stream of

time, I came across a remarkable thought expressed by the Psalmist, of whom I know that he was under inspiration, which is, "If I ascend up into heaven, thou art there. If I make my bed in Sheol, behold thou art there" (Ps. 139:8).

We all know that God is alive in heaven. Thus we can easily follow David's statement that He is alive there, and being omnipresent, would reach alive into the Sheol. He certainly would not be or go alive to the grave, where they cannot hear, feel, see, talk and walk! Thus Sheol here, is the place of the dead, but lo, they are "living dead." They are most certainly such whose bodies have already been eaten by worms of the earth, and whose bones have already been burned up by chemical actions. While the bodies of the dead have thus been dissolved, still there will be many souls who shall continuously experience "where the worm dieth not, and the fire is not quenched." But that is another matter, to be discussed later.

Amos, living much later than David, searchingly and under inspiration, came even nearer to this truth. He says, "Though they dig into Sheol, thence shall mine hand take them; though they climb to heaven, thence will I bring them down" (Amos 9:2). In any case, observe that they are alive, though they are already physically dead.

As God's anointed king, David was sorely oppressed by enemies. These were the worst kind of enemies. They were treacherous ones. Wishing to be rid of them, note David's prayer, "Let death seize upon them, and let them go down quick into Sheol: for wickedness is in their dwellings, and among them" (Ps. 55:15). I have to concede, David already knew more about Hell than the Jehovah's Witnesses do. Imagine, David shows that even after death has seized upon them, their souls go alive to the Sheol; and, it is a place where such souls as they fittingly dwell and have suitable company. David figured shrewdly that once they were dispatched there, they would not bother him. This was good reasoning, wonderful discernment of the destiny of the wicked. But first of all, it was God's revelation.

While Eccl. 9:5,10, which the Jehovah's Witnesses like to use so much, conclusively shows that all sense perceptions of the body are gone in the grave, there being no feeling whatsoever, David already was aware, as taught by Holy Spirit, which I now know is a lot better than being taught by the *Watchtower Society*, that there "is pain in Sheol." While sorely afflicted he could meaningly cry out in the 116th Psalm, verse 3, "The sorrows of death compassed me, and the pains of Sheol got hold of me; I found trouble and sorrow." He obviously did not expect oblivion in Sheol, but trouble and sorrow and pain. How different from the grave does he depict Sheol! More importantly, how fully he connected the torment and torture of "dying thou shalt die" with the continuance of the soul in Sheol!

Associating pain with the Sheol, David gave eloquent witness that he had begun to understand the doctrine of Hell as being a place of eternal punishment in torment. However, he did not clearly enunciate it. Why? It had not yet been fully revealed to him. However, already he looked upon death and the grave as the gates of Hell (Luke 16:23,24), and already he expressed the hope that these gates would not prevail against him (Matt. 16:18). The Holy Spirit was already planting this hope in the hearts of men.

Speaking in the same vein as Isaiah had spoken, Amos warns Israel, "I have overthrown some of you, as God overthrew Sodom and Gomorrah, and ye were as a firebrand plucked out of the burning: and yet have ye not returned unto the Lord" (Amos 4:11). With the brush of true comprehension Amos depicts this whole nation as being on the road to Hell, and of burning in Sheol, but as being arrested on its course by the grace of God and plucked out of burning for salvation. On their way to death and the grave, they were also on their way to Hell. Amos already understood the destiny and fate of the wicked.

Slowly now, as I continued reading God's word, the Bible, I was beginning to see things by way of discernment rather than by way of indoctrination. The fate of the dead, so long shrouded in my befuddled and brainwashed mind, was coming clear. I now discerned that the Jews spoke of *Sheol,* and the Greeks of *Hades.*

By this time, however, I had become intensely interested. You already are guessing what was happening, are you not? I asked myself, What did Jesus say it was? What did He call it? To my surprise I found that *He* called it Hell, or better, Gehenna. Why did He call it Gehenna? As a Jehovah's Witness I was taught to lay emphasis on this being the name of a place outside of Jerusalem, in the valley of Hinnom, in which the trash and garbage of the city of Jerusalem was burnt up. A perpetual fire was kept there. Was Jesus talking about a dump?

I could no longer go along with what Jehovah's Witnesses were being taught by the IMAGE, the WATCHTOWER SOCIETY — not after what I already had learned, as you have read so far. Hinnom, valley of Hinnom! Where did I hear that before in my reading in the Bible? Had I not just a little while ago read about it? Well, to the Bible Dictionary! Ah, there it is.

The valley of Hinnom is first mentioned in Josh. 15:8 and in Josh. 18:11. In the days of the kings of Judah the valley Hinnom was the scene of worship by torturing children to death with fire (2 Chron. 28:3; 36:6). Still later they built a shrine for worship to a god called Molech, the fire god. This type of worship was a derisive farce set up by the devil himself to ridicule the emerging doctrine of Hell as a place of eternal punishment in torment, by portraying it as if it was but a passing stage. There was nothing eternal about it at all!

That is precisely what I as one of Jehovah's Witnesses had been doing, raising all sorts of flippant points to laugh at Hell. I shuddered. Oh, Lord, forgive me.

Looking further into the Bible Dictionary, I discovered that much later the king Josiah, who was a faithful man, razed Molech to the ground in the valley of Hinnom. That is how the valley of Hinnom was turned into a dump.

Satan's ridicule of Hell, enacted daily in passing through the fire before Molech, and earlier the throwing in of live humans into the flames thus depicting the torment of its flames to be of a fleeting nature, was now replaced by faithful Jews as a dump into which they threw garbage, trash and the dead bodies of criminals.

To refute Satan's ridicule of Hell as a place of eternal punishment in torment, Jesus by usage approved the word which had come to describe the place that the devil had misused as the valley of Hinnom, namely "Gehenna." The Lord thus tore the veil of ridicule and mystery away from what had been practiced in the valley of Hinnom. It was not, as the Jehovah's Witnesses so conveniently assert, only a reference to a place for garbage disposal. Jesus was not here talking about a dump; he was speaking of Hell.

Jesus Gives It the Touch of Reality

This was getting breathtaking now. I followed the formulation of the doctrine of Hell as being a place of eternal punishment in torment, not just a fleeting pain of passing through a fire. In Matthew I learned that Gehenna (Hell) is really Christ's doctrine. He himself mentions it in Matt. 5:22, 29, 30 as Gehenna; Matt. 7:19,23, where separation from Christ is the result of eternal punishment in torment; Matt. 8:12 where (Gehenna) Hell is the condition outside of the feast showing that such recognize their being excluded proving that all the while they are conscious of not being at the feast. Matt. 11:22-24 where Hell (Gehenna) is depicted as having degrees of punishment, consciously classifying different people and types, is another point. In Matt. 12:31,32 I noted the Lord Jesus discussing Hell as punishment eternal for the unforgivable sin.

That Gehenna is not only a dump outside of Jerusalem as we Jehovah's Witnesses were taught to depict it, came clear to me in reading Matt. 13:40-42. Here it is described as a "furnace of fire." Notice the similarity of language in describing it as a furnace in the belly of Molech (2 Chron. 28:3, 36:6). How like the language of Isa. 66:24 is the Lord's description of Gehenna (Hell), in Matt. 18:6; Mark 9:42,43-48. The conscious punishment here for the first time is called by our Lord, eternal. Other similar statements are made by the Lord Jesus in Matt. 22:13, Matt. 23:15 and in this latter chapter the 31st verse. Observe how the Lord describes the "hellish" nature in lost man, which indubitably leads to Hell, which reminds us of David's same observation in Ps. 55:15.

Again I came across the Lord's use of the term Gehenna in Matt. 23:31. Still another use is gleaned from Matt. 25:30, and followed by even a more pungent use of it in verse 46.

From these Matthew, and parallel Mark and Luke passages, I piled up to my complete satisfaction overwhelming evidence that the Lord Jesus taught the doctrine of Hell as a place of eternal punishment in torment. I could not help observe that He called it emphatically, without sugar-coating it with our 20th century supersensitiveness, "unquenchable fire," "outer darkness," a place of "gnashing of teeth and wailing," and a point of no return to forgiveness, and finally, "better never to have existed" than to be in it.

The Doctrine of Hell as a Place of Eternal Punishment in Torment Is a Doctrine Once Delivered to the Saints

All kinds of human reasoning, all kinds of misuse of Scripture notwithstanding, I have come to the firm conclusion that the Bible teaches Hell — not as a grave — but as a place of ever-lasting conscious punishment.

The doctrine of Hell as a place for such punishment, I now see, thus not only comes to us as it evolved in the writings of the prophets, but is plainly accredited to us by Jesus Christ Himself.

Does believing that make me morbid? Does it make out my God a fiend? Does it make our Lord Jesus despicable? Nay, nay. To understand the seriousness of our plight as men in eternal damnation, however, *is to appreciate the magnitude of God's mercy*. That, it came so clear to me, is what Paul means in Rom. 9:21-23. If there were no eternal punishment in tor-ment in Hell, it suddenly struck me with great force, then we would not have needed a Saviour. But the Lord Jesus came to us as our Redeemer because there was this frightful destiny ahead of us all, as condemned souls who had become "vessels of wrath" fit only for destruction. How clear that becomes in His sayings!

If man were like a beast, as Jehovah's Witnesses and other cultists like to aver and eagerly vie to prove by misusing Scripture, then man would not be lost. As soon as he died, he would perish and that would be the end of him as a self-conscious being. He would never recognize himself anywhere. His thoughts, words and acts, performed in this body would not in Judgment be resurrected, would not need to come into Judgment before God. Only as a beast, before he died, he would have begotten children and thus the race would live on in them and after his KIND. That is what happens in the animal king-dom, to which Jehovah's Witnesses compare man, as far as his destiny is concerned. If man dies like a beast, goes to the same place as a beast, then he IS NOT LOST. He would live, then live on in his offspring.

But, if man was created "in the image and likeness of God," His Maker (Gen. 1:26,27), and not like the beast after the image of his KIND (Gen. 1:24,25), then man's destiny is an eternal one. That is quite another matter, a far more serious matter (Matt. 10:28).

"Dying thou shalt die" over so long a spell of time, has shrouded in darkness our possession of "an immortal soul." We fail to appreciate that our destiny was and is, immortality! Our Lord Jesus tore the veil from our forgetfulness. How? The apostle says of His work, in part, "Who hath abolished death, and hath brought life and immortality to light through the gospel" (2 Tim. 1:10).

Why the emphasis here on "immortality and life" brought to light? Because these important facts about man and his destiny had long been shrouded in *death, grave* and the unseen *Sheol* and *Hades* darkness. The doctrine of Gehenna, or Hell, as a place of eternal punishment in torment contrastively, as taught by our Lord Jesus, brought that eternal fate, as never before, to light. Here are two sides of our eternal lot: "vessels of wrath" and "vessels of mercy" who once were meant to be "vessels of glory." The vessels of mercy receive LIFE in Jesus Christ in glory, as the "vessels of wrath" receive immortality of a living death.

Not only did our Lord Jesus bring forth to view the eternal destiny of Hell which awaits unrepentant sinners, but as never before, he brought forth our hope for LIFE as it had been meant to be lived, in glory! This pinpointed the enormity and scope of the act of mercy to be accomplished by the Lord Jesus right here on earth. In bringing to light for those who believed on Him, Jesus opened the way of escape from eternal punishment in torment and damnation.

The Gospel of Salvation

How I praise God, who showed us our great need by the coming of the Son, and in showing it, brought us so "great a salvation."

Chapter 7

"HELL IS THE GRAVE," SAY THE JEHOVAH'S WITNESSES AND OTHER CULTISTS

Jehovah's Witnesses have undergone a complete soul-washing. This process has been total. It was accomplished already in the first generation of the movement between 1876 and 1916. This was engineered under the able leadership of Charles T. Russell. He developed the reasonings which conjured up the new doctrines in the place of the doctrines "once delivered to the saints," or "the form of sound words" handed down to historic Christianity by our Lord Jesus Christ, the apostles and prophets.

Techniques of Heresy

It was in the period of 1876 to 1916 that Charles T. Russell developed certain techniques which have become peculiar to the Watchtower system as represented by the Jehovah's Witnesses today. The pattern etched out was this: Set up an overall statement of a doctrine. Give it a form which sounds good and different. What form that doctrine was to take, was for Russell to say, as he had become the sole arbiter. The Watchtower Society, his *image,* as later revived between 1918 to 1942, inherited this position.

When a pattern had been set, he put up a goal. In order to buoy up his doctrine, he developed the technique of "running to and fro" in the pages of the Bible and of tearing suitable passages out of context and using these arbitrarily in ever-changing combinations. Two things were achieved by this technique. One, it destroyed the acceptance by faith of those doctrines "once delivered to the saints." This was done by raising doubts about them in the minds of the prospective converts. Two, by means of "reasonings" or "reason" the true doctrine was torn to shreds and replaced with the new doctrine.

If the Jehovah's Witnesses today preach a doctrine which differs from what the Bible shows Christianity to be, it is largely due to their close adherence to Russell's credo. What was that?

"Come and Reason With Me"

Russell loved to quote Isa. 1:18, "Come now, and let us reason together, saith the Lord: though your sins be as scarlet, they shall be as white as snow; though they be red like crimson, they shall be as wool." This passage, he taught, showed that "reasoning" of man should be used in understanding the truth of the Scriptures.

Of course, Scripture means something entirely different here. God pleads with His people to accept the unchanging way of salvation as described in His unchanging Word. God wants man to change. But God's Word and truth never changes.

But it is this credo, "Come now, and reason with me," which has promoted the setting up, over, and above the Bible the so-called "present truth" published by the Watchtower Society. It is this technique of "reasoning" which every Jehovah's Witness is taught to accept and employ. It is in this way and manner that they draw converts into their net.

Doctrines Should Be Solid Fundamentals

Doctrines are very important to a Christian. Someone once said, and in this connection it bears repeating, "Doctrines are the rungs of the ladder which leads to heaven."

When were the doctrines which historic Christianity teaches established? Of the early church it is said in Acts 2:42, "And they continued steadfastly in the apostles' doctrines and fellowship and in breaking of bread, and in prayers." Not only did they believe the doctrines taught them by the apostles, but it is said of these early believers, as Luke reports in Acts 5:28, "Behold, ye have filled Jerusalem with your doctrine."

Paul rejoices in the Christians at Rome when he says in Rom. 6:17, "But God be thanked, that ye were servants of sin, but ye have obeyed from the heart *that form of doctrine* which was delivered you." Here, then, was already a definite "form of doctrine" delivered. How did the Roman Christians receive it? By reason? Or by faith? Paul says "from the heart"; by faith, not by reason.

False Doctrines Appear

However, not all in Paul's time remained in this proper receptive mood in regard to doctrines. We read of Paul's definite instructions in Rom. 16:17, "Now I beseech you, brethren, mark them which cause divisions and offenses *contrary to the doctrines* which ye have learned; and avoid them."

It was against "sound doctrines" that the onslaughts of heresy were made in the first century. Dr. Edgar Goodspeed, in the foreword to his 1900 edition of the translation of the New Testament says that one third of the writings in the text of the New Testament are concerned with the battle contra heresy in doctrines.

Thus, whatever else we may think about the cults, and in this case about the Jehovah's Witnesses, they are truthful when they boast that their doctrines have been taught since the days of the apostles. They were then, and are now, consistent improvisations of "reasonings" contra revelation of solid "sound form of words" handed down by Jesus, the apostles and prophets. In the main, heresy's technique then, as now, was to break down the "sound form of words" and make them fluid and changing. That *was* and *is,* the Modus Operandi of heresy. As you examine heresy's doctrines then, and those of Jehovah's Witnesses now, it will soon appear that theirs is not "the sound form of words" to which Timothy was admonished to hold fast (2 Tim. 1:13).

Spirit of Approach to the Jehovah's Witness Doctrine of "Hell Is the Grave"

It is in this spirit and with this knowledge that we must approach the Jehovah's Witness doctrine that HELL IS THE GRAVE. This doctrine is taught by them in the place of the Christian doctrine that Hell is a place of eternal punishment in torment.

What is their doctrine on this point? Having examined closely the development during Old Testament times and having before us the full revelation of Hell by our Lord Jesus, we now know that it was He who "brought life and immortality to light" (2 Tim. 1:10). In the development of the Christian doctrine, which came by stages of revelation, not reasonings, such words as Sheol, Hades and finally Gehenna and Tartarus are used. As you look at these words, note how these terms are promiscuously used by the Jehovah's Witnesses to create doubt about the Christian doctrine. They are juggled and sometimes lumped together as one, to buttress the Jehovah's Witness doctrine.

Jehovah's Witnesses' Textbook Speaks

We get the authentic and full statement of the Jehovah's Witness doctrine HELL IS THE GRAVE, from their overall textbook, MAKE SURE OF ALL THINGS, as stated on page 154:

Hell, a definition.

"False religion teaches that hell is a place where the wicked suffer a two-fold punishment; the pain of loss, and the pain of sense. The pain of loss consists in the eternal separation of the sinner from God and the realization that the failure to reach heaven is due to his fault. The pain of sense consists in the torment of unquenchable fire. It is claimed that the body by itself is incapable of pain; it is the soul that suffers.

"This unreasonable doctrine contradicts the Bible, the truth of which has been confused by misrepresenting in translations of the original meaning of three distinct Greek words and one Hebrew word. Sheol, in Hebrew, and Hades, in Greek, were originally used by the Bible writers to represent gravedom, or the common grave of mankind. Gehenna, in Greek, was used as a symbol of annihilation or everlasting death in unconsciousness from which there was no awakening. Tartarus, in Greek, meant a degraded or debased condition only for rebellious spirit creatures during their conscious lifetime with the certainty of annihilation awaiting them at the time of their execution. These original words have been discriminately translated 'hell,' 'hell-fire,' 'grave,' 'pit' and 'death.' The English word 'hell' is taken from the Anglo-Saxon 'helan,' literally meaning 'to conceal.' Hence, the English word 'hell,' to conform with the original meaning, scripturally applies to gravedom, the common grave of mankind, good and bad alike, in an unconscious state without suffering or pleasure. After Jesus introduced the truth about life and immortality, only the willfully wicked were spoken of as being in 'Gehenna.' The expression Hades (translated hell) being applied to the dead in God's memory, those with opportunity or hope of a resurrection.

ORIGIN

"The false conception of eternal torment after death was introduced early in apostate Christianity, and by the fourth century after Christ was firmly entrenched in false religion. It is based on Satan's lie in Eden."

Note at the close of this quotation an overall statement. This illustrates their technique. Jehovah's Witnesses use many Scripture passages, torn out of context, to buttress the above overall statement. This is done in an adroit manner and gives Bible color to their cross statement of denial of the historic Christian doctrine that Hell is a place of eternal punishment in torment. In this overall statement they include every ingredient to subvert the true doctrine by reasonings. You will see this most clearly in what follows.

Examples of Jehovah's Witnesses' Reasonings

In the first column they use Rom. 5:12, 3:23 and 6:23. These passages are used to lend color to their interpretation of death and grave. Instead of showing "hell" to be the common lot of all mankind in death and grave, these really point up, as Paul intends to show in Romans, that ALL have sinned, that ALL fall short of the glory of God, no longer being "vessels of glory" for which purpose they had been created in "the image and likeness of God" (Gen. 1:26,27).

Only half of the transition verse of Rom. 6:23 is used by them in their quote. This is done artfully to cover up its true point. They quote only "for the wages of sin is death." In this way they ignore "but the gift of God is eternal life through Jesus Christ our Lord."

Their failure of explicitly using this transition verse of Rom. 6:23 *in toto,* can immediately be used to show their method of twisting God's word. It presages what is coming. Be on guard!

How does it show this? I asked myself, Why is the second clause left out? The reason is evident. The second clause in application, proves that both the good and the bad live after death, as "vessels of mercy" and "vessels of wrath." Read John 5:24, "Verily, verily, I say unto you, he that heareth my word, and believeth on him that sent me, hath everlasting life, and shall not come into condemnation; but is passed from death to life."

It is this truth, which the Jehovah's Witnesses wish to hide. According to this passage of Scripture a believer instantly passes from death to life, as he is saved. From earliest times, millions of such saved ones have died and have been put into the grave. Did Jesus lie about their present state? Are these unconsciously "in the grave of all mankind"? That is what

Jehovah's Witnesses say in their overall statement of doctrine. If they are alive, is it their body, or is it the soul?

Note how this misused passage (Rom. 6:23), when placed in context, can be turned against their false improvisation.

Was Jesus Left in Sheol?

The next set of passages they misuse are: Ps. 16:10 and Acts 2:27: "For thou wilt not leave my soul in the Sheol," and "Because thou wilt not leave my soul in Hades."

They use these passages to bear up their doctrine, that Jesus Christ was not bodily resurrected. In their thinking He came forth only in the Spirit. They claim that His body was dissolved and that He assumed or created a body for each occasion of His appearance after the resurrection. This is, of course, a flat contradiction of Luke 24:36ff.

But let us now turn the tables on them for their misuse of these Scriptures. In both passages it is shown that the soul of Jesus was not left in Sheol-Hades, which is the place of the unseen dead, as we learned the ancients called it. Jesus' soul was not left in the common grave of all mankind! How was this Scripture fulfilled?

Read the inspired account by Peter, "For Christ also hath once suffered for sins, the just for the unjust, that He might bring us to God, being put to death *in the flesh* [not soul] but quickened by the Spirit: by which He also went and preached unto the spirits in prison" (1 Peter 3:18,19).

Note, His spirit was quickened and not left in the grave. Note also, not in the form of flesh, but in the spirit and in all consciousness did He preach to the spirits in prison. Indeed, as promised in Acts 2:27 and Ps. 16:10. His soul was not left in Sheol-Hades.

But far more important to us, who depend upon this marvelous evidence for our future resurrection, His body was resurrected on the third day, and forty days later He ascended on high to heaven with it.

This fact is crucially important to us, as Paul rightly asserts when he says, "Wherefore he saith, When he ascended up on high, . . . what is it but that he also descended first into the lower parts of the earth? He that descended is the same also that ascended up far above all heavens, that he might fill all things" (Eph. 4:8-10).

When he descended to the lower parts of the earth, as we noted previously, "he preached unto the spirits in prison," and when he ascended on high "he took captivity captive." Only those who are conscious can be imprisoned. At this time the Jews already believed in Paradise, and they called it Abraham's lap. That is why they fully understood the Lord's depiction of Lazarus in Abraham's lap, to mean Paradise, and Dives place to mean "hell."

As the Lord preached to the captives in Sheol-Hades, so would historic Christianity by its example of testimony preach to those alive. This statement is followed to show the arrangement for such preaching of the good news. It is, as has been shown in a previous chapter, against this arrangement that the Jehovah's Witnesses have rebelled. For that reason they have become totally blind to this great doctrine.

From what has just been explained, note, how the Jehovah's Witnesses can only walk a mile in Scripture support for their error, whereas we go right on two miles and then some.

Make Sure of All Things Affords Us Another
"Ripping" Example

Here is another example of ripping a text in twain. In the second column, page 155 of MAKE SURE OF ALL THINGS, we come upon another citation of a half-verse. Luke 12:5 is quoted by them to bear up the doctrine that Gehenna is annihilation. This passage reads in the KJV, "But I will forewarn you whom you shall fear: Fear him, which after he hath killed hath power to cast into hell: yet I say unto you, Fear him."

This passage is deliberately ripped in two in order to destroy its true meaning. Let us read the other part of Luke 12:4, which is by them cunningly omitted: "And I say unto you my friends, be not afraid of them that kill the body, and after that have no more that they can do."

By reading verses 4 and 5 together, which the Jehovah's Witnesses endeavor to thwart by focusing your attention solely upon verse 5, this passage proves that Gehenna is Hell, and not the grave, but far more serious a fate than is physical death! To prevent your seeing this, the astute Watchtower Society uses only verse 5 in its official textbook. This is deliberate subversion.

What really does this ruse teach us? It teaches us first of all to read the Scripture which the Jehovah's Witnesses have torn out of context to uphold their false doctrine and then to read the context itself. Never fail to do that. The context usually shows up the misuse the Watchtower Society has made of that Scripture. It can also become an eye-opener to a Jehovah's Witness right in front of you.

Going Alive to Sheol

Another passage is cited in MAKE SURE OF ALL THINGS. They quote Num. 16:33, "They, and all that appertained to them went down alive into the pit (Sheol), and the earth closed upon them; and they perished from among the congregation."

This passage as above quoted no more or no less, is actually marshaled to uphold their doctrine that HELL IS THE GRAVE. The context, however, of the entire 16th chapter of Numbers shows that these were treacherous enemies of the congregation and that their punishment was so sudden that it completely took them out of sight of the congregation. In other words they did not die in the ordinary way and were not buried in the ordinary way of sinners, but the Sheol swallowed them up alive. They did not go through the ordinary gates: death and a grave.

Jehovah's Witnesses will say this is not so. To prove that it was so, let me quote David's inspired plea for the same thing to happen to his treacherous enemies. He actually prays, "Let death seize upon them all and let them go down quick [like the Korahites in Numbers 16:33] into Hell [Sheol]: for wickedness is in their dwellings, and among them" (Ps. 55:15).

Wickedness, as you read in the context of Num. 16:33, was in the dwellings of the Korahites. It was truly among them. In this manner they were suddenly taken and blotted out as a pest, by going alive without death and grave, into Hell.

Hiding the Grave

Much ado is made by the Jehovah's Witnesses of Job 14:3. On page 156 of MAKE SURE OF ALL THINGS, they quote, "Oh, that thou wouldst hide me in the grave, that thou wouldst keep me in secret, until thy wrath be passed, that thou wouldst appoint me a time, and remember me."

Again, please observe their technique. That is what I want to fully impress upon you. This verse, too, is torn out of its context. Why? This is done in order to prove that the meaning of the Hebrew word Sheol is always grave. This is done to buttress their false doctrine that HELL IS THE GRAVE.

I invite you now to use with me the Christian technique of debunking heresy. What happens when you read the whole 14th chapter of Job? Let us read it and see. . . .

It is actually a comparison of man to flowers, trees, etc., and of man enclosed in God's wrath. The statement is then made that when a tree is chopped down, or dies, its hope to sprout out anew and live again lies in water reaching its roots. Like animals, trees and flowers, man's body is condemned to return to dust to decay. But here is where the likeness ends. Unlike them, man does not come back as himself in the body. Why not?

To crown this we read in the 10th verse, "But man dieth, and wasteth away: yea, man giveth up the spirit [breath of lives: Hebrew] and where is he?" In the grave? Dead? Unconscious?

Comes back Job's inspired answer, "If a man die, shall he live again?" What did Job expect to lose when he died? As the context shows, he expected to lose his body or sense consciousness, as did the tree and the flower. But he did not expect to lose his soul. With the faith of the true Old Testament believers, who were highly regarded by God, as Paul shows in Heb. 11, Job sings out the great truth concerning Sheol, "All the days of my appointed time will I wait, till my change come." If Job was expecting to be unconscious in the common grave of mankind, then for him time would be no more. Time: days to come, waiting through them, implies if anything, consciousness! (Rev. 6:9-10) .

There is more to come. Job continues in the 15th verse, "Thou shalt call, and I will answer thee." Whom will the Lord call? The body alone? No, more than that. Job says, "I will answer thee." Who is I? It is the person Job, soul and body, who will answer the Lord.

The 14th chapter of Job closes with this clear indication of what happens in the Sheol. Speaking of man and his demise Job depicts man's end in the flesh and portrays the loss of his body. Job further shows man's inability to keep track of the sensual world once his body has died and he has lost his sense perception. It is exactly as we read in Eccl. 9:5,10, "For the living know that they shall die: but the dead know not any thing, neither have they any more a reward; for the memory of them is forgotten. . . . Whatsoever thy hand findeth to do, do it with all thy might; for there is no work, nor device, nor knowledge, nor wisdom in the Sheol [grave implied by context] whither thou goest."

Even though the body is dead, unable to know and do anything about the life on earth, Job speaks in the 22nd verse, "But his flesh upon him shall pain and his soul within him shall mourn." Who is described here? This is the man who died without hope. This man is not like Job. Although the fire of chemical reaction have consumed the bones and the worms have gnawed the flesh away, for such there still is pain.

As for the destiny of Job, what was it? Job had faith. He expressed it in the 14th and 15th verses. He says here that he will wait for the Lord to call him.

He knows the Lord will call his soul and body and spirit together again. That is why he has peace and rest. His flesh does not burn in reflection on him as it burns upon the soul of one who knows it will get back again the body once it has gone to Hell. As far as his sense perceptions are concerned, Job's case with the Lord rests, because he has faith in the Lord and his call. That is why his soul is not now tortured and tormented with what is to come, but is tranquil and restful. But note this outstanding factor here, both Job and the man described in pain, are described as being conscious! And that after death!

What a beautiful description of the Sheol is that found in Job 14. But to destroy it for you, the Jehovah's Witnesses deliberately tear from its context a small verse, verse 13. In this way they hope to rivet your attention on what *they* want you to see. They hope thus to prevent you from seeing what the Lord caused Job to write there these many centuries ago.

Common Grave of Mankind?

Continuing our examination of the Jehovah's Witnesses' textbook MAKE SURE OF ALL THINGS on Hell, we find Jehovah's Witnesses misusing Isa. 38:10,11, on page 156. They quote, "I said, in the noontide of my days, I shall go to the gates of Sheol [die and be buried]: I am deprived of the residue of my years. I said, I shall not see Jehovah, even Jehovah in the land of the living: I shall behold man no more with the inhabitants of the world."

To what use is this passage put by the Jehovah's Witnesses? It is used to show that dead men are in "the common grave of mankind," unconscious. But note again, what the context teaches out of which this passage was torn.

The context begins with the 9th verse and ends with the 20th. Observe how the reading of the context furnishes you with the Christian techniques for debunking heresy. Read this passage for yourself before continuing.

Now that you have read the context, let us examine it. Hezekiah had been very ill. During his illness he learned a lesson taught him by Jehovah. What was that lesson? He learned not to live in the flesh, gratifying the bodily senses, which could only result in bitterness (verse 17). Rather, he learned to deliver his soul (self-consciousness), to deliver it now while he was alive in the flesh, from the corruption of the body. Having been delivered in his living from sin of the body and in the soul, he says, "For thou hast cast all my sins behind thy back."

He says that in this new state of affairs he can truly live, and see Jehovah, the great God in whose image and likeness he was created. "The living, the living, he shall praise thee, as I do this day: the father to the children shall make known thy truth" (Isa. 38:19). This is a great truth! This is life . . . this living in the land of the living! Let the flesh, which goes on to corruption in the grave die *now,* as Hezekiah learned, so that your soul may be delivered from its works and already unencumbered by it now, can soar in the spirit to live forever!

That is what Isa. 38:10,11 teaches when read in its context. The Jehovah's Witnesses do not want you to see that. That is why the Watchtower Society rivets your attention to just verses 10 and 11. In this manner you become blind to what Hezekiah really learned during his illness.

Conclusion

Every passage the official textbook of the Jehovah's Witnesses, MAKE SURE OF ALL THINGS, used on pages 154-164, to prove HELL IS THE GRAVE, and there are many, can easily be refuted by using the Christian technique of debunking heresy. Let them quote, then stop them at the end of quote, get your Bible, and read the context.

Always, when you are confronted with the crude procedure of cultists to rip a passage out of context, lovingly put it back into context again.

Do not let Jehovah's Witnesses and other cultists in your hearing and presence bandy God's word about. Do not permit them to perform a juggling act before you. Stop them. Read the passage they misuse, then continue to put it back into its right place right before their eyes. *Defend the word of God,* and in so doing you will "earnestly contend for the faith once delivered to the saints." In that manner, you will repel the enemy's subtle onslaught against your faith, and may be instrumental in winning lost souls for Christ. It is as simple as all that.

Chapter 8

WHICH IS TRUE: HELL IS A PLACE OF ETERNAL PUNISHMENT IN TORMENT, OR HELL IS THE GRAVE?

Do Not Accept Doctrine by Reasoning

Never rationalize a doctrine of historic Christianity with its opposite heretical doctrine in comparison! If you do so, you unconsciously give room to the doctrine of heresy in your thinking. Heretical doctrines have remained alive because defenders of doctrines of historic Christianity have done so in the past. Why is this so? Why has the controversy continued without conclusion when in speaking about the Christian doctrine of the deity of Christ, the apostle could close out all argument about the matter by saying "that no man can say that Jesus is the Lord, but by the Holy Spirit" (1 Cor. 12:3)?

All doctrines "once delivered unto the saints" have remained dominant within the precincts of historic Christianity, because they are accepted by faith as the truth revealed by our Lord Jesus, the apostles and prophets. It was sufficient for Timothy to have the apostle Paul admonish him, "Hold fast the form of sound words, which thou hast heard from me, *in faith* and love which is in Christ Jesus. That good thing which was committed unto thee keep by the Holy Spirit which dwelleth in us" (2 Tim. 1:13,14). Why then, have these doctrines remained dominant? Because the Holy Spirit upheld them within the believing hearts of Christians ever thereafter, as generation came, and generation went.

Doctrines of Heresy Brought In by Demons

To say that there is a "theology" of the cults is a gross misnomer, and shows a complete lack of understanding of the cults. Doctrines "of demons" came in early to oppose true Christian doctrines. What are these doctrines? These are the views of man or men, and not of God, which are believed by others because they become convinced by specious "reasonings" which tickled their ears. Looking for something new many listen to what is said about new doctrines. Finally, they accept them. Why? They like human reasonings better than to exercise faith in the Lord and His word. They are followers of men in a natural way, and accept "hearsay" more readily than revelation.

Heretical doctrines are only possible as such, apart from revealed truth, in the position of error in opposition to truth. Men raise doctrines in order to pervert true doctrines. In this manner they employ the techniques of demons, or of Satan, whose title means "opposer." They use the Scriptures in the way the devil does, quoting wrongly in order to deceive. Thus it is inherently impossible to discuss the doctrines of the cults rationally by comparing them with the doctrines once delivered to the saints. Here is why it will fail.

Two Kinds of Knowledge

In other words, there are two kinds of knowledge: (1) true knowledge as revealed by Christ Jesus, the apostles and prophets, and (2) false knowledge in the form of conclusions through the process of faulty "reasonings" or reasoning from false premises. How can that be shown conclusively?

For thirty years I was one of the Jehovah's Witnesses. I not only had accepted their doctrines, but was quite effective in teaching them to others, winning several hundred into the cult. Not only was I able to instill these false doctrines into the thinking of new converts, but to teach whole congregations to go out and win others. Thus the fact that I could successfully teach their doctrines and cause others to embrace them proves that I did know them.

Thus I worked for the propagation of heresy. In this same manner as do all good Jehovah's Witnesses, so also I worked for salvation. It was with me a very serious matter, as it is with many Jehovah's Witnesses today. In the course of time, alas, I never received assurance of salvation. Increasingly, this worried me. A heart attack laid me low, and very much like many other men before, in sickness I was arrested in my foolish way. After rising from my sick bed I was a different man. In the face of death and the grave, I had come free from sin and death.

By 1952 I despaired completely of implementing that experience, and in prayer that night of April 18, I abjectly repented my wrong course of life of thirty years. I frankly asked to be saved, to "have my soul within me delivered," as Hezekiah called it. What I had not been able to do in thirty years of hard work, the Lord did for me that night. He saved my soul. I came free.

Lord Takes Hold to Teach New Kind of Knowledge

How was I saved? Was I saved by the reasonings of some man? No, I was saved by faith in the Lord Jesus. Note, only then did the hand of the Lord take hold of me. By making the situation he caused me to be put into circumstances where "the water of truth" in the past seven years has totally washed away all errors. By His grace I not only have found salvation, but also light and truth. I have subsequently come into a new kind of knowledge, learning to appreciate and understand fully the doctrines of historic Christianity.

The Lord has thus placed me into a unique position. I have now, by His grace, complete comprehension of two kinds of knowledge. Being born again, the Holy Spirit works and dwells within me, fructifying the knowledge of the doctrines of historic Christianity. Thus the doctrines of Christianity are now upheld by the Holy Spirit in my heart by faith. In my memory, sharper than ever, I retain the doctrines of heresy which I so indelibly stamped into it. I have now come to maturity "in Christ" and thus I can, right within me, review both sets of doctrines; and I confess that in every instance the Holy Spirit convinces me of the excellency of the doctrines of historic Christianity. Thus the Holy Spirit has become *the* power to uphold the true doctrines in my heart. Not only has the battle been joined in the past seven years since I came free, but it has been won by revelation and light and truth.

One can only talk out of the fulness of his heart, and describe only what has happened. Be not surprised therefore, if I have used in writing this book the pattern as it was spun within me to bring me to the light. Note the plan? In Chapter 6, I portrayed the doctrine of Christianity of Hell as a place of eternal punishment in torment and in Chapter 7, I allowed the Jehovah's Witnesses through their textbook, MAKE SURE OF ALL THINGS, to do their best to assert that HELL IS THE GRAVE. Which of the two shines in the greater excellency? Behold, and see, and experience how the Holy Spirit will uphold the true doctrine in your heart.

Recapitulating the Truth

The wrath of God came upon man when he sinned. His life,

instead of living unto the Lord, changed to dying unto the Lord. The body, in torture and torment of "dying thou shalt die," was returned to dust (Gen. 3:14), out of which elements it had been formed (Gen. 2:7; Isa. 43:7; Job 10:9), and his spirit, or God-consciousness, was returned to the Lord (Eccl. 12:7). Life unto the Lord ended and dying unto the Lord began.

The body, after death, was put into the grave. Death and the grave thus were the two outward evidences that man had died. The body was interred and decayed; the spirit had returned to God. But the soul, now without a body to express itself, where was it? If it had built up its spiritual expressions, its living unto God in the spirit, then, of course, it stands to reason that it would return to God. But what if it had lived only in the body, using only the flesh facets of the "breath of lives"? (Gen. 2:7).

What Did Jacob Think of Hell and the Grave?

All Bible writers knew what was put into *queber*, the "grave." All writers knew that man died. Jacob certainly knew that through death and the grave man entered Sheol, the place of the unseen dead. Unseen by him, of course, he could not yet distinguish what happened to those that did good, and what happened to those that did evil.

Gen. 37:35 shows at least how much he knew about Sheol. Jacob says there, "And all his sons and all his daughters rose up to comfort him, but he refused to be comforted; and, he said, For I will go down into SHEOL unto my son in mourning...." This sounds like the same language employed by Job later, in Job 14:22, describing the conscious state of a man in Sheol!

It is quite evident that Jacob in saying he would go unto his son did not mean the grave, or "the common grave of mankind." This could not be. Jacob believed the report of his sons that Joseph was devoured and digested by wild beasts and therefore was not buried in a grave. Besides, nobody *goes* mourning into the grave. Adam was sentenced to die and be placed into the grave, dead. Furthermore, nobody can go to another's grave. But the souls do go to Sheol — some in peace, some being wicked, without peace and rest. Abraham was definitely promised by the Lord, in Gen. 15:15, "And thou shalt go to thy fathers in peace; thou shalt be buried in a good old age."

Where Were Abraham's Fathers?

Where did Abraham consider his forefathers to be? If he had

thought of them as being in the "common grave of mankind" then it would not at all have mattered to Abraham whether he went to them in peace, or to Jacob whether he went mourning to his son. It mattered only — and this is the point — because they considered their forefathers to be in the Sheol, the place of the unseen dead, and not in the "common grave of mankind." They knew that their bodies had decayed and had long since been eaten by worms in the grave; but their souls were thought of as being in the Sheol.

The Sheol of the Old Testament (translated Hades in the New Testament) came definitely to mean the place of the unseen dead souls. It was thought that upon all of these was the wrath of God, which enclosed them. Of this wrath, Job says, "Thou prevailest forever against him, and he passeth: thou changest his countenance, and sendest him away" (Job 14:20). Where and how? "But his flesh upon him shall have pain, and his soul within him shall mourn" (Job 14:22).

That the wrath of God abides upon all flesh Moses shows in Ps. 90:7, "By thy wrath are we troubled." The wrath of God presses in on all flesh. Man has become a "vessel of wrath" fit only for destruction.

In other words then, it is through the gates of death and the grave that man loses his tabernacle, or body. His soul becomes naked before God (Gen. 3:9,10). In his soul, now, in Sheol-Hades, man mourns his loss.

Isaiah Comes to See Hell

Sheol then came to be regarded as being for some a place of rest, and for others a place of torment.

Revelation was slowly getting brighter and brighter in Isaiah's time, as men began to appreciate vaguely, the lot of the wicked. In Isa. 66:24 we read, "And they shall go forth, and look upon the carcasses of the men that have transgressed against me; for the worm shall not die; neither shall the fire be quenched; and they shall be an abhorring unto all flesh." Eternal punishment comes to the fore here — eternal punishment for the wicked — in torment.

Leaving Behind God's Word, Jehovah's Witnesses
Love Reasonings

While this wrath of God is upon all flesh, God's love devised a way to transform these "vessels of wrath" into "vessels of mercy." Why? So that they might learn to know the riches of

His glory which He intended for them when he originally created them in "His image and likeness." The measure of the degree of this eternal punishment upon the vessels of wrath and its severity for all time, is accentuated by the enormity of the sacrifice God made, in sending His beloved Son to become the Saviour. Truly, both life and immortality came to light by this act of mercy: life for the "vessels of glory" unto God, punishment for the "vessels of wrath."

The Jehovah's Witnesses like to reason that way. They like to say that GOD IS LOVE. He cannot punish a creature consciously forever. They imply, that because GOD IS LOVE, he is constitutionally incapable of punishing the vessels he has fashioned in His image in eternal torment of Hellfire. If this is true, if God cannot, because of divine nature do this, then I ask the Jehovah's Witnesses, "Why did He go to so great a length to save these lost souls by sacrificing His Son? Why so great an offering to save such souls if they were dead and unconscious anyway?"

Wrath to Come

The Lord's coming obviously saved lost souls not only from the wrath of God already upon them, which had caused them to die and be buried and their souls to become naked (sans body). In Matt. 3:7 and Luke 3:7 John the Baptist warned humans to flee from "the wrath to come." He must mean something occurring in the conscious life after death and burial.

When is this "wrath to come"? Isaiah already says "the day of the Lord cometh, cruel both with wrath and fierce anger" (Isa. 13:9). In Romans 2:5,6, Paul warns men against the coming revelation of wrath in the day of Judgment of God, as we read, "But after thy hardness and impenitent heart, treasurest up unto thyself wrath against the day of wrath and revelation of the righteous judgment of God; who will render to every man according to his deeds."

Is this something to look forward to with equanimity? No. It is a foregone conclusion that *all* souls must face the wrath to come on Judgment day. Paul says, "For we must *all* appear before the judgment seat of Christ; that every one may receive the things done in *his body* according to what he hath done, whether it be good or bad" (2 Cor. 5:10). Is this a perfunctory judging of the body, at worst resulting in annihilation? Paul did not think so, for in the 11th verse he says, "Knowing therefore the *terror of the Lord,* we persuade men; but we are made manifest unto God; and I trust also are made manifest in your own consciences."

Escaping the Wrath to Come

As *all* in the day of resurrection hear the voice of Jesus and come forth (John 5:28,29), many will come forth with the horrible bodies they conjured up in their wickedness, and their souls within them, will stand naked before the Judge.

In Romans 2 Paul shows that the "vessels of mercy" will receive the glory and honor they sought in a glorious body in immortality (7th verse), or in truth and fact in LIFE unto God. This then is a coming to eternal LIFE. Clearer still are Paul's words, "For we know that if our earthly house of this tabernacle were dissolved, we have a building of God, a house not made with hands, eternal in the heavens. For in this [earthly house body] we groan, earnestly desiring to be *clothed upon* with our house which is from heaven" (2 Cor. 5:1-2).

If, after this house or body is dissolved and a new body in the resurrection is forthcoming, what is the destiny of the righteous? It is unto God, and as Paul says, "If so be that to be clothed we shall not be found naked [without the garments of salvation]" (2 Cor. 5:3). But to come forth in the day of resurrection in the old body of flesh, hideous according to a wicked soul, will mean to remain a "vessel of wrath"; and being naked such a one will be ejected to "depart into everlasting fire prepared for the devil and his angels." Such a one is a "vessel of wrath," fit only for destruction.

Note what Paul says of them in Rom. 2:8,9, in contrast to what is said of eternal life in glory in verse 7: "But unto them that are contentious, and do not obey the truth, but obey unrighteousness, indignation and wrath, tribulation and anguish, upon every soul of man that doeth evil; of the Jew first and also of the Gentiles."

Notice the contrast which there will be in the day of judgment for the righteous and the unrighteous. In verse 7, there is promised to the righteous a body in glory, eternal life in immortality. In verses 8 and 9 there is no mention of a new body, nothing new; the old one with torment, torture is continued in all eternity.

There is then a wrath to come! There is to be a day of judgment in which will be decided the finale or destiny of the judged to be either LIFE in a new glorious body unto the Lord, or DEATH in an old body made hideous with sin in absence from the Lord.

Judgment to Come

The wrath of God then, which caused man to die and be buried, will have an outcome in immortality. This eternal destiny will be irrevocably fixed when all shall appear in the resurrection (John 5:28,29) before the judgment seat in the same manner Adam and Eve once personally were summoned before God in the garden of Eden. On that occasion (Gen. 3:18-19), they were sentenced "dying thou shalt die." Adam dreaded that hearing. So did Eve. They hid; they cowered behind trees, seeking cover.

How much more so then, is the day of judgment to be dreaded by the wicked and unrepentant! All will be called forth by the Lord — all will be summoned. Every soul will get a personal hearing, and in this process can fall into the hands of the living God (Heb. 10:31). Again in Heb. 12:29 Paul says "for our God is a consuming fire."

If all souls have been dissolved in the common grave of mankind, as the Jehovah's Witnesses aver, why does Paul say in 2 Cor. 5:11, "Knowing therefore the terror of the Lord, we persuade men; ..." Why would Paul spend his entire life to persuade men to come unto salvation, if a judgment upon them were not the prospect of the future? This judgment to come will result in a terrible thing to many, and in something blessed for others. It will result in eternal punishment in torment in hellfire, or it can result in a life of glory in immortality. Which do you seek, Rom. 2:7 or Rom. 2:8,9? (Cf. also Matt. 5:21; John 5:22; Rom. 14:10; Heb. 9:27; Matt. 12:41; Heb. 10:7 and James 2:13).

The Great Portrayal of a Soul, Come From Heaven

All the witnesses we have marshaled so far have been men, albeit inspired men. But now comes the Lord.

It is said of him, "And no man hath ascended up to heaven, but He that came down from heaven, even the Son of Man which is in heaven" (John 3:13). He came down from heaven, but even now is in heaven; and He actually will appear from heaven, quite soon now, in His Second Coming!

What does this presage for us? Here for the first time man,

the Son of Man, and the Son of God, was in mystic union both as man and God on earth. In Isa. 9:6, "For unto us a child is born, unto us a son is given. . . .". We see this miracle projected and described. Born as a man, Jesus Christ came as and in fashion of a man into the world. He lived the life of a man from the cradle to the grave. He experienced all a man ever experiences. Yet, He also was the Son of God, says Isaiah here. So truly was He God, that the government of the universe was upon His shoulder.

Not only did He come from heaven, as He says in John 3:13, but He is going back there. Here is *the one* who for all purposes of our discussion here, in evaluating the excellency of the Christian doctrine under discussion, can authoritatively lift the veil of the unseen for us. Up to His time SHEOL-HADES had been only understood to be the state of the unseen dead. For the first time, and we can be present, the Son of Man has lifted that veil!

Are you stirred at what is coming? What are death and the grave? Are they Hell? The Pharisees believed in Sheol-Hades but could not define them. Others, like the Sadducees who in this respect were much like the Jehovah's Witnesses of today, said HELL is the GRAVE, or "the common grave of mankind."

The Veil Cast Aside — The Inside of Sheol No Longer Unseen

The revelation came. A marvelous confession of who Jesus is, given by Peter, furnishes for us the verdant background. We read, "And Simon Peter answered and said, Thou art the Christ, the Son of the living God. And Jesus answered and said unto him, Blessed art thou, Simon Bar-jona: for flesh and blood hath not revealed this unto thee, but my Father which is in heaven. And I say unto thee, That thou art Peter and upon this rock I will build my church; and *the gates of hell* shall not prevail against it" (Matt. 16:16-18).

This at once raises the question: What are the gates of hell?

Let us open our Bibles at Luke 16 and read a few remarks of the Lord as He is in the process of lifting the veil from Sheol-Hades, and as he brings "life and immortality to light" (2 Tim. 1:10): "And it came to pass, that the beggar died, and was carried by the angels into Abraham's bosom: the rich man also died, *and was buried*; and in hell he lifted up his eyes, being in torments and seeth Abraham afar off and Lazarus in his bosom" (Luke 16:22,23).

The rich man *died and was buried* (in a grave) and it says this is the way he entered hell. Death and Hades (grave) then, are the "gates of hell." If they are the "gates of hell" they cannot be hell. The grave then is not hell, as the Jehovah's Witnesses contend.

Lazarus Not in Hell

Another distinction made by the Lord should be noted here. Lazarus died. His soul was immediately carried by angels to Abraham's lap. Also notice that the direction from the rich man in hell, was up — the rich man "lifted up his eyes." In Jesus' day the term "Abraham's lap" was understood to mean Paradise, which though unseen, as was hell, was distinct from it.

The soul of the righteous then, does go upward! It does not go downward, where hell is. Eccl. 3:21, shrouded for ages in mystery, here finds authoritative definition. The soul of the righteous goeth upward. The soul of the wicked, who lives like a beast gratifying his sense perceptions or body, then goeth downward, falling, falling farther and farther away from God. These terms "up" and "down" are clustered with rich symbolic meaning.

What a revealing picture we have here. Sheol-Hades up to now shrouded in mystery, is peopled with conscious souls! There is no need for guesswork any longer.

New Word Used to Describe Hell

Sheol-Hades is a term which had been used to refer to the place of all the unseen dead. It now appears from what Jesus reveals that SHEOL-HADES is no longer an adequate term. He, at least, had distinguished between Paradise (Abraham's lap) and hell, which up to now had not been differentiated. New distinctive terms would therefore have to take the place of those general terms. Unless this is so, then truly as the Jehovah's Witnesses aver, Jesus was merely giving a parable which told nothing about the beyond.

Here now comes the real proof that Jesus was revealing something about what is beyond — what is the state of conscious souls of men who had left the earthly scenes as Dives and Lazarus had done. It is obvious that the words Sheol and Hades were no longer adequate to describe the revelation pertaining to the destiny of souls. Thus the Lord Jesus uses another word! It is a word which is so graphic and pungent, that it will never be misunderstood by those who accept Him in faith. It is a word which would have within its ethnological roots the connotation of its fearful meaning. The word is GEHENNA. In use of this word GEHENNA Jesus Christ shows, that HELL IS NOT THE GRAVE (Sheol-Hades-Queber) but is GEHENNA.

Without equivocation Jesus shows that there is a punishment far more worse than death and the grave. In Matt. 10:28 he says, "And fear not them which kill the body, but are not able to kill the soul; but rather fear him which is able to destroy both body and soul in GEHENNA (hell) ."

The body and soul are separated by death. In the grave the worms gnaw up the flesh and the fiery process of chemical reaction burns up the bones. That is bad. But the Lord here shows something far worse, far more severe than this physical death!

What is it? For the first time the Lord Jesus gives us a beyond-the-veil description of the fearful implications of soul death. We read in Mark 9:43-46 and 48, "And if thy hand offend thee, cut it off: it is better for thee to enter into life maimed, than having two hands to go into GEHENNA (hell) , into the fire that never shall be quenched: where their worm dieth not, and the fire is not quenched."

If Paradise — or as the Jews termed it in Jesus' day, "Abraham's lap," in which souls rest in peace — is in heaven and apart from hell, and is fixed by a great gulf, then Hell, in which souls are tormented in pain and anguish, is indeed a PLACE. It cannot be the GRAVE, if both death and the grave are its gates! To go down into the grave by death is bad enough; but if one dies faithful such a one will fall into Abraham's lap. But to go down into the grave by death, and to fall into hell is worse, because such soul is irrevocably lost in Hell and dies continually in separation from God. In Paradise are such souls who have lost their bodies, but as "vessels of mercy" await the day when they shall receive a body of glory in immortality in the day of resurrection. In hell are such souls who remain "vessels of wrath" and who in the day of resurrection receive their old bodies with the new ingredient of immortality in them, for a living death of total separation from God, in a body of shame and contempt.

Wicked Soul Sees Death

Thus the Lord portrays for the first time how souls see death! When you see death like that, it is the end of all hope that a resurrected body which is sinful will ever become a "vessel of glory" in life in a body of glory in immortality, which is what we as "vessels of mercy" today are stretching ourselves out to find (Rom. 2:7). The possession of a body of shame and contempt in resurrection seals the fate of such a "vessel of wrath" forever, and condemns such a one in immortality of soul — "dying thou shalt die" — to eternal total separation from God. Is it not better to go into the grave with one hand, than to go into GEHENNA with two? That is the point the Lord makes.

It is said of Enoch, "He did not see death." It is the combination of death and the grave, as the gates of hell, which shall not prevail against the "vessels of mercy." Did not Jesus promise "verily, verily, I say unto you, if a man keep my sayings, he shall never see death" (John 8:51)?

Not to See Death

What does this statement mean? Those who are included in this statement will never see death as those who go to GEHENNA (hell) see it, as those who receive back their old body of sin fit only for shame, contempt and destruction, see it. The moment the souls of such are called out of hell, and the bodies are called out of the grave (sea or grave on earth) (Rev. 20) and reunited, at that moment of awakening (John 5:28,29) they will again see death staring them right in the face, as they are told to stand at the left hand of the Lord. Death stares them right in the face then. GEHENNA, a lake of fire, a vast place, is just ahead. Their fate is sealed the moment they appear in their old bodies now with the ingredient of immortality in them. THAT IS seeing death in shame (nakedness) and contempt in a body in immortality.

A Glimpse Into the Future

As this day of judgment, which is also the day of the Lord, approaches, we look with interest upon Rev. 20:12-13. It says there, "And I saw the dead, small and great, stand before God; and the books were opened: and another book was opened, which is the book of life: and the dead were judged out of the things written in the books, according to their works. . . . And death and Hades [grave, or the gates of Hell] delivered up the dead which were in them: and they were judged every man according to their works." Notice here the gates of Hell swing open in reverse this time, as "ALL THAT are in the graves shall hear His voice" (John 5:28). That is the last time these gates will function — for it is said, "And death and Hades [grave] were cast into the Lake of Fire [Gehenna]..." (Rev. 20:15). And if any man was not found written in the book of life, he was cast in the Lake of Fire [Gehenna].

Why is this? Because, and here is the proof, in the day of resurrection when *all* shall come forth, the good and the bad, coming out of death and grave and hell and heaven, *immortality* as the nature of man comes into view. For those whose names are written in the Book of Life, glory and immortality (Rom. 2:7) ; for those whose names have not been written in the book of Life, a body of *death,* vile, in shame and contempt and immortality. Since such no longer can die in the body, death and the grave, along with them, are thrown into GEHENNA, the vast place and domain of DEATH, and such will SEE IT forever as their mode of life.

Annihilation or Eternal Torment: Which?

The Jehovah's Witnesses and certain other cultists, foolishly teach that this event denotes annihilation. Is it true? Note "the gates of hell" are closed now that judgment has been pronounced. With resurrection bringing back (or reviving again, which is what that term means) body and soul into unity then, plus the ingredient of immortality added to it in resurrection, such souls as lack the IMAGE AND LIKENESS OF GOD which is newly impressed upon those who are "in Christ," are fit only for destruction in perpetuity out of sight of God. Gehenna, in which alone they are fit to live, is now tightly locked. There is no way out of it. It is just a perpetual death in "outer Darkness" suffering the unquenchable fire of God's wrath, in a domain so vast that it is termed a "lake." It has no place of either entry or exit. Is this annihilation?

Again, if this second death (which we have seen is forever), or the actual closing of Gehenna (hell), means annihilation and complete unconsciousness, how is it that we read in Revelation 21:8, "But the fearful, and unbelieving and the abominable, and murderers, and whoremongers, and sorcerers, and idolators, and all liars, shall have their part in the lake which burneth with fire and brimstone: which is the second death"? Fire and brimstone are mentioned here. That is the same wording as in Rev. 20:10, "And the devil that deceived them was cast into the lake of fire and brimstone, where the beast and the false prophet are, and shall be tormented day and night for ever and ever."

Let us see what happened to the beast and the false prophet. We read in Rev. 19:19 and 20, concerning the beginning of the judgment, this, "And I saw the beast and the kings of the earth, and their armies, gathered together to make war against him that sat on the horse, and against his army. And the beast was taken, and with him the false prophet that wrought miracles before him, with which he deceived them that received the mark of the beast and them that worshipped his image. These both were cast *alive* into the lake of fire burning with brimstone." If, as the Jehovah's Witnesses and some other cultists say, this transpired at the beginning of the millennium, Rev. 20:5, then is it not obvious that when in the end of the millennium, as we read in Rev. 20:10, the devil is cast in the same lake of fire, it is there said both the beast and false prophet are still alive in there in the lake of fire, so much so that they are tormented day and night, and have been alive for 1,000 years? If those cast into the lake of fire are alive, then the second death (which is what Hell, or Gehenna, is) means to be in the place of the living dead, the land of the dead separated from God forever. Then it does not mean annihilation.

Lifting of the Veil by Jesus Proves Hell to Be a Place of Eternal Punishment in Torment

Our Lord Jesus gave us a full view of man's horrible fate as "children of wrath." This has been a great boon to us. If anything, it gave us an insight as we never had before, that all men are lost. The Lord Jesus handed us a lifeline by showing us the enormity of the fate that awaited us as "children of wrath." Death and grave (Sheol-Hades), or the common grave of mankind are as nothing compared to Gehenna!

We are lost, fellow men, for by nature we are "children of wrath" (Eph. 2:3). We can be saved from our fate only when we are born again in the spirit. Accept by faith the lifeline which is in the hand of the Lord Jesus. Let His image and likeness be impressed upon you, in which "image and likeness of God" you were created, but which you lost through sin. You shall then, in the resurrection, be a "vessel of glory" in immortality. You shall *live* in the land of the living, as Hezekiah realized after his conversion (Isa. 38). Otherwise, if we die in our sins, our doom as "vessels of wrath" is sealed: for in the resurrection we shall awaken in bodies of shame and contempt, of *death,* and shall see the land of living no more (Isa. 38) for we shall be sent to Hell.

Invitation to Take Hell Serious

As one of the Jehovah's Witnesses, believing and teaching this awful error that HELL IS THE GRAVE, I also was on my way to Hell and perdition. I was proud of my achievements as a Kingdom Publisher, as one of the Jehovah's Witnesses. Twenty-one years of full-time service, a quarter million books sold, 463 new converts baptized, indelibly impressed the seal of achievement (onto my hands). Completely obsessed with the doctrines of heresy, my brain was filled with them as I bore the mark of this kind of thinking (on my forehead). I had become smug and self-satisfied. My barns were filling up in the Theocracy of works. But what, if as it almost happened when a heart attack laid me low, the Lord should require my soul of me — in this condition!

When I realized my mortal danger, with all of its implications, I came to the Lord. I did not even come with a plan aforethought. I just threw myself upon the mercy of God. The grace of God became mine in one night of prayer. Forgiveness came. Assurance came of salvation, as a wondrous gift, unearned, undeserved, rich and free!

Therefore, by the grace of God, I am not crying out now as did that rich man after he departed through the gates of hell: death and the grave, from out of hell! If I did, that would be rather futile. But I am crying out as one who walked right up to the brink of hell, and then was plucked as a brand out of the fire. I am crying out to Jehovah's Witnesses still living. Turn from your fatal delusion! Leave behind the errors of the WATCHTOWER SOCIETY. Turn now, while your soul is still within your body. Change your course right now, ere your body enters the gates of hell: death and grave. Come to Jesus Christ. Believe on Him. Be saved from this WRATH TO COME. Believe His sayings. He meant them! Be saved from perdition to come. If you do YOU SHALL NEVER SEE DEATH. You will REALLY be in that vast throng of MILLIONS NOW LIVING WHO SHALL NEVER DIE!

Chapter 9

MAN CREATED IN THE IMAGE AND LIKENESS OF GOD

Coming away from the discussion of Hell, its eternal implications, its present danger to us, you will find, as did I, that the discussion of the doctrine of an immortal soul is a sort of anticlimax.

That is because in the order of cause and effect, sin is the cause, and Hell is the effect. The fact is that sin is the overtone of life and death: for in order to sin one must be alive; then in death *sin* can no longer be performed. Death then could be a condition in which one cannot sin, is restrained from doing so, and still be alive. How?

The apostle shows that the Christian who dies in or with Christ, shall live with Him. He also shows that this dying takes place in this life; and to the extent it takes place, to that extent such an one *already lives with Christ.* The very use of this picture projects the existence of a realm of reality of *life* and *death,* as two contrasting conditions: of Obedience and Life, or Sin (or transgression) and Death, both in the conscious realm.

Jehovah Has Immortality

Since man was originally made and created in the image and likeness of God, which he subsequently lost as a result of sin, the question now came to me, What is this image and likeness in which man was created in the first place? In this principle of cause and effect, since in the last three chapters of our discussion we have seen that the effects are *eternal,* let us examine the cause by finding out who man is.

But before I could do that, I had to find out who God is. Here is what I found.

Describing God, Paul says of Him in 1 Tim. 6:16, "Who only *hath* immortality." We look upon a more lucid portraiture of God by our Lord Jesus Himself in John 5:26, "For as the

Father hath life *in himself* [immortality]; so hath he *given* to the Son to *have* life *in* himself."

In what way did the Father give the Son to *have* life in Himself? Jesus answers, "Therefore doth my Father love me, because I lay down my life, that I might take it again. No man taketh it from me, but I lay it down of myself. I have power to lay it down, and I have power to take it again. This commandment I have received of my Father" (John 10:17,18). This being so, Paul answers for us the above query and in his answer lies the direct proof that man *has an immortal soul.* Paul says, "Because he hath appointed a day in which he will judge the world in righteousness *by that man* whom He hath ordained; whereof he hath given assurance unto all men, in that he had raised him from the dead" (Acts 17:31).

Coming of Jesus Proves Man Has an Immortal Soul

Of the Lord's coming to earth, bodily as man (Col. 2:9) Paul says, "But is now made manifest by the appearing of our Saviour Jesus Christ, who hath abolished death, and hath brought *life and immortality* to light through the gospel" (2 Tim. 1:10). As we have seen, in the former chapters, this brought to light that man has an eternal destiny: *life in glory and immortality,* or *death in shame and contempt and in immortality.*

By actually becoming a man Jesus portrayed anew how a man was created by God in His image and likeness thus having an immortal soul.

In this revelation of the God-head in a human body (Col. 2:9), living as a man, we see the creation of man re-enacted, the impress of the image renewed, coming forth as composed of: body and spirit. The apostle Peter in 1 Peter 2:24 says, "Who in his own self bare our sins in his own body on the tree, that we, being dead to sins, should live unto righteousness; by whose stripes ye were healed."

Why did Jesus bear our sins in His body? "For ye were as sheep going astray, but now are returned unto the Shepherd and Bishop of your souls" (1 Peter 2:25) comes the answer. It shows that our souls were lost, no longer knew the way of *life* to God, but were on the way of *death* away from God.

Jesus Died to Save Our Souls First

The immediate danger to man was the losing of his soul.

Jesus died in the body to save our souls which without Him would be eternally lost as we died. Losing at death our *bodies* returning to the grave our souls would continue to die, farther, farther away from God. There was no anchor for our souls. Once we lost the body tying us to terra firma, we were lost without it.

We needed an anchor first, to stop us from falling and going astray. When our Lord Jesus died as a man on the Cross, He changed all of this. For not only did He die; He was resurrected, and in doing so, He became the anchor of our souls. He caused us to be anchored against the day of judgment. As Paul says of us, "I pray God your *whole* spirit and soul and body be preserved" (1 Thess. 5:23).

Peter says, "Wherefore let them that suffer according to the will of God commit the *keeping* of their souls to him in well doing, as unto a *faithful Creator*." The death of our Lord Jesus in His body projects a full hope, so strong, that Paul could say of it in Heb. 6:9, "Which hope we have as an *anchor of the soul,* both sure and steadfast, and which entereth into that within the veil." Such a soul is not tossed to and fro in hell, but is saved now with the sure promise of a *new and glorious body* in the day of resurrection. Such a soul does not come in judgment to receive its old body in immortality in the day of resurrection, to have its fate sealed forever in *Gehenna*. The soul of such a one has been *saved* from the fate of a "vessel of wrath." His soul has been *saved* not only by the death of Jesus Christ in the body but by His resurrection in the body to a *life of glory* and immortality.

The Whole Man

If there is a whole man, then when is a man not whole? In our dealings with man, we deal either with him bodily, or with his range of thoughts, or with his aspirations. But God, knowing all aspects of man, deals with him differently.

In this manner then we have the testimony of God in His word, furnishing us with proof of what constitutes a *whole man*. God's word exerts itself in this manner upon man. The Holy Spirit knowing the man's frame, unerringly, directs the effectiveness of God's work upon *the whole man*. That is the way to look at it. "The word of God is quick, and powerful, and sharper than any two-edged sword, piercing even to the dividing asunder of soul and spirit and of the joints and marrow, and is a discerner of thoughts and intents of the heart" (Heb. 4:12). The whole man is, according to the Holy Spirit, body and soul.

How Was Man Created?

With these opening remarks in mind let us now look at the facts in the case of man. Let us look on the report of the Bible. How was he created?

First off, we note that animals were created first. As reported by the Holy Spirit in Gen. 1:24-25, "And God said: Let the earth bring forth the living creature *after his kind,* cattle, and creeping. thing, and beast of the earth *after his kind* ... and cattle *after their kind,* and everything that creepeth upon the earth *after his kind*: and God saw that it was good."

What is the outstanding feature of the above creation report by the Holy Spirit, caused to be written by Moses? It is this. God created all these lower creatures *after their own kind.* In other words, each kind had its own pattern, or image of the species.

Next we come to the report of how man was created. Is he too, created only *in the image of his own kind,* as are all animals? Let us see. We do have the facts you know, put down for us so long ago by the Holy Spirit who was an eye-witness and participant. Let us read this report. We find it in Gen. 1:26,27, "And God said, Let us make man *in our image, after our likeness*: and let them have dominion over the fish of the sea, and over the fowl of the air, and over the cattle, and over all the earth, and over every creeping thing that creepeth upon the earth. So God created man *in his own image, in the image of God* created he him; male and female created he them."

What is the outstanding fact in this report? It is this: man was created *in the image of God!* Here is riveted for us, for all time, the vast gulf which exists between animals and beast, and man or humans.

Created in the Image of God

This creation of man with an immortal soul, or immortality, was a gift of God to man. It was a gift which He did not give to the animal world. They, the animals, too received a gift: life. But it is not the kind of life which is inherent. in man, *immortality!* It is that which God created and gave to man alone. Never forget that. *That is his image.*

So far we have read the blueprint in Gen. 1:26-27. Now let us go into the details — the worksheet of creation, so to speak.

The Holy Spirit furnishes us this in Gen. 2:7. It reads quite tersely, yet revealingly, "And the Lord formed man of the dust of the ground, and breathed into his nostrils the breath of life [Hebrew: *ruahh* — plural, 'breath of lives'], and man became a living soul."

What did *God create* here? The body? The soul?

First off, note that God formed man's body out of already existing materials, in the same manner a potter forms a vessel. True, He was making this vessel in His likeness. Yet, He formed man from the ground, thus already testifying before the world began (John 3:16) of the coming of His Son, in whom would dwell the God-head bodily (Col. 2:9).

What then did God *create* in man? God created man's soul. How? The worksheet given us in Gen. 2:7 says that God did so by "breathing into his nostrils the breath of life." The Hebrew word *ruahh* is a plural word, meaning actually, "breath of lives."

Once the body of Adam was formed, and the breath of life, or better the "breath of lives" was breathed into Adam's nostrils, the account says, "Man became a living soul"; that is, one capable of living unto God, in fellowship and in eternity.

It is very important for us to pause here and ask, according to Gen. 2:7, Just how did God create man? In Gen. 2:7 it says, "And the Lord God formed man of the dust of the ground, and breathed into his nostrils the breath of life; and man became a living soul."

What does this show? It shows graphically, that the outer man, the body, and the inner man, the soul, were here mystically fused into one and that by a creative act of God. Here uniquely, for all time, was created an individual who throughout all eternity would remain HE, his identity forever intact.

The body of this man was not created in the sense that it was made out of nothing. Gen. 2:7 says it was formed out of the dust of the ground, or from existing matter. But the inner man, the soul, was created. It was not taken from something which existed. The individual Adam, or the soul, was created by God's breath.

How is that shown elsewhere? Let us read 2 Tim. 3:16, "All scripture is given by inspiration of God, and is profitable for doctrine, for reproof, for correction, for instruction in righteousness." The Greek term here for "given by inspiration of God" is actually *theopneustos* or God-breathed. In other words, God breathed out His word.

In what way does this explain *ruahh* or the "breath of lives" in Gen. 2:7? We read in Ps. 33:6, "By the word of the Lord were the heavens made, and all the hosts by the breath of His mouth." Could this mean God breathed creatively all the hosts of heaven into existence?

The Jehovah's Witness would immediately here counter, "That may be true of angels. They are spirits, like the wind. Breath, wind, spirit, all have the same connotation."

Firmly we must reject that by quoting Job 33:4, "The Spirit of God has made me and the breath of the Almighty hath given me life." This is Job talking, not an angel. Job was created as JOB, by the breath of the Almighty to live! In the same way Adam was created by the breath of God to eternal life.

Pondering over this, the true essence of 2 Tim. 3:16 dawned upon me. In 2 Tim. 3:16 we read that God's word was God-breathed. Of it, God's word, it is said by Jesus, "Heaven and earth shall pass away, but my words shall not pass away" (Matt. 24:35), and Peter says in 1 Peter 1:23,24,25, "Being born again, not of corruptible seed, but incorruptible, by the word of God, which liveth and abideth forever ... but the word of the Lord endureth forever." If the word of God, I opined, *theopneustos,* or God-breathed as Paul calls it, is immortal, then why not the soul God created with His breath?

Can a Distinction Between Soul and Body Be Shown?

If a distinction between soul and body can at all be made, Scripture must show that a point of severance exists. Reading Gen. 35:18, "It came to pass, as the soul was departing (for she died) that she called his name Benoni." Does this Scripture show a point of departure of the soul from the body?

It came to me, now thinking along lines of a Jehovah's Witness, if I had to prove such a departure or severance of soul from the body, I would actually have to have Scripture proving an entering of the soul into the body. Was there Scripture, apart from Gen. 2:7, now under discussion?

I came upon 1 Kings 17:21, "He stretched himself upon the child three times and cried unto the Lord, and said O my Lord God, I pray thee, let this child's soul come into him again." Could this be a valid description?

A Jehovah's Witness would reply, the return of the soul designates the beginning of the circulating of the blood of the child, which is his life.

This was a puzzler. Reading on, verse 22, "And the Lord heard the voice of Elijah; and the soul of the child came into him again, and he revived." The blood of this child had not been spilled, or poured forth out of its body. So, it was not the blood that came back into it. It was the soul, which came back into it again, not the blood.

But a pet Jehovah's Witness demarche came to my mind. Was this not the same as in the case of Lazarus whom the Lord resurrected? You do not there read of anyone reporting, nor do you read of the Lord explaining, where his soul was as he lay dead for four days?

Why does John 11 not mention such an explanation? It is because no one asked Lazarus whether his soul was conscious or unconscious. Everyone was so thrilled and awed with the glory of God manifested in this resurrection that no one was flippant enough to ask Lazarus about that. The Scripture is here mute on that score in the same way as in 1 Kings 17:23. In these passages it gives voice not to what the soul was doing while out of the body, but to the glory of God who could put body and soul together again.

Herein lies the crux of our discussion. God can, and does, not only form the body of man, but also creates his soul, and He IS able to fuse them into one, by either the power of Creation as in Gen. 2:7, or of resurrection as in John 11 or 1 Kings 17.

As man became alive, we note, he also came alive in the spirit. He could think, reason, associate with God, all things which did not happen to the beasts, who only could come alive in the blood in their bodies. Man came into his own and became God-conscious. Note the divergence from the beast? Both beast and man have life in the body through blood. That is the limit of the beast though. But man, possessor of an immortal soul, emerges into God-consciousness! How did this take place in Adam's case?

Adam Exercises God-Consciousness

The day came when Adam surveyed all beasts. As a result of this, he gave each a name. In this survey he soon discovered that there was among them no helpmate for him. Also he talked with God in the cool of the evening. Thus man was exerting himself in two distinct directions: through blood in the body toward the animal world and through his soul in

God-consciousness toward God. Man's soul, giving him the consciousness that he had to come to terms not only with flesh on earth but also with God in heaven, thus gave eloquent evidence as to its destiny.

As the body of man became a vessel of glory, a soul glorious to God, being complete for life within itself for eternity, man in obedience would have a *life* of glory in immortality. "The spirit of man is the candle of the Lord, searching out all inward parts of the belly" (Prov. 20:27).

From the very beginning of man's existence, did the Lord light up man's spirit. Adam surveyed the beasts, and he reasoned himself to the conclusion that there was no suitable helpmate or companion among them for him. God put man to sleep and gave him Eve. Upon wakening Adam immediately discerned what God had done. He said, "This is now bone of my bones, and flesh of my flesh; she shall be called Woman, because she was taken out of man" (Gen. 2:23).

Adam recognized in Eve "bone of my bones, flesh of my flesh." Having been created an immortal soul Eve *was* a separate being. She had become by act of creation a living soul in her own self-consciousness.

It was in this manner that new souls were multiplied. We read, "And God blessed them and God said unto them, be fruitful, and multiply, and replenish the earth" (Gen. 1:28). Souls would continuously be multiplied with the multiplying of bodies as they became self-conscious by an *act of God*. This would be, as it was in Gen. 2:7, first the forming of the body from existing things, then the placing of the soul in the body by God.

Job asks, "Did not he that made me in the womb, make him? And did not *one* fashion us in the womb?" (Job 31:15). God kept forming vessels out of existing materials, each time placing in the body a new immortal soul.

Looking at Creation of Man From the View of Dissolution

Let us now approach this subject from still another view. Unfortunately, there is another side. It is the dissolution of man. What happened when man sinned? We read, "In the sweat of thy face shalt thou eat bread, till thou return unto the ground; for out of it wast thou taken; for dust thou art, and unto dust shalt thou return" (Gen. 3:19).

What part of Adam had been taken out of the ground?

The soul? No. The body. But when the body dissolves, what happens to the rest of the whole man?

We read in Eccl. 12:7, "Then shall the dust return to earth as it was: and the spirit shall return unto God who gave it." So the spirit of man, made by God, returns to God, as the body returns to the dust of the ground out of which it was formed.

What Happens to the Soul, If It Is Immortal?

But what about the soul, the self-consciousness of man? Is it too dissolved? If it is, then it is not of the substance of immortality. Let us see.

Paul says in 2 Cor. 5:10, "For we must all appear before the judgment seat of Christ; that every one may receive the things done in his body, according to that he hath done, whether it be good or bad." Who appears before this judgment seat? Just the body? No. The whole man: body-soul. *All hear the voice of the Lord* in the day of resurrection and their soul will receive a glorious new body.

Is not the body our earthly tabernacle? What, if it is dissolved into dust?

Why, if such a soul does not receive a tabernacle from heaven, but instead, one from earth, is it called naked? (2 Cor. 5:1-4). John actually saw souls without bodies, earthly, or resurrection bodies — not yet clothed (Rev. 6:9,10). When they, the souls of the dead coming out of the great tribulation (verse 9) cried out (verse 10), we observe that the Lord gave them robes (verse 11), so they would not be naked and could rest. Obviously, without cover of a glorious new resurrection body, such souls find no rest until the day of resurrection.

Then there are the souls of those of former ages of whom Paul writes in Heb. 12:22,23, "But ye are come unto mount Zion, and unto the city of the living God, the heavenly Jerusalem, and to an innumerable company of angels, to the general assembly and church of the firstborn, which are written in heaven, and to God the judge of all, and to *the spirits of just men made perfect.*"

Again we read in another chapter, Rev. 20:4, a report by John. He says, "I saw souls of them that were beheaded for the witness of Jesus."

Where did the souls of these men go? In Old Testament times it was believed they went into Sheol-Hades. But then when the Lord Jesus came, Paradise and hell came to view: Paradise, a place of peace and rest, and hell, a place of no peace and rest.

Description of Souls

In Paul's wonderful experience related in 2 Cor. 12:2-4 he actually describes a soul, "I knew a man in Christ above fourteen years ago (whether in the body I cannot tell; or whether out of the body, I cannot tell: God knoweth); such a one caught up to third heaven. And I knew such a man (whether in the body, or out of the body, I cannot tell: God knoweth); how that he was caught up into Paradise and heard unspeakable words, which it is not lawful for a man to utter." Here we have a description of a soul's experience in Paradise.

The soul of a man, then, is immortal.

Fate of the Soul

If in this life a soul lives only to gratify its sense-consciousness, or the flesh, it comes under the law of sin. Its wages is death. When it dies, it loses its sense-consciousness as the body decays in the grave (Eccl. 9:5,10) — to await the day of resurrection when the old body with the ingredient of immortality comes forth to judgment.

If in this life a soul lives to express itself in the spirit, or in its God-consciousness as living unto the Lord, it learns to walk and to talk with God. Such a soul will never see death in the day of resurrection, as then it will receive a body of glory in immortality. Resting in Paradise, such (as we have seen in Rev. 6:9,10) can talk, feel, cry, etc., even though their bodies have been slain and have been dissolved long since.

Many men from Abel on have lived after the spirit in their fallen bodies. Of such we read in John 1:12, "But as many as received him, to them gave he power to become the sons of God; even to them *that believe* on his name." Such, living like Abraham, lived after the spirit. How do we know? We read, "But they now desire a better country, that is, a heavenly: wherefore God is not ashamed to be called their God: for he hath prepared for them a city" (Heb. 11:16). In spirit they saw the day of Jesus in faith and rejoiced.

Eternal Life in Glory, or Immortality in Shame and Contempt

What power is here at play. It is the power of God. It is a tremendous power. It enables us in a quickening effectiveness, as it did Abel, to live a new life in and after the spirit. Such in times past in faith, and we today by the Holy Spirit working in us, were born again, producing the fruits of the Spirit (Gal. 5:22) in the place of the fruits of the flesh.

This being the case, the one soul expressing itself in the flesh and another soul expressing itself after the spirit, we can see the potentials for war. Thus, early in man's existence, soon after his fall, the soul became the scene of this warfare. Whether one lives solely to gratify the body of flesh, or lives the way of the spirit determines the destiny of the soul, as in faith it hopes for redemption to come in the Redeemer promised from Gen. 3:15 on.

If a man lives solely to gratify the flesh, then at death he will, without a body anchoring him to the earth, be lost in hell — falling far away from God. Within itself it will contain the memory of all the feelings, thoughts, and deeds it committed in the body of sin. This will cause torment and torture. As to its future, it has no hope. Such a soul continues what already it has been doing while still in the body *"dying thou shalt die"* (Ezek. 18:4). Because of the prevalence of sin it will be unable to enter the land of the living, Paradise.

If a man's soul has lived after the spirit, then he has slowly learned to use the power of God. Such a man bears fruits of the spirit, by which he becomes stabilized in spiritual living. As we shall see in chapter 10, Christ becomes for such a one the anchor, who being thus in Christ, is anchored until the resurrection when his soul puts on a body of glory in immortality. Such a soul, though separated from the body, through the quickening power of the spirit can, while waiting upon Christ and the day of resurrection in Paradise, observe, feel, talk, touch, live in the spirit (Rev. 6:9,10).

The Soul a Battleground

With the soul thus being immortal, and the arbiter between spirit and flesh, or two worlds within man, the soul truly would be the *glory of God*. But with sin having entered into the soul, all offspring of Adam, since all were created in possession of an immortal soul, have become a battlefield between the flesh and the spirit. The very fact, that this has been so all down through the corridors of history, is *eloquent proof* that man has an immortal soul!

This battle in the soul in this life after the image of Adam, is well described for us in Gal. 4:22,23, "For it is written that Abraham had two sons, the one by a bondmaid, the other by a free woman. But he who was of the bondwoman was born after the flesh [body]; but he of the free woman was *by promise.*" This brings immediately to mind two kinds of human beings.

There are on the one hand those who cater exclusively to their fleshly bodies. When they die, the opportunity for their souls ever to become "vessels of glory" fades forever, as they fall into hell awaiting resurrection of their bodies in immortality. Those who live after the spirit, being mindful as had been Abraham of the promise of God to furnish salvation (as early as Gen. 3:15) when they die they rest and repose in Paradise awaiting the glorious day of resurrection. This day is now no longer a mere hope. It is unconditionally guaranteed by the death and resurrection of our Saviour God, Jesus Christ.

Abel and Cain, Jacob and Esau, Isaac and Ishmael, the fleshly Jew and the Christian, the man in Christ and the heretic, come to view in successive generations as classic examples of this struggle of flesh and spirit for supremacy in the soul. But after all is said and done, there comes the seal to all of this in the statement of Paul in Phil. 2:10. "That at the name of Jesus every knee should bow, of things in heaven, and things on earth, and things under the earth."

Are those who are placed under the earth, in graves, at their death, really dead? Their bodies, yes, but not their souls. If they were really dead when put into the grave, that is, if their souls are unconscious or have been annihilated, how can they bow the knees to Christ? How can they worship, if they are dead? Yet, those under the earth shall bow their knees in worship to Christ, or be thrown into the lake of fire (Rev. 20:4).

Body of Sin an Impediment of the Soul

In Ps. 6:5 David cries out, "For in death there is no remembrance of thee: in the grave who shall give thee thanks?" Why does David say this? David knew that he who lives a wicked life by way of death and the grave winds up in hell (Luke 16:22,23), where no one praises the Lord. This vexed and puzzled him. Knowing this, he cried out for us to read in the 4th verse, "Return, O Lord, deliver my soul: O save me for thy mercies' sake." He actually prays to be rid of his sinful body, groaning in pains and sorrows of hell, in the *dying thou shalt die* torment, so that his spirit can soar unto God.

We live in Paul's hope: "Therefore we are always confident, knowing that, whilst we are at home in the body, we are absent from the Lord" (2 Cor. 5:6).

To those souls who live after the spirit (this was already true at the time of Abel) the body becomes an encumbrance. They have often prayed for its dissolution in death. If they possessed no immortal soul, wherein they could be totally God-conscious forever, they would have been very foolish indeed to want to be rid of the body.

All godly men, along with such particular examples of fact as Enoch, Moses, Elijah, etc., never saw death. God called himself their God; and God is not a God of the dead, for He condemns these to hell; but He is a God of the living. By stating concerning such men that He is their God, the Lord testifies eloquently that these men do have immortal souls. Viewed from this side of the veil, we may look upon them as dead, but God proclaims them to be in the land of the living.

What is the land of the living? What part of man is in it? The body? No, for these are awaiting a body of glory in the resurrection. Their souls? Yes, for having lived after the ways of the Spirit, this has quickened their souls. In their souls, they are alive to God.

In Matt. 17:1-9 we observe Moses, Elijah and Jesus in earnest conversation. Were Moses and Elijah real? It is a fact that Jesus was real. If he was real, so were Moses and Elijah. He was not shadow boxing! They were all real enough to Peter who saw them, for he wanted to build a tabernacle for each of them. God spoke in the 5th verse too. They were alive to him, to the Lord, and to Peter. Why not to us?

Where did they come from? Were they conjured up by witchcraft, as was Samuel by the witch of Endor? No, the veil was drawn aside for a while. The disciples saw Moses and Elijah alive, not dead. Elijah and Moses were alive! This being the case, they must have resided in the land of the living.

In this transfiguration scene we have another factual behind-the-scenes look afforded us by the Lord Jesus. Graphically, He shows what has happened to the souls of just men made perfect, to the men of old who sought a heavenly country. This scene is every bit as authentic as is the description of the rich man and Lazarus. Both scenes reveal something of what has happened or happens to the soul, to those saved, and those lost. In the story of Dives and Lazarus, in Luke 16, incidentally, we see Abraham alive too.

What force these revelations give to the words of Jehovah, "I am the God of Abraham, Isaac and Jacob"! He is indeed the God of all the living souls!

From the highest authority then, we have incontrovertible proof that the soul within man is immortal.

Chapter 10

"MAN IS A SOUL," SAY THE JEHOVAH'S WITNESSES

A Natural Doctrine Because of Unbelief

Once Charles T. Russell had left behind in unbelief, the Bible doctrine of Hell as a place of eternal punishment in torment he laid himself wide open for soul-washing. But this came as an anti-climax to his rebellion from historic Christianity. Once you deny Hell, then the doctrine of the immortality of the soul must go, and soon the doctrine of God and the deity of Christ likewise become untenable in your thinking.

How clear that came to me now! It caused within me a firm resolve never to play down the doctrine of Hell as taught by the Lord Jesus, the apostles and prophets. Those who do not fully understand the sad and eternal lot of lost souls will never appreciate the magnitude of God's love for them in Christ. This great love of God, in sending His Son, will draw lost souls into letting Christ come into their hearts as a new strongman, whose brilliant presence will drive out the spirit of fear and condemnation, and the way of flesh, sin and death. Only a knowledge of the full extent of the condemnation from which a Christian has escaped, makes the believer cry out jubilantly, "Now there is no condemnation to them which are in Christ Jesus!" Thus the strongman Christ Jesus takes ascendancy in our hearts in a new life "who walk not after the flesh but after the spirit" (Rom. 8:1).

That man was created with an immortal soul is a spiritual doctrine coming from God. That man is a mortal soul, as is the beast, is a natural doctrine. One is of "spirit and truth," and the other of "hearsay and reasonings."

How does a natural doctrine gain credence? At first you may not pay much attention to what the Jehovah's Witnesses say about the soul; but as they return with books, booklets and magazines, their words slowly sink in. You become conditioned to their man-reasoned premise that man *is* a soul. First you do not know exactly what they mean by this, and you begin to tolerate it. By constant repetition their lie becomes plausible. Next they begin to refer to their books as authoritative helps. In these books they slowly teach you how to misuse God's word to prove their conclusions and their natural doctrine. To the extent that you accept their books as interpretations to that extent you are weaned away from rightly using God's word.

The moment you learn to misuse God's word to prove some doctrine men have reasoned out, from that moment on you cannot accept the facts of the Bible by itself, or its spiritual doctrines, or its fundamental theme and center. You begin to cling desperately to what the Watchtower says. You will only use such portions and combinations of Bible texts, as do the Watchtower Society. You will no longer absorb the spiritual side of God's word. The letter, the verse, the torn out passage from context, are all you can absorb of the Word of God (2 Cor. 3:6).

Make Sure of All Things, *Furnishes Techniques for Wrongly Dividing God's Word*

For a million Jehovah's Witnesses, and in a degree more or less according to the stage of their indoctrination for ten million others undergoing Jehovah's Witness brainwashing, their text-book *Make Sure of All Things* is their doctrine Bible. In this book the Watchtower Society has condensed man's natural doctrines, and has glibly subordinated the spirit of Scripture to the letter. This is done deliberately (2 Cor. 3:3,4), and to put in its place in the hearts of these converts a ministry of the letter (2 Cor. 3:6). The method is here for you to see.

To prove conclusively that this technique exists I will show by using their very own texts. I will uncover for you to see the deceit and carnal malpractice. Simply read the verses of the context which they omit. These usually point up the spiritual side of the text which the Jehovah's Witnesses are misusing. If you do so, doctrines of men will fade away as the spiritual vista opens. Harmony in your thinking will usher in peace. This will be incomparably satisfying and right. It will not lead to frustration as do Jehovah's Witness doctrines. That is what had happened to me. Once I was steeped in their doctrinal errors. Now, no longer using their literature, but solely using God's word, the word of truth has washed away all Jehovah's Witnesses' errors. Herein to me lies the proof that the Jehovah's Witness doctrines are errors.

I now have no feeling of nearness to Watchtower men. It used to mean so much to me. Now, in its place, I have a sense of nearness to God — to God Himself, in whose image and likeness I was made. This image I lost but now, being in Christ, I recognize it within me once again. Now knowing of my soul within me, which is increasingly becoming enlightened by the spiritual side of God's word, I know I am being led on the pathway of seeking *life* in glory and immortality (Rom. 2:7). In the place of a sense of being adrift, I have found in Christ an anchor for my soul, and practicably, I am now learning how to put on divine nature. Thus I am consciously moving towards my heavenly home on high. I know now I can always be there in Christ. Death and the grave have truly lost their sting. Jehovah's Witnesses, on the other hand, are still totally occupied with death and the grave, believing their flesh and blood are the soul. (This they express by saying that man *is* a soul.) In brief, you can see the vastness of change which came to me, as I left Watchtower men and their teachings behind and Christ came into my heart.

The Devil's First Lie (John 8:44)

The doctrine that "man is a soul" is the devil's first lie. In Genesis 3:4 we read, "And the Serpent said unto the woman, Ye shall not surely die."

As Eve stood before him, having an immortal soul, Satan tricked her to believe that she would never be dissolved or die. He ignored the point of man's structure, body and soul. Satan knew that man had an immortal soul. He led her to believe that her body too was immortal — that the body of Eve would not dissolve and die. From that day on, idol worshippers, supporting this, the devil's first lie, have always tried to preserve bodies.

Back there, Satan went even one step farther in his lie by saying, "For God knoweth that in the day ye eat thereof, your eyes shall be opened, and ye shall be as God, knowing good and evil" (Gen. 3:5).

Of course, Satan's lie, that man would not die, was soon exposed. It is true that on the day of sin and sentencing, Adam and Eve were not executed. It is this which has brought about credence to Satan's lie. But Eve did die. The body and the soul separated. Her body so beautiful to look at, disintegrated. Her spirit returned unto the Lord.

Satan Improvises on His First Lie

Astutely Satan soon latched on to the fact that man died. Wanting to discredit God, Satan began to bring into question the immortality of the soul. He put forth the view that man himself *is* the soul, and that when man dies, the soul also dies. Soon the idea of natural man prevailed and the conclusion became general that man in this respect is like a beast. Man was thus encouraged to live to gratify his flesh. In that way he would get the full measure out of his life. Satan moved viciously in to eradicate the Scriptural concept of the "image of God" in man, hoping to accelerate its loss.

Soul Washing Begins

How was this done? By soul-washing humans. Once the idea of an immortal soul was washed away, men could be taught to reason out Satan's new doctrine, that *man is a soul.* That done, men's reasoning process could be brainwashed to a narrow channel of revelation and indoctrination. Long afterwards came the Watchtower Society. They have become past masters and teachers of the above age-old natural doctrine about man.

How narrow a channel did the Watchtower Society create? Let me show you by quoting from their official textbook, *Make Sure of All Things,* page 349 on the soul:

"A soul, heavenly or earthly, is a living (or sense-possessing conscious intelligent) creature or person. A soul, heavenly or earthly, consists of a body together with the Life principle, or life force actuating it. An earthly soul is a living, breathing, sentient creature, animal or human. Earthly souls, human and animal, have an organism of flesh kept living by means of blood circulating in their system (Hebrew: *Nephesh*; Greek: *psyche*)."

Spirit

To explain away the spiritual doctrine of the immortality of the soul, the Jehovah's Witnesses render their own definitions. *Ru-ahh* which means "breath of lives," in which creative act God created the soul in His image, as I have shown in Chapter 9, is explained like this on page 357 of *Make Sure of All Things,* under the subheading of Spirit:

" 'Spirit' is translated from *ru-ahh* in the Hebrew and *pneuma* in Greek. The simplest or elementary meaning of both original words are to describe something windlike, that is, something that is not visible but nevertheless produces visible or perceptible results. Both are drawn from root verbs meaning 'to breath' or 'to blow.' 'Spirit' as used in the Bible has at least seven senses or applications of meaning to describe something windlike, viz., as applying to (1) Jehovah God, (2) Christ Jesus, (3) Angels, (4) Life force, (5) mental disposition, (6) inspired expression and (7) active force of God. This variety of applications is possible in that all are windlike, all are invisible to the human eye and yet all effects that are visible, as the elementary meaning of the original words indicate."

Animal Souls and Human Souls Alike?

Under the subheading "soul," on page 349, Numbers 31:28 is quoted, "And a levy of tribute unto the Lord of the men of war which went to battle: one soul of five hundred, both of the persons, and of the beeves, and of the asses, and of the sheep." This passage is used to prove that animal souls and human souls are alike.

The context of chapter 31 of Numbers, however, shows that a war levy of 1000 persons per tribe was taken. From the 25th verse on, a division of the spoils is projected. Among other things, the spoils included living things. This description has nothing whatever to do with the quality of animal or human souls. It only makes distinction between animate and inanimate things for division purposes.

Does the Soul Die?

Rev. 8:9 and 16:3 are quoted in *Make Sure of All Things*, to prove that the soul dies, or better, is mortal. Note the Scripture in both places. These passages describe creatures that live in the sea. No significance should be placed on the word "soul" in the translation of this text, since it means merely a living thing.

Is Likeness With Adam the Soul?

They then quote 1 Cor. 15:45, "And so it is written, The first Adam was made a living soul, the last Adam was made a quickening spirit." Here is an old Jehovah's Witness trick designed to confuse the soul with the body.

We can easily show the meaning of this passage by reading its context. "Howbeit that was not first which is spiritual, but that which is natural; and afterward that which is spiritual.

The first man is of the earth, earthy; the second man is the Lord from heaven. As is the earthy, such are they also that are earthy; and as is the heavenly, such are they also that are heavenly. And as we have borne the image of the earthy, we shall also bear the image of the heavenly" (1 Cor. 15:46-49).

Passage 45 quoted thus proves in context the very opposite of what the Jehovah's Witnesses claim for it. It tells us that the human race is patterned in appearance, in its body in the image of Adam. But even in that structure (note Gen. 2:7; Isa. 43:7) the body was formed first, then the soul was created in "the breath of lives." Even here the earthly came first, then the spiritual. The second Adam is the Lord from Heaven, or God, come to impress His image anew on men. This is a heavenly image, and not an earthly one, as is Adam's in sin and death which now reigns in our race of flesh and blood. As a quickening spirit He leads us fully into his image and in the day of resurrection we who are so quickened will receive a body of glory. This body will be a heavenly one, and not the old earthly one which those will inherit in the resurrection who remained lost.

Paul says, "Now this I say, brethren, that flesh and blood cannot inherit the Kingdom of God." Why? "Neither does corruption inherit incorruption" (1 Cor. 15:50). If one then, as the Jehovah Witnesses here aver, was resurrected in the image of Adam, in a body which is earthy, such a one would not then have put on incorruption. For corruption or condemnation would still characterize that body, even though resurrected (John 5:28,29) and reunited with the soul.

Herein lies proof of another sort. The body of flesh and blood cannot inherit the incorruptible, no more than can the soul receive a body of glory in immortality if while in this body of corruption it became lost to things of the spirit. But the soul living after the spirit, or in Christ Jesus, can and does inherit a heavenly tabernacle (2 Cor. 5:1-4).

God Alone Hath Immortality

In order to confuse the above truth, the Jehovah's Witnesses cite 1 Tim. 1:17 in *Make Sure of All Things*: "Unto the King Eternal, immortal, invisible, the only wise God, be honor and glory forever, Amen!" With the torn-out passage they wish to show that God alone hath immortality. However, the above text says nothing of the kind.

Is the Soul in the Grave?

On page 351, column 2, the Jehovah's Witnesses quote Isa. 14:9,15, 19-20. I will now demonstrate to you to the full a favorite Watchtower trick. Verse 9 reads "Sheol [hell] from beneath is moved for thee to meet thee at thy coming. . . ." That is all they quote of verse 9. Still, verse 9 contains more, as follows, ". . . it stirreth up the dead for thee, even all the chief ones of the earth; it hath raised up from their thrones all the kings of the nations!"

Why have they omitted this second portion of verse 9? Because it shows that the dead were stirred up at his coming to Sheol. They were moving about.

But that is as nothing in this deception. Why, in their quotation do they omit verses 10-14, and then jump to the 15th verse? It is because these interim verses show conclusively that the dead in Sheol are very much alive, the very thing they endeavor to disprove in the hacked-up quotation of a part of verse 9.

Let us read the 10th verse, which Jehovah's Witnesses want us to overlook. "All they shall speak and say unto thee, Art thou also become weak as we? Art thou become like unto us? Thy pomp is brought down to the Sheol [grave] and the noise of thy viols: the worm is spread under thee, and the worms cover thee."

In these verses we are met by those already dead: and they talk, ask questions, evaluate their fate, etc.

If verses 19,20, which they quote in *Make Sure of All Things,* are read in conjunction with the 9th to 18th verses, most of which they delete, we see that the lot of one in Hell is here described in full. It is obviously, and irrevocably described as conscious everlasting punishment of such souls, beyond the grave and beyond death of the body. Obviously, death and grave are only the gates that lead to Hell.

The Soul That Sinneth, It shall Die

On page 352, column 1, we come across another gem of Watchtower trickery. Here Ezek. 18:4 and verse 20 are quoted: "Behold, all souls are mine; as the soul of the father, so also the soul of the son is mine; the soul that sinneth, it shall die."

First of all note that they totally ignore verses 5 to 19 in this quotation. Deleting arbitrarily, they jump to the 20th verse which reads, "The soul that sinneth, it shall die. The son shall not bear the iniquity of the father, neither shall the father bear the iniquity of the son: the righteousness of the righteous shall be upon him, and the wickedness of the wicked shall be upon him."

Why do they omit and completely ignore verses 5 to 19? It is because therein are given the wonderful conditions under which each and every soul can live after the Spirit in the flesh, and then can go to rest at the time of death and the grave to await resurrection of *life* in immortality, and will not see *death* in a body of shame and contempt in immortality, when it comes forth. In those verses is set forth the case of a just father, who walks with God, who begets a son who becomes unjust and is a sinner, who in turn begets a son who is adjudged just. Three generations are here portrayed. The one who was wicked dies in his iniquity; the other two, who also die, shall live.

Yet all die — one dies in iniquity — the other two in righteousness. What is their destiny?

The 20th verse, misused and misquoted out of context by the Watchtower Society in order to hide this revelation of salvation to come, gives the answer. "The soul that sinneth, it shall die. . . ."

A total picture of what is here portrayed emerges in verses 21-24. The Jehovah's Witnesses deftly ignore this.

The Lord asks in the 23rd verse, "Have I any pleasure at all that the wicked should die?" Why does the Lord ask this? Even then there were many in Israel who ignored their future state after death. We read in the 25th verse, "Yet ye say, The way of the Lord is not equal." Such who then, and who now, raise this question of complaint, shout "The Lord cannot punish and torture a soul forever, because that would be unjust."

Is the Lord really unequal or unjust in His decree of death for the wicked? The Lord answers in the 25th verse. "Hear now, O house of Israel; Is not my way equal? are not your ways unequal?"

Who Is Responsible for the Destiny of the Soul?

Who is responsible for the destiny of the soul of the wicked, or of the righteous? To show conclusively who is responsible the Lord portrays the case of the wicked who turns to righteousness, and the righteous who turns to wickedness. Each individual himself is responsible for his own course of action in this life in the flesh, and whether his soul shall be continuously separated in the same manner as his body, *dying thou shalt die,* finally to be resurrected in the old body with the ingredient of immortality. The individual is responsible whether he shall continue in *death* in a body of shame and contempt, or whether his soul shall have impressed upon it once again the image of God, our Lord Jesus, and receive in resurrection a body of glory in immortality *to live.* Of such who choose the Lord in this life, the Lord says in the 27th verse, "he shall save his soul."

From what shall he save his soul? "From dying," says verse 28. The full burden of soul-death, eternal punishment in hell, lies upon each individual, says verse 29. If an unequal lot results in one's living in heaven, and another's in Hell, who is unequal? Is it the Lord? He says No in verse 29. You are responsible.

In the 30th verse the Lord promises to judge everyone. This will take place in the day of judgment. Even though all Israelites addressed here were dying, and long since have returned to the dust, they are nevertheless admonished to turn and repent, cast away their transgressions, and make over their heart and spirit. The Lord has no pleasure in their death as is, and much less as it will be if they die in their iniquity unrepentant, with their soul continuing on to a destiny of "Dying thou shalt die" forever.

"The soul that sinneth it shall die." This was not spoken of the body, but of the soul. The body is already condemned to return to dust. Body-death ends in death and the grave. But the soul of the sinner continues dying in hell in eternal separation from life with God. This fate becomes finally sealed when the wicked in the resurrection receives back his own body, vouchsafing for the process of *dying thou shalt die,* forever.

God has sentenced all mankind after Adam to "dying thou shalt die" "for dust thou art, and to dust thou shalt return." Ezekiel 18 shows clearly that whereas death came to all who are in the flesh, for all flesh is included in the sin of Adam and his condemnation, death upon their souls comes only in accordance with each individual's own life while in the flesh. Why? Because Jesus Christ died for us and has thus become the anchor for all souls who accept him and who already before his coming accepted him by faith. Who, then, is unequal? Surely it is not God. It is men who will not repent.

Everybody dies after Adam in whose image we are born.

But the soul does not die if the *image of God,* Jesus Christ, is once again impressed upon it. Each soul lives or dies, thus, according to its own life in the body. This discussion of Ezekiel very obviously proves the very opposite of what the Watchtower intends to show.

For they, the Jehovah's Witnesses, in accepting the devil's lie that man shall not die, had to wash away the image of the soul, and convince men that the soul is non-existent in death and in the grave. This is done to hide the fact that man died spiritually, in the soul, falling away from God in continuous and eternal separation. Satan will have been proved a liar as sinful souls clothed once again with their sinful bodies of shame and contempt see *death* in immortality in Hell. Transgressors *will die* forever and ever, thus disproving the devil's lie.

The Lord verifies it: "For I have no pleasure in the death of him that dieth, saith the Lord God: wherefore turn yourselves, and live ye" (Ezek. 18:32). Those who come forth in *death,* soul and a body of dishonor reunited in the resurrection, certainly do not give God pleasure. Upon them is His wrath.

Man a Brute Beast Soul?

On page 352 in the first column of *Make Sure of All Things* the Watchtower Society quotes 2 Peter 2:12, "But these, as natural brute beasts made to be taken and destroyed, speak evil of things they understand not; and shall utterly perish in their own corruption." This verse is supposed to prove that Peter teaches that "the creature soul is mortal, destructible and corruptible."

You are watching another Watchtower conjured up red herring streak across a great spiritual truth. It is deliberately drawn across the second chapter of second Peter. This is done in order to hide the fact that Peter here speaks of "false prophets," heretics, and of the fate of wicked and corrupt souls. Peter says in verse 3, "And through covetousness shall they with feigned words make merchandise of you; whose judgment now of a long time lingereth not, and their damnation slumbereth not."

First of all Peter says, such are already judged since they embrace not Christ; condemnation of old abides on them. Peter even states that their damnation is a reality, not even deferred. In fact, they are on their way to Hell.

Those who are heretics, false teachers, or brute beasts are

described in this second chapter as "unstable souls." Their characteristics are: "they speak great swelling words of vanity, they allure through the lusts of the flesh, through much wantonness, those that were clean escaped from those who live in error" (2 Peter 2:18).

The Watchtower Society early embraced such errors, or heresies. Now they uphold them in *Make Sure of All Things.* If you follow their main thrust, HELL IS THE GRAVE, and you agree that you have "no immortal soul," they will say you have come free. To what have you become free? You have become free to become a Kingdom Publisher of the authoritarian New World society. You are thus overcome by a corruption of truths, and made to join their error. Once you have been so overcome, you are in bondage to their teachings in the Watchtower. In performance, you become merchandise to them. Out of the books of *the image,* come forth "great swelling words" and works of men, in place of the word of God.

Peter pungently describes such in this second chapter, in verses 19-22, "While they promise them liberty, they themselves are the servants of corruption: for of whom a man is overcome, of the same he is brought in bondage. For if after they have escaped the pollutions of the world through the knowledge of the Lord and Saviour Jesus Christ, they are entangled again therein, and overcome, the latter end is worse with them than the beginning. For it had been better for them not to have known the way of righteousness, than, after they have known it, to turn from the holy commandment delivered unto them."

Artfully bandying about the name of Jesus Christ, mouthing terms of salvation or being saved, they lay themselves open to condemnation in Hell, as shown in verses 4-6.

Verse 22 shows they act like dogs or swine towards salvation — or like brute beasts. Such still say, wallowing in errors of old, that they are beasts, die like beasts, go to the same place as beasts. This 22nd verse shows, since they act like beasts, they are treated as such, in that they are taken, chained and delivered into darkness, being reserved for the coming judgment. Then, appearing in their old bodies with the ingredient of immortality quite evident, which they denied in this life, *they will be imprisoned* in the prison house of the Universe, the Lake of Fire, to roam under restraint like beasts, forever and ever.

This passage, and this entire chapter, shows once more the

very opposite the Watchtower intends it to show. It shows the lot of the souls who are lost.

Soul Is the Seed

When the body dies and is buried, the soul either goes to Paradise or to Hell. In Hell it keeps on dying eternally; in Paradise it rests in the anchor of Jesus Christ.

Luke 21:19, "In your patience possess ye your souls!"

1 Peter 4:19, "Wherefore, let them that suffer according to the will of God commit the keeping of their souls to him in welldoing, as unto a faithful Creator."

Rev. 20:4, "And I saw thrones, and they sat upon them, and judgment was given unto them: and I saw the souls of them that were beheaded for the witness of Jesus, and for the Word of God, and which had not worshipped the beast . . . and they lived and reigned with Christ a thousand years."

How did these souls get to Paradise, in heaven? In what way do they become the seed for a new glorious body?

1 Cor. 15:35-38, "But some man will say, How are the dead raised up? and with what body do they come? Thou fool; that which thou sowest is not quickened, except it die; and that which thou sowest, thou sowest not that body that shall be, but bare grain, it may chance of wheat, or some other grain [perhaps tares]; But God giveth it a body as it hath pleased Him, to every seed [soul] his own body."

From the 39th verse on, in 1 Cor. 15, the illustration of the soul as the seed or grain, is elucidated.

Adam, the first man, was made a living soul. The whole soul dwelt in a body *formed* out of the dust of the ground. By sinning, Adam lost the image and likeness of God. His offspring all now came forth in Adam's condition, although created of God as immortal souls.

Then came the last Adam, the very image of God Himself, the express image of Him, Heb. 1:3, who was made a quickening spirit, his soul living in full harmony with God the Father. He died, but He was not left in the grave. He brought about atonement. This same body, since His soul had not sinned, came forth the third day. His body was a body of flesh and bone when he died. It was, what Paul here so wonderfully shows, in resurrection, to become a glorified body. He concludes this to be the destiny of all who believe in Jesus Christ: "As we have borne the image of the earthy [Adam] we shall also bear the image of the heavenly. Now this I say, brethren, that flesh and blood cannot inherit the kingdom of heaven; neither corruption inherit incorruption."

If a soul dies clothed with Christ's righteousness upon it, or with His image impressed upon it, it carries with it the life of Jesus Christ, and in the day of resurrection inherits a body of glory in immortality to life.

But if a soul dies in the image of Adam, in dissolution, *sans* the image of God, it cannot inherit in the resurrection the image of Jesus Christ in His body. It depends exactly on the kind of seed that is planted. If it is the old body in whose features the image of God was long marred, it comes forth to a resurrection of damnation (John 5:28,29). Thus, if the soul dies wicked, it is corrupted as we read in 2 Peter 2:2, which is what Jehovah's Witnesses hide. It cannot therefore, inherit an incorruptible or untarnished body of glory. In its case, it sees death, where the "worm ceaseth not to gnaw and the fire remains unquenched."

The soul of man is immortal. Apart from God, His image and likeness become marred and lost. The soul then because of this, remains in torment and torture. If it has once again been impressed with God's IMAGE AND LIKENESS, by putting on Christ, it lives forever unto God.

The soul then is apart from the body. It was not formed from existing material as was its body. This soul is immortal. God delights in those souls who live unto His glory (Isa. 42:1; Heb. 10:38; Lev. 26:11; Isa. 1:14).

What kind of soul do you have?

Chapter 11

IMMORTALITY OF THE SOUL BROUGHT TO LIGHT BY JESUS CHRIST

Immortality Comes to Light Again

Death and the grave, man's exit gates from earth from Abel on, long shrouded the destiny of the soul in darkness. In fact, because of this darkness into which souls vanish, it has been easy for heretics and false teachers to wash it entirely out of existence.

All of that, however, need no longer be true. Matters have changed. Listen to Paul's statement of that change. Who brought immortality to light as far as souls are concerned? Was it some philosopher like Plato? Or Socrates? No, nothing like that. "Who hath saved us, and called us with an holy calling, not according to our works, but according to his own purpose and grace, which was given us in Christ Jesus before the world began" (2 Tim. 1:9).

What purpose and grace is this, which had its antecedence before this world of man began? As Paul says in Romans, it is to be vessels of mercy (Rom. 9:23). What again is the glory of God in Christ Jesus? It is his immortality, his "dwelling in the light which no man can approach unto, whom no man hath seen, nor can see: to whom be honor and power everlasting, Amen" (1 Tim. 6:16). Man made in this image who was in this manner to be a vessel of mercy (Rom. 9:23) alas, subsequently became a vessel of dishonor!

Disobedience changed man. Because of this, man's body disintegrated at his death in the grave and his spirit returned to God who gave it (Eccl. 12:7). Since revelation was incomplete his soul disappeared in a shroud of darkness in the Old Testament Sheol-Hades.

What Happened to the Soul?

Just what happened to this immortal soul? Many a writer and seer of the Old Testament wrote about the mystery of the whereabouts of the soul. This we have already discussed in Chapters 9 and 10 in this book. It becomes obvious to us in this account that the souls of many, because wicked and impenitent, went to hell. However, others because of their seeking God in this life, though under wrath and thus afar off, in death resting in Paradise were and are held in escrow, so to speak, in Heaven (Rev. 6:9,10). They rest against the day of resurrection in which such souls will receive a new glorious body. In God's thinking, and that is all important, though once under wrath, they have become vessels of mercy (Rom. 9:22).

But what has changed their status from being under wrath to vessels of mercy? Better still, when did this event transpire? What event would end death and bring life and immortality of soul to light again — something so long shrouded in utter darkness?

Read "But is now made manifest by the appearing of our Saviour Jesus Christ, who hath abolished death, and hath brought life and immortality to light through the gospel" (2 Tim. 1:10).

An Authentic Revelation on the Whereabouts of the Soul

The appearance of our Lord Jesus Christ on earth, as the Son of man, brought to light this authentic revelation of the destiny of man's soul. He had come from behind the veil. Life and immortality in both facets are revealed to us in the second chapter of 2 Timothy. The 20th verse speaks of "vessels of honor" and "vessels of dishonor." Our Lord thus reveals that life and immortality of the soul are prevalent in the great beyond either in a destiny of dishonor, or one of honor!

This, of course, is in harmony with Daniel's prophecy of so long ago, when the end of all is discussed. "And many of them that sleep in the dust of the earth shall awake, some to everlasting life, and some to everlasting shame and contempt" (Dan. 12:2).

Let us examine the course of the appearance of our Lord Jesus Christ as man. We will see depicted for us in this life of the Son of Man, from the cradle to the grave, how Jesus revealed and brought life and immortality to light. If this is so, and our examination proves this, then there never again will be a question in our minds as to what and where the soul is. Once and for all, we will be able to prove the excellency of the Christian doctrine of the immortality of the soul, over the doctrine of heresy that "man *is* a soul," as the Jehovah's Witnesses say.

The Drama of a Soul in Life and Death

A great drama is depicted for us in Phil. 2:5-8: "Let this mind be in you, which was also in Christ Jesus; Who being in the form of God, thought it not robbery to be equal with God: But made himself of no reputation and *took upon him* the form of a servant, and was made in the *likeness of men* and being found in fashion as a man, he humbled himself, and became obedient unto death, even the death of the cross."

What constituted the man Jesus? Was it body and soul?

That can best be evaluated by what happened to him when he died on the cross.

(1) He poured out his soul unto death by shedding his blood (Isa. 53:12). Before he died, he asked his father to receive his spirit (Luke 23:46) (Ps. 31:5).

(2) When the Lord died on the cross, what did he give up and lay down? He Himself said in John 10:15, "I lay down my life for my sheep," or, my total humanity. The apostle John describes the totality of this sacrifice in 1 John 3:16, where he says, "Hereby perceive we the love of God, because he laid down his life for us. . . ." The Son of God, John says, laid down his total life as man.

Jesus actually partook of our human nature. He died for us as a man. We live in him again, by partaking of his divine nature.

Although he was of divine nature, he took unto him, in this act of appearing on earth, human nature. As God, or of divine nature, he eventually sacrificed his human nature. Paul explains this further in Heb. 2:14 for us when he says, "Forasmuch then as the children are partakers of flesh and blood, he also himself likewise took part of the same; that through death he might destroy him that hath the power of death, that is, the devil."

How Could He Partake of Our Nature?

However, since he also had divine nature, he could say of this great event of sacrifice, "Therefore doth the Father love me, because I lay down my life, that I might take it again. No man taketh it from me, but I lay it down of myself. I have power to lay it down, and I have power to take it again. This commandment I received of my Father" (John 10:17,18).

How could that be? Let us look for an illustration which at once could clarify this for us. We have such an illustration in Melchesidec, King of Salem, to whom our Lord is compared. He also was "without father, without mother, without descent, having neither *beginning of days,* nor end of life; but made like unto the Son of God" (Heb. 7:3). Now that is an interesting proof offered as to the deity of Christ, in conjunction with his appearance as Son of Man!

All throughout the 7th chapter of Hebrews, we see Paul make this vital point. This point culminates electrifyingly, "By so much was Jesus made surety for a better testament. And they truly were many priests, because they were not suffered to continue *by reason of death*; but this man, because he continueth ever [Son of God], hath an unchangeable priesthood. Wherefore he is able to save them to the uttermost that come unto God by him, seeing He ever liveth to make intercession for them. For such a High Priest became us, who is holy, harmless, undefiled, separate from sinners and made higher than the heavens" (Heb. 7:22-26).

Here now we have the Son of God, come in the flesh, who took upon him the form of a servant, and was made in the likeness of men. Here was God! What a drama!

How did the Lord take unto himself the form of a servant and the likeness of man? Was it by materializing in human form just as he often did in Old Testament times? Isaiah gives the answer in Isa. 9:6, "For unto us [1] a child is *born,* [2] unto us a son is *given.*" Two natures come here to view.

Jesus was miraculously conceived and born, as a child. Why as a child? Because it is as children that human life begins. That is what Paul means in Heb. 2:14, "For as much as the children are partakers of the flesh and blood, he also took part of the same...." The human nature of the Son of God, was *born.*

But divine nature was not born here; it cannot be. Neither was it begotten in Jesus thirty years later when the Father acknowledged Jesus as His Son, as the Jehovah's Witnesses teach. It is "unto us a son is *given,*" not begotten, begun or born. In the Son "given," here is divine nature fullblown as the Son of God. Note the description: "... and the government shall be upon His shoulder: and His name shall be called Wonderful, Counsellor, the Mighty God, the Everlasting Father, the Prince of Peace" (Isa. 9:6). Could this be said of anyone who was less than divine?

The History of the Lord Jesus as Man

Let us trace the Lord's history as a man. As a man, he began to grow from childhood in his human nature. How was that growth conditioned? "And the child grew and waxed strong in spirit, filled with wisdom; and the grace of God was upon him" (Luke 2:40). He was directing his life to wax strong in the spirit, in his God-consciousness. Consequently, he was filled with wisdom, instead of with fleshly lust. And, as a result, "the grace of God was upon him." That is exactly what would have happened to Adam and to Eve, had they not turned their souls towards gratifying their bodies of flesh. This would have resulted in eternal life to Adam and Eve, in their bodies, as implied in Gen. 2:16,17.

Luke 2:46-47 records another remarkable incident in the growing-up process of Jesus as a man. Note that in this incident the complete spiritual unity and fusion of his two natures comes into play — and that at the age of twelve! His divine nature, of course, was showing through here. (How wrong the Jehovah's Witnesses are to teach that his divine nature was begotten when he was thirty years old!) Also his human nature was already at the age of twelve, attuned to his divine nature. What does this event emphasize? It shows the remarkable growth of his soul toward total God-consciousness at this stage. Poor parents of Jesus, who lived more in the flesh, "And they understood not the saying which he spake unto them" (Luke 2:50).

Still, at the age of twelve, his time had not yet come to fulfill his divine mission. For that reason "he went down with them, and came to Nazareth, and was subject unto them; but his mother kept all his sayings in her heart" (verse 51). Thus Jesus grew from a child to a man. It took all of thirty years. Of this entire period the Holy Spirit says, "And Jesus increased in wisdom and stature, and in favor with God and man" (verse 52).

Luke 3:21-38 records the next report on the man Jesus. Jesus was baptized when thirty years old. God the Father publicly acknowledged Him then as His Son, or God the Son, whereas men had supposed that he was the son of Joseph, etc. His entire life on earth reveals him to be both the Son of God and the Son of Man. We see the two natures, divine and human, in mysterious harmony and interplay. They are here in full view. Let us keep them in full view throughout this discussion. Let us not lose sight of them for one moment. For the deity of Christ is the key to salvation!

The God — Man — or Creator — Soul

The Lord, as Son of man, was thirty years old when his remarkable ministry began. From then on we see a gradual revelation of his coming death. Like all men since Adam, the Son of man was born to die.

Slowly, we begin to see a life unfold of a man pleasing to God. In this process the Lord will have to lay down his life, and then he will take it up again. How could that be? Can a soul take up a new life pleasing to God, after his body has disintegrated in the dust? That will be answered for us, at last, in this forthcoming drama!

Here actually is mention of resurrection of the body. Except in miracles, of temporary duration, that had never happened before. The force of such miracles was blunted, because eventually the one involved died again. Something else, an enduring resurrection here came into view. Here is something stupendous!

Note the first concrete development of things in that direction in what transpired at the temple, as recorded by John 2:13-18. The events portrayed there culminated in a startling revelation. "Jesus answered and said unto them, Destroy this temple, and in three days I will raise it up. Then said the Jews, Forty and six years was this temple in building, and wilt thou rear it up in three days? But he spake of the temple of his body" (verse 19-21).

In the 22nd verse it is said that his disciples remembered this *when he was risen,* and they believed the word which Jesus said. Do we believe it? It was a sign of coming events.

Immortality of a Soul Proved by a Sign

The Lord's disciples were not looking for a sign, for they believed his words. However, the unbelieving Pharisees kept looking for one, and thus the Lord gave them one. "This is an evil generation: they seek a sign: and there shall no sign be given it, but the sign of Jonas the prophet" (Luke 11:29).

What was the sign of Jonah? It is recorded in Jonah 1:17: "Now the Lord had prepared a great fish to swallow up Jonah.

And Jonah was in the belly of the fish three days and three nights."

Was Jonah dead? His body may have been to all intents and purposes. But he cried out during that time and prayed, "And the Lord spoke unto the fish, and it vomited out Jonah on dry land."

In what way was this experience of Jonah to become a sign to the Pharisees? Only if we tie it in with what Jesus said in John 2:19-21, does it become that. The sign would be the *bodily resurrection* of the Lord, after being three days and three nights in the grave. This the Pharisees failed to understand and see. Believing in resurrection, as they professed, they failed to recognize in Jesus the sole "way, the truth, and the life," of all who are embraced in Christ, the redeemed of all ages from Abel on, and all who remain condemned. Jehovah's Witnesses are like the Pharisees in professing to believe in the resurrection while they do not recognize Jesus as the sole way, truth and life. They foolishly expect today, salvation by being in the so-called New World Society. The sign of Jonah is thus lost on them.

Our Lord was here prophesying His bodily resurrection!

There came the fateful day when Jesus, the son of man, died on the cross in agony. He had shown how to live the life of man, from the cradle to the grave. His death on the cross was a humiliating one (Phil. 2:4-9). What was to happen to him now that he hung on the cross? It is important for us to know. For this will tell us what happens to the soul of man when he dies. In the life and death of Jesus is the first full revelation of this long shrouded secret.

Beclouding a Fact

We read, "And when Jesus had cried with a loud voice, he said, Father, into Thy hands I commend my spirit, and having said that, he gave up the ghost" (Luke 23:46).

Here is a very important revelation. Watchtower distortion creeps in here, to blind the Jehovah's Witnesses to the purport of this last statement of our Lord. In their New World Translation of the Greek Scriptures, the translation committee translates Matt. 27:50, "Again Jesus called with a loud voice, and ceaseth to breathe." The Greek word here translated "breathe" is *pneuma,* which most other translations render "spirit."

Why do the Watchtower Committee translate *pneuma* in

Matt. 27:50 as they do? It is because they want the Jehovah's Witnesses to believe that man's spirit is nothing more than the breath of his body and that it does not survive after his death. Thus they say Jesus simply ceased breathing.

However, and they hope the Jehovah's Witnesses will not notice this, they are caught in their own arbitrary ways. Turning upon the parallel passage of Luke 23:46 they translate the same Greek word *pneuma* "spirit." Why this inconsistency, particularly since the same event is recorded? They do this because it would have glaringly exposed their error for the Lord to say, "Into your hands I commend my breath." They had to render it "spirit," to cover their deceitful use of God's word.

What does *pneuma* (Greek) and *ru-ahh* (Hebrew) mean? Is it "spirit," or "breath," which? *Ru-ahh* is a plural word, and literally means "breath of lives." As we have seen in Gen. 2:7, God created the soul in man, by giving him the "breath of lives." This breath of lives, brought sense-consciousness to the body God had formed out of the existing material of the earth. There was also the other facet. This breath of lives was in man's case God-breathed. For man it made God-consciousness possible. It endowed man with an immortal soul. Also when Jesus gave up his spirit to God, he gave up his life in his body.

A little later a man by the name of Joseph, from Arimathea, came to Pilate and begged for the body of Jesus. He laid the body in a sepulchre hewn out of stone, obviously to return to the dust from which it had come (Luke 23:50-55).

From the above we now know what happened to the body of Jesus. What about his soul? This is important. Was His soul dissolved when his blood poured out of his body? Or was it dissolved when He gave up His Spirit to God?

The soul of Jesus was quickened by the spirit in death.

The inspired apostle gives us the answer. He says, "For Christ also hath once suffered for sins, the just for the unjust, that he might bring us to God, being put to death in the flesh, but quickened by the spirit" (1 Peter 3:18).

Here we have it! The Lord's soul, without body, was quickened by the spirit. It was alive! Read for yourself what happened to Jesus: "By which he also went and preached unto the spirits in prison" (verse 19). Minus body, which lay in the tomb, he was nevertheless alive.

So that is what happens to the soul. "The souls of just men," where are they? They obviously are not visible to our view, because they have no *body*, which we can see. But now we do know what happens to their soul in Paradise.

Shall his soul remain in Sheol, a common grave of mankind?

This drama goes on. As we wait breathlessly, our mind's eye is drawn to a prophetic utterance of David, made so long ago, which we find in Ps. 16:10. It reads provocatively, "For thou wilt not leave my soul in hell [Sheol], neither wilt thou suffer thine Holy One to see corruption."

Hell, here of course, in Hebrew is Sheol, the Old Testament term referring to the place of the unseen dead. But what about the Holy One not suffering corruption? Upon the separation of soul and body, the body soon disintegrates. But we know that a soul does not dissolve. Here was a soul which was not corrupted, which was innocent of wrong-doing. Yet it had died, in this, that its life in the body had been snuffed out. How could such a body, though dead, remain uncorrupted? Only if it were immediately resurrected! That is the crux of Ps. 16:10.

Resurrection Is the Clue to Understanding of Immortality of Soul

As we linger on the threshold of resurrection, we are reminded of an event which is recorded in John 11:34-44. Of the many facets of truth here recorded, note this outstanding one, "Said I not unto thee, that if thou wouldest believe, thou shouldest see the glory of God" (verse 40). What was the glory of God? It was the creative act of God in man, creating man a composite of body-soul. Here Jesus, as Son of God, was to show the glory of God, when as a *whole* man, body and soul, He came back from the dead.

When Jesus asked them to remove the stone of the tomb, Martha made a very important statement, "Lord by this time he stinketh: for he hath been dead these four days" (verse 39).

The resurrection of Lazarus concerns us and our ancestors, whose bodies suffer corruption in the grave. It promises that, even after the body is corrupted, we shall have a bodily resurrection in God's time, to reveal the glory of God, his creation of a *whole* man: body and soul, even though it has been marred by death and its inevitable results. That is what Jesus meant in saying, "Said I not unto thee, that, if thou wouldest believe, thou shouldest see the glory of God?" namely God's power to put man together again as a vessel of glory: body and soul.

"And when he had spoken, he cried out with a loud voice, Lazarus, come forth. And he that was dead came forth, bound hand and foot with grave clothes: and his face was bound about with a napkin. Jesus said unto them, loose him, and let him go" (43-44).

How a Soul Penetrates From Death to Life

Let us go back now, after this informative digression, to our drama. The time has come. It is early in the morning of the first day. Women who loved Jesus came, and the body of Jesus was gone! Grief-stricken, they were interrupted by two men with a strange question, "Why seek ye the living among the dead? He is not here, but is risen: remember how he spoke unto you when he was yet in Galilee, saying, the Son of man must be delivered into the hands of sinful men, and be crucified, and the third day rise again" (Luke 24:1-8).

Prodded like this, they remembered the words quoted by the angels, for that is who these two young men were. Still it was hard for them to fully realize that the Lord had been raised in his body. As we follow the events in the narration of Luke 24 we can appreciate the experiences of the disciples.

In the Gospel of John we are shown a specific instance in the case of Thomas. He simply could not believe it. Thomas went so far as to say, "Except I shall see in his hands the print of nails, and put my finger in the print of the nails, and thrust my hand in his side, I will not believe" (John 20:25).

Eight days later Thomas was present with the assembled disciples. Jesus came through the wall, saying, "Peace be unto you." Looking at Thomas he said to him, "Reach hither thy finger, and behold my hands; and reach hither thy hand, and thrust it into my side; and be not faithless but believing" (John 20:26,27).

In abject submission Thomas exclaimed, "My Lord and my God."

The Glory of God

It is in the resurrection of Jesus that we see the glory of God upon man again, which is: body and soul, creatively put together again.

Why do the Jehovah's Witnesses deny this bodily resurrection of Jesus? Why do they say he arose in the Spirit and manufactured the various bodies used by materializing?

They had no way of going farther with their natural doctrine than this. If they believed in the deity of Christ, as I do now, they could have walked the second mile with Christianity. But they deny it. Unless you believe the doctrine of God, that Jesus is both the Son of God and the Son of Man, and that he died, and was resurrected, you cannot appreciate the extent of the salvation which has come our way.

A Man Going to Heaven

Jesus long ago promised that he would go to heaven as a man, in toto: body and soul. That had never before been done. Souls have gone to heaven (Rev. 6:9-10).

The whole process of this phenomenon is explained by the apostle Paul in Eph. 4:9-10, "Now that he ascended, what is it but that he also descended first into the lower parts of the earth? He that descended is the same also that ascended up far above all heavens, that he might fill all things."

Our High Priest Is the Son of God

What a rebuke this inspired statement is to the Jehovah's Witnesses! We all know that Jesus died; and here we are told he was resurrected to be the same as he was, and ascended to heaven the same as he was: body and soul. We are told he will return exactly like this (Acts 1:9-11).

Following the description of Jesus as the Son of Man in John 3:13 we are told in the 17th verse, that at the same time Jesus also was the Son of God.

To appreciate this fully let us read once again Heb. 7:26-28. "For such a high priest became us, who is holy, harmless, undefiled, separate from sinners, and made higher than the heavens; who needed not daily, as those other high priests, to offer up sacrifice, first for his own sins, and then for the people's: for this he did once, when he offered up himself, for the law maketh men high priests which have infirmity; but the word of the oath, which was since the law, maketh *the Son,* who is consecrated forever."

There we have it. The Son of God in his divine nature was to become the high priest who offered up himself, as the Son of man; or who gave his complete human nature as a sacrifice, and was to carry this sacrifice in toto to heaven. That put sin and death to an end for all time in those who believed in Him, and brought life and immortality to light.

By denying the deity of Christ the Jehovah's Witnesses have again lost sight of life and immortality.

Jesus Christ the Glory of God!

As we look now upon Christ, we see the Son of God and the Son of man mysteriously one. As this Christ is the center of the Bible.

As we look fully upon Christ, and believe, death vanishes, and everlasting life begins. The flesh fades, and we are born again, or, as was He, quickened in the spirit. And like Him, we busy ourselves by preaching to the prisoners in the flesh.

Let us say, "Come, look upon Christ, our Saviour and God: repent, believe, be born again, live in Christ."

Chapter 12

JESUS CHRIST IS THE SON OF GOD

What Proves Jesus to Be the Son of God?

Great emphasis is laid by the Jehovah's Witnesses, who deny the deity of Christ, on the Father's declaration in Matt. 3:17. "And lo a voice from heaven, saying, This is my beloved Son, in whom I am well pleased." They say that this declaration proves that Jesus Christ was, at the stage of this declaration, spirit begotten to become the Son of God; and as an embryo His New Creation would grow to maturity, while He lived on earth as man. Then, so they say, upon his death as a man his body was annihilated, and He was resurrected in the Spirit as possessor of divine nature, or a new Creation.

It was not only the declaration by the Father, which was heard when Jesus stepped out of Jordan's waters, which proved Jesus to be the Son of God. It was His subsequent resurrection from the dead which demonstrated beyond a shadow of doubt that Jesus *is* the Son of God, equal to God. The Apostle Paul introduces him to us in Rom. 1:3,4 as follows, "Concerning his Son Jesus Christ our Lord, which was made of the seed of David according to the flesh; and declared [determined] to be the Son of God with power, according to the spirit of holiness, by the resurrection from the dead." The power of God made manifest in His resurrection presents Jesus to us as our Saviour-God.

Few men recognized Jesus as the Son of God while he was in the flesh. Paul says in 1 Cor. 2:8, "Which none of the princes of this world knew: for had they known they would not have crucified the Lord of glory." But many men, *after* His resurrection, recognized Him as the Lord of Glory. By the Lord's grace, I am one of the millions.

The real proof of the deity of Christ was not given by word, or declaration, for it was not given credence. Telling proof of Christ's deity was furnished in our Lord's dying and in His subsequent resurrection by the power of God. This power carries it right into the heart of the believer, lending to the believer power to live and die with Christ. That power changes things. We read, "For to this end Christ both died, and rose, and revived, that He might be Lord both of the dead and the living" (Rom. 14:9).

What Is the Extent of This Power?

Peter clarifies the extent of this power in Acts 10:36 by saying, "The word which God sent unto the children of Israel, preaching peace by Jesus Christ (he is Lord of all)." This means that he was not only Lord of the living, but also the dead. You find this word spoken to Israel in Isa. 57:19. The preaching of the peace, predicting it both for the living and the dead, is found in numerous places, such as Dan. 7:14; Matt. 28:18; Rev. 17:14; Rev. 19:16. This is really the gospel, made so by the power of God in the resurrection of Jesus Christ.

As shown in chapter 11 it was by the Lord's life, his subsequent death and his triumphant resurrection, that the state of both the living and the dead was for the first time illuminatingly revealed. Having both lived and died, which embraces both the living and the dead, Christ triumphed in coming forth to life again in his resurrection. In this way He revealed Himself to be not only God of the living, as had been His title as a result of the act of creation, but now, God of the living and the dead, becoming so by his power of resurrection.

That by his resurrection He became God of the dead and the living, is proved in its *ultimo ratio* by His becoming the Judge of both the living and the dead in the last day. We read this confident declaration in Rom. 14:10. "But why dost thou judge thy brother? Or why dost thou set at naught thy brother? For we shall all stand before the judgment seat of Christ."

The life, death and rise of Jesus Christ brought to light that He is the Lord of glory. By the power of His resurrection He stands brilliantly revealed as God of the living and the dead. That is indeed good news. That is the gospel!

This latent power of the gospel, extending over the living and the dead, is expressed in a spirit of love, and a spirit of power (2 Tim. 1:7). We see its positive character for the living believers well described by Paul in the spirit of love, "For I am persuaded, that neither death, nor life, nor angels, nor principalities, nor powers, nor things present, nor things to come, nor height, nor depth, nor any other creature, shall be able to separate us from the love of God, which is in Christ Jesus our Lord [Greek: *Kurios*]" (Rom. 8:38,39).

It is also pressed in on both the dead and the living in a spirit of power, for it makes certain the appearing of all the living and the dead before the judgment seat of Christ our Lord (Greek: *Kurios*).

The Dual Nature of Jesus Christ

An authoritative statement is found in Isa. 45:23. There Jehovah, the covenant God of Israel, says of Himself, "I have sworn by myself, the word is gone out of my mouth in righteousness, and shall not return, That unto me every knee shall bow, every tongue shall swear." Paul quotes from this positive statement in Rom. 14:10-12, applying it as coming from the Lord Jesus Christ. It is not limited to the living only as was in Isa. 45:23, but to both the living and the dead, as follows, "For it is written, as I live, saith the Lord, every knee shall bow to me, and every tongue shall confess to God. So then every one of us shall give account of himself to God."

This is the spirit of power inherent in death and resurrection. It determines, beyond refute, that Jesus Christ is the Son of God in the divine trinity: Father, Son and Holy Spirit.

In the account of Phil. 2:6-9, which the Jehovah's Witnesses must twist out of shape to uphold their unitarianism, as we shall see in the next chapter, we come face to face with the dual natures of Jesus Christ. More than that, we see the miracle of two natures fused into one personality. Only God can do that, for God is one in three persons: Father, Son and Holy Spirit. Here He is one personality in two natures!

In verse 6 Jesus is depicted as very God. Note, He does not give up His being God. No, He "took upon him the form of servant," says the 7th verse. In other words, He added this nature of man to His divine nature. He blended them into one personality.

How could that be? Let us look once more at Isa. 9:6. "For unto us a child is born, unto us a son is given. . . ." What a wealth of insight lies revealed in this Scripture! It reveals to us the mind of the Lord in the matter.

Can you understand it? Please remember we are not discussing here a doctrine of man. You are here face to face with the doctrine of God!

If it were about man, we would not have too much difficulty. "For what man knoweth the things of a man, save the spirit which is in him?" (1 Cor. 2:11).

But Phil. 2:6-9 and Isa. 9:6 are not about a man. They were written about and reveal to us, God. To understand them at all, we must have the Spirit of God. Paul says, "Even so the things of God knoweth no man, but the Spirit of God" (1 Cor. 2:11).

Let us face it. If we cannot understand the doctrine of God, which is a spiritual doctrine, if we cannot discern Jesus Christ as Lord (Greek: *Christos Kurion*), then read what Paul writes, showing why we cannot discern it. He says in 1 Cor. 12:3, "...and that no man can say that Jesus is Lord (*Christos Kurion*) but by the Holy Spirit." There we have it. Only the Holy Spirit, the third person of God, can reveal that to you (John 16:13,14).

The Watchtower Society knows the power of that statement. They came face to face with it in the Greek manuscripts, when they discovered it in 1 Cor. 12:3b, "and that no man can say *Christos Kurion*." They had declared in the foreword of their New World Translation, that "wherever the Greek word *Kurios* and *Theos* appeared they would translate them Jehovah." Notice, in this case, as in many others, they broke their own rule and did not translate *Christos Kurion* as "Christ is Jehovah," but left "Lord" stand. The Unitarian lie had to be covered up. Those who do not have the Holy Spirit not only fail to understand that Jesus is God. They also deny it.

A Child Is Born

But now enough of the headquarters of natural man's religion. We go back to this fascinating revelation of Isa. 9:6, "A child is born." By birth as a child Jesus Christ became the Son of man, the Son of David, the son of Abraham, etc. See how many prophecies about the Messiah already fall in line? It is, however, also said in Isa. 9:6, "a Son is given." As you read on in Isa. 9, look at the God-like titles there! His deity leaps to view in them in this manner: Son of God, the Mighty God, Lord, Jehovah, El, Elohim, etc.! These are different from the titles used in referring to Him as being born a child! How the fusion of His two natures shine in the titles accruing as both Son of man and Son of God in one person. The prophecies of all the past portray and verify it.

All of this becomes clearer and glows with greater luster in the mystic fusion of two natures, as radiated in Christ's life, death and resurrection riveting for all time their transcendent, external union. This, Paul describes as the Son being the brightness of the Father's glory (Heb. 1:3) in the same way as brightness is related to the sun.

Note more of the pregnant meaning put by Paul into Phil. 2:8-9, "And being found in fashion as a man, he humbled himself, and became obedient unto death, even the death of the cross. Wherefore God also hath highly exalted Him, and given Him a name which is above every name."

By His death and resurrection Jesus is revealed as God, as the Son of God. Paul shows this in Rom. 14:10-12.

Jehovah the Hidden God — Jesus the Revealed God

Jehovah hid His face from sinful man. There was the barrier of sin. Yet, Jehovah's purpose for man remained unchanged, as Isaiah says in Isa. 45:23, "That unto me every knee shall bow, every tongue shall swear." The limitation of this divine purpose reaches its climax in the all-embracing statement: "That at the name of Jesus every knee should bow, of things in heaven, and things in earth, and things under the earth, and that every tongue shall confess that Jesus Christ is Lord [Greek: *Kurios*] to the glory of God the Father" (Phil. 2:10,11).

Here again in Phil. 2:11 the Unitarian minded Watchtower Society had to do some twisting and juggling in their New World Translation. Although they had ruled that wherever *Kurios* or *Theos* appeared in the Greek, they would translate it Jehovah, they left "Lord" stand here too. They did this because like all sinful men, they like the "hidden God" better than the revealed Saviour! If they had followed their intentions it would have read "and that every tongue shall confess that Jesus Christ is Jehovah." That would have proved right the historic doctrine of God of Christianity, and would have proved wrong their Unitarian doctrine that Jesus is a created being. So they chose to be inconsistent.

A Name Above That of Jehovah

Would this name even be above the name of Jehovah? It certainly was above every name ever given to both of His natures, now fused into one, until all becomes subject to God — Father, Son and Holy Spirit — in the end of judgment, as shown in 1 Cor. 15:27-28. Let us see.

In Isa. 45:23 Jehovah says, "And unto me every knee shall bow...." Note the context. Israel and her surrounding neighbors are discussed. It is therefore in the present and future tense that Jehovah tells these nations, who were in existence then, and would be for some time in the future, that "every knee shall bow" to him. But, he does not reveal all to them. He hides the most important part to them, as to how "every knee shall bow." Jehovah hides Himself from these nations from afar. The Holy Spirit causes Isaiah in the 15th verse to write of Jehovah, "Verily thou art a God that hidest thyself, O God of Israel, the Saviour."

Jehovah had not fully revealed Himself. This He would do in the Saviour, who is the Son of God. He would reveal Himself as the Father in the Son, in the sense that a Son inherits His father's name, estate, glory, etc., and continuing would add new luster to His Father. In what way would this be done? John reveals that to us in a striking portrayal of the Trinity in John 1:18. "No man hath seen God at any time; the only begotten Son, which is in the bosom of the Father, he hath declared him."

Thus the hidden God, who withdrew from sinful man when he transgressed His law, who hid from man from the days of Adam to John the Baptist, now revealed Himself in the only begotten Son of God.

The Lord of Glory Is Jesus

Forgetting those amidst the Jehovah's Witnesses who simply will not "Let God be True," let us look at the revealed Lord of Glory! It is particularly in His death and resurrection that Jesus is revealed as the Lord of Glory — or God (1 Cor. 2:8). "Emmanuel," or as the Holy Spirit translated it in Matt. 1:23, "God with us," is his name. "They shall call his name Emmanuel, which being interpreted is God with us." That is also what the Lord is called in Isa. 7:14. In Matt. 1:21 his name is given as Jesus, which in Hebrew is *Yashua,* or as the 21st verse of Matt. 1 says, "for he shall save his people from their sins." He, then, is the "hidden God," hidden in the bosom of the Father (John 1:18) to come forth as the Saviour (Isa. 45:15), prophesied long ago. As Saviour, then, Jesus Christ is identified as the Son of God — or God.

This chain of proof, that the Son of God is "God with us" (Matt. 1:23) in the flesh, extends backwards into the Old

Testament to Isa. 9:6 and forward into the New Testament to 1 Tim. 3:16, "And without controversy great is the mystery of godliness: God was manifest in the flesh, justified in the Spirit, seen of angels, preached unto the Gentiles, believed on in the world, received up in glory."

The significance of the name Jesus over against that of Jehovah, as exemplified in meaning of Saviour-God over against Creator-God, is further brought to light by the statement made in 1 Tim. 3:16, "Preached unto the Gentiles." Note, Jehovah of Isa. 45:23 speaks only of Israel as being saved; and of Egypt and Ethiopia, and the Sabians or Gentiles, being enslaved.

How that was all changed after the resurrection of Jesus Christ! Then we read of Him, "In his name shall the Gentiles hope" (Matt. 12:21). Peter could add, "Neither is there salvation in any other: for there is none other name under heaven given among men, whereby we must be saved" (Acts 4:12). That is the reason why his "name is above every other name" (Phil. 2:9).

Jesus and the Father Are One

If Jehovah was the God of Israel and they were His peculiar people, then Jesus is revealed as *Yashuah,* meaning Jehovah-Saviour, because He is He who fills "all in all," as we read in Eph. 1:23. Who then is the God of our Lord Jesus, who is called the Father of Glory (Eph. 1:17) when Jesus is dying and being resurrected becomes again the Lord of Glory? (1 Cor. 2:8).

The God of our Lord Jesus is a triune God: Father, Son and Holy Spirit (Matt. 28:18,19; Heb. 9:14). Coming out of the bosom of God (John 1:18) everything in heaven and earth becomes subject to Him. As this subjection is achieved (Phil. 2:10,11) over all who either find salvation, or eternal damnation in Judgment, there comes the time when the Son Himself becomes subject to God. Why? So that God (the triune God: Father, Son and Holy Spirit) may be "all in all" (1 Cor. 15:27,28).

How wonderfully here in 1 Cor. 15:27,28 is elucidated the doctrine of God — Father, Son and Holy Spirit! Having come out of the bosom of God in the first place as the Son of God, the Lord of Glory returns to the bosom of God when He has accomplished His mission as Saviour-God. Once again we see God: Father, Son and Holy Spirit, become "all in all."

In the more ancient sense, and originally, in the sense of

Creation it is said, "For of him, and through him, and to him are all things: to whom be glory forever. Amen" (Rom. 11:36). Recall that the act of creation being all these long ages an accomplished fact, is reported as having been achieved by God: Father, Son and Holy Spirit. Note the triune aspect accomplished by creation becomes in Paul's distinctive: (1) *"For of Him,* (2) and through Him, (3) and to Him are all things." This is a present aspect; always *present,* as shown in the last clause *are* all things.

Jesus, God's Heir

This continuity of creation in being is brought out in Col. 1:15-16. Here Jesus as the heir — or the begotten one, is credited with having built all things. Of the Father He is eternally begotten, and He created or built "all things." Who now built "all things"? Note, Paul in Heb. 3:4 says, "For every house is builded by some man, but He that built all things is God"; this is the God of the Bible: Father, Son and Holy Spirit.

How is explained this subjection of the Son unto the Father, when it has subjected all in heaven, in earth, and under the earth, either in salvation or condemnation? In Dan. 7:9 we read: "I beheld till the thrones were cast down, and the Ancient of days did sit, whose garment was white as snow, and the hair of His head like the pure wool: His throne was like the fiery flame, and His wheels as burning fire." Here is a wonderful description of the Ancient of days.

Now looking at the Son of God in heaven, we locate, and we identify him in Rev. 1:13-15 as the Son of man. Let us read the description of him: "And in the midst of the seven candlesticks one like unto the Son of man, clothed with a garment down to the foot, and gird about the paps with a golden girdle. His head and his hair were white like wool, as white as snow; and his eyes were as a flame of fire; and his feet like unto fine brass, as if they burned in a furnace and his voice as many waters." Note the similarity in description. The Son returned to the bosom of the Father? Of the God of Jesus Christ it is said in Isa. 44:6, "Thus saith the Lord. . . . I am the first, and I am the last, and beside me there is no God." Jesus, speaking in Rev. 1:17 says, "Fear not, I am the first and the last." Is this not the same God?

In Ps. 93:1,2 we read, "The Lord . . . thy throne is established of old; thou art from everlasting"; and in Ps. 90:2 we read,

"From everlasting to everlasting thou art God." Of Jesus we read in Micah 5:2, "But thou, Bethlehem Ephratah, ... out of thee shall He come forth unto me that is to be ... whose going forth have been from of old, from everlasting." Is this not the same God?

All-embracing, in every aspect, note the following comparisons between God and Christ:

God		Christ
	As Saviour	
Ps. 106:21		Luke 2:11
Isa. 43:11		Acts 4:12
	As Creator	
		Col. 1:16
		John 1:3
		Heb. 1:2
	As Lord of Lords	
Deut. 10:17		Rev. 19:16
	As the Rock	
Ps. 18:2		1 Cor. 10:4
2 Sam. 22:2		
Deut. 32:4		
	As Our Strength	
Isa. 26:4		Phil. 4:13
	As Omnipresent	
Jer. 23:24		Matt. 28:20
Ps. 139:7-10		Matt. 18:20
	As Pierced	
Zech. 12:10		Rev. 1:7
	As I Am	
Exod. 3:14		John 8:58
	As Our Redeemer	
Jer. 17:10	Ps. 130:7,8	Rev. 2:23
2 Chron. 6:30		Titus 2:13,14

As a Rock of Offense and Stumbling Block

Isa. 8:13,14		Rom. 9:32-33
		1 Peter 2:8
	As Judge	
Ps. 96:13		John 5:22

God		Christ
	As Shepherd	
Ps. 23:1		John 10:14
		Heb. 13:20
		1 Pet. 5:4
		John 10:16
	As Light in New Jerusalem	
Isa. 60:19		Rev. 21:23
	As Coming with All Saints	
Zech. 14:5		1 Thess. 3:13
	As Jehovah (the name)	
Exod. 6:3		Rom. 10:11,13
Joel 2:32		Acts 16:31
Isa. 40:3		Matt. 3:1-3
		John 1:23
	As Our Hope	
Jer. 17:7,13		1 Tim. 1:1
	As Builder of All Things	
Ps. 102:25		Heb. 1:10
		Col. 1:16
		Heb. 3:4
	As Unchangeable	
Ps. 102:27		Heb. 1:12 (8)
		Heb. 13:8
	In Forgiveness	
Exod. 34:7		Mark 2:5-12
	As the Holy One of Israel	
Ps. 71:22		Acts 3:14
Isa. 41:14		
	As the Light	
Ps. 27:1		John 8:12
	As Lord of Glory	
	King of Glory	
Ps. 24:7-10		1 Cor. 2:8
	As Hiding Place	
Ps. 32:7		Col. 3:3
Isa. 32:2		
	As Living Waters	
Jer. 17:13		John 4:14
	As Worshipped of Angels	
Neh. 9:6		Heb. 1:6

God	As Glory	Christ
Ps. 29:1		John 17:24
Ps. 29:3		Luke 9:26
Jer. 13:16		James 2:1
Ps. 115:1		2 Peter 3:18
Isa. 42:8		Rev. 1:6
	As El Elohim	
Isa. 40:9,10		Rev. 11:15
Ps. 47:7,8		Rev. 19:16
Ps. 45:6		1 Cor. 15:24,25
	As Jehovah of Hosts	
Isa. 6:1-3		John 12:41
Isa. 8:13		1 Peter 2:5-8
	The Great I Am	
Isa. 43:10		John 8:24
		John 13:9
		John 4:36
		Mark 13:19
	Adonai	
Ps. 110:1		Acts 2:34-36
		Matt. 22:41-45

These above comparisons are only a fraction of what can be quoted from Holy Writ in parallel passages showing that Christ is God. Cumulatively they show conclusively that God and Christ are one God: Father, Son and Holy Spirit.

The Jehovah's Witnesses Embrace the Unitarian View of God

Notwithstanding this overwhelming evidence, the Unitarian minded Jehovah's Witnesses insist that Jesus was not "the Son of God" in its true meaning, namely of His God: Father, Son and Holy Spirit. They insist, (1) that he was the Son of God by creation, (2) and then by human birth, (3) and then by spirit begetting in a resurrection in the spirit, or through three lives.

They embrace the old Socinian fallacy that Jesus died for Adam as an exact replica of Adam, as they put it. They try to prove this by misapplying, "A tooth for a tooth, an eye for an eye, a life for a life." This has absolutely nothing to do with the atonement! This is a law given to deal with covenant viola-tors and murderers. Quite another norm comes into play where atonement is concerned. Speaking of the atonement for man, our Lord Himself gives us the true picture and setting in John 12:23,24, "The hour is come, that the Son of man should be glorified. Verily, verily, I say unto you, except a corn of wheat fall into the ground and die, it abideth alone: but if it die, it bringeth forth much fruit."

Atonement Is Evidence of Deity of Christ

Here then is the true evaluation of the atonement! It is the death and resurrection of the Son of man, which brings to view the glory of God, namely of the Son of God — of our God: Father, Son and Holy Spirit. It is here where becomes a reality the statement of the Lord in John 10:30, "I and my Father are one." Here we see the Saviour-God. In other words, in the act of procuring salvation, Jehovah and Christ, or Father and Son, are seen as one, every bit as much as they were in the act of creating all things. Again they will be seen as one when all things pertaining to the results of salvation and judgment have been brought into subjection to God: Father, Son and Holy Spirit (1 Cor. 15:27,28).

As the Son of God, Jesus lays down His human nature as the Son of man. As the Son of God in His resurrection He takes this life back again, to perpetuate the mystic union of the two natures, the divine and the human, until the end when all things shall again be subject to God, as all in all, when the mystic union of both natures comes into the fullness of God in eternal glory (1 Cor. 15:28).

This whole act of atonement is wonderfully described for us by the Lord Himself in John 10:17,18: "Therefore doth my Father love me, because I lay down my life, that I might take it again. No man taketh it from me, but I lay it down myself. I have power to lay it down, and I have power to take it again. This commandment have I received of my Father."

The Jews Deny the Deity of Christ

The Jehovah's Witnesses deny that Jesus ever claimed that He was God. Keenly aware of what the Lord was saying, the Jews understood Him well enough. They knew He was telling them that He was God. Just read John 10:33-39. Jesus chided the Jews by saying in effect, If your fallible and sinful judges were called gods, much more I, who am one with the Father and free from sin, claim the title, The Son of God. This entire comparison is clinched in verse 38 where it is stated that the Son is in the Father and the Father in the Son. This remark brilliantly illuminates Christ's assertion in the 30th verse, "I and the Father are one."

The Jehovah's Witnesses Prove Too Much!

No distortion by the Jehovah's Witnesses of the allusion to "gods" can dim the luster of John 10:30 and 38. Twist it they may, but only to their undoing — because in using it in this distorted manner, *they prove too much.* They run up against the fact that worship of servants, angels or other creatures is wrong. The term "God" elicits honor and worship; even though it may (in the plural sense only) have conveyed the idea of "mighty one."

All such "gods," on the contrary, are commanded to worship him (Ps. 97:6). This same advice was given to the devil by the Lord (Matt. 4:10). If these judges were Gods in the same way Jesus was the Son of God, which is what the Jehovah's Witnesses attempt to prove, then worship was due them. For Jesus, as the Son of God, did receive worship (Heb. 1:6; John 20:28; Rev. 5:13; Rev. 5:8; Phil. 2:10,11; Luke 24:52; Matt. 28:9). Thus in going overboard in making the Son of God to be like the judges and prophets whom the Jews called "gods," the Jehovah's Witnesses come close to agreeing that creatures should be worshipped. Peter refused worship himself (Acts 10:26). The angel refused worship (Rev. 22:9). On the other hand, if Christ is a created being, which is what the Jehovah's Witnesses are trying to prove in their twisting of John 10:33-39, then worshipping Jesus is creature worship (Rom. 1:25). But Christians, true Christians everywhere, worship Christ as God the Son (1 Cor. 1:2; Rev. 1:17).

Look at the Center of Salvation

Looking away from this sad confusion, let us again look squarely at the center of our salvation. It is, we find, in the atonement and shines brilliantly as the brightness of the sun. Christ dies, but by the power of God, rises again. Truly, here is proved the deity of Christ. "I have power to lay down my life, I have power to take it up again."

Is this just a man laying down his life? No, for "None of them can by any means redeem his brother, nor give to God a ransom for him" (Ps. 49:7,8).

Who, then, can redeem man's soul? Only God can do this. The Psalmist says, "But God will redeem my soul from the power of the grave: for He shall receive me" (Ps. 49:15).

We read in Acts 20:28, "Take heed therefore unto your-selves, and to all the flock, over the which the Holy Spirit has made you overseer, to feed the church of God, *which He hath purchased with His own blood.*" That this blood is that of our Lord Jesus is proved by Eph. 1:7, Col. 1:14, 1 Peter 1:19 and Rev. 5:9.

Thus all make-shift and torturous rendering of Watchtower men in their New World Translation, their clever scheme of putting several suggested renderings alongside each other on Acts 20:28, come to naught.

Thus, effectually, in this mystic union of His two natures, as the Son of man and the Son of God, Jesus Christ makes atonement. No man could do it. Not even a perfect man could do it. It had to be God, as the Psalmist said in Ps. 49:15.

Melchisedec

Likened unto Melchisedec in Heb. 5-7, note in Heb. 7:28, that it is the Son of God who is made high-priest *forever.* This Melchisedec is likened to the Son of God in Heb. 7:3: "Without father, without mother, without descent, *having neither begin-ning of days, nor end of life; but made like unto the Son of God.*" As the Son of God Jesus is our God. And effectively as Son of God, He is the second person of the Trinity. Here we see once more the Triune God: Father, Son and Holy Spirit. This is declared of Him in Heb. 9:14, "How much more shall the blood of Christ, who through the eternal Spirit offered Himself without spot to God, purge your conscience from dead works to serve the living God?"

Beyond the shadow of doubt the Son of God is foreshadowed in Melchisedec. Then in 1 Tim. 3:16 Christ is revealed as God appearing in the flesh, or made manifest, and in such a way that the Godhead dwelled in him bodily (Col. 2:9).

The Masterpiece

This is superb, culminative proof, you say? Not at all! These are only avenues of proof leading to the masterpiece of the New Testament. Look at Heb. 1. Here is the quintessence of proof. In the very first six verses of Hebrews we see ten facts offered in quick, breathtaking succession, presented about Christ, which could never be postulated about a mere man — not even about a perfect one.

Note how verse 3 postulates that Jesus alone has accomplished redemption of the race. No sinful man, not even a perfect man, could redeem a whole race of sinners. A finite sacrifice of one perfect man, could never accomplish it. It took an infinite sacrifice of the Son of God to bring atonement to all mankind. This is put in verse 3, "When he had by himself purged our sins."

Only as the Son of God, or God, could Jesus occupy the highest position next to the Father; sharing with God the Father the eternal throne of God: Father, Son and Holy Spirit. In Rev. 22:1 we read, "The throne of God [not thrones] and the Lamb." There is only one throne. This transcendent fact is stated with finality, "He sat down at the right hand of the Majesty on high" (Heb. 1:3).

Jesus Himself said to the devil in Matt. 4:10 that only God is to be worshipped. God says of the Son in Heb. 1:5, "Thou art my Son," and in colloquy, "I will be to Him a Father, and He shall be to *me* a son." Because of this intimate Father-Son relationship verse 6 commands, "Let all the angels of God worship Him."

Why should the angels worship Him? Verse 4 gives us the reason: "Being made so much better than the angels." Note, Jehovah's Witnesses, here falls flat the statement of Watchtower men made on page 85 of *Make Sure of All Things,* namely, "Jesus is to be worshipped as a glorious spirit." As a Jehovah's Witness you will come back and say that secondary worship is only meant. Let me then quote page 177 of *Make Sure of All Things,* which condemns secondary worship, and on page 178, your Watchtower men aver that even bowing before men and angels is forbidden.

Jehovah's Witnesses note, the double standard of your Watchtower rulers! In the charter of the Watchtower Society they say they are organized to give public Christian worship to Almighty God and Christ Jesus — in other words, identical worship. Yet they tell you, Jehovah's Witnesses, that Jesus is a creature. If He really is a creature then they are enticing you to creature worship. They are making you worship Christ as God's first creation. Christians worship Jesus Christ because He is God. That, Jehovah's Witnesses, is a fact stated in Heb. 1:6.

Men in the past, particularly the theocratic Jews, and now the theocratic Jehovah's Witnesses, called men "gods" to disprove that Jesus is God (John 10:35). But God, in verses 1 and 2 of Heb. 1, calls Jesus "Son." This is in contrast to men who in times past spoke unto the fathers for him and who were servants. God says that in the last days He spoke by the Son. That is why Jesus Himself postulates His difference of position and nature, in John 10:36.

As Son of God He died. Jesus is called His heir. How can He be the heir? Only because He is uniquely the Son of God, therefore He is the heir. Conclusively we read this in Heb. 1:2, Christ is the "heir of all things." This proves that He died as God-man.

Look at the Aspect of Creation

Leaving behind his position of Saviour, and of God, and of Heir and an object of worship in which He is here in Heb. 1 depicted as God, let us look at the aspect of creation. Immediately we note this startling statement in verse 2: "By whom also he made the worlds." This is in exact harmony with John 1:1-3, "All things were made by Him."

But there is more to His power of creation. Not only was He a master-craftsman, to which the Jehovah's Witnesses limit the range of His power, but more extensively. In John 1:3 we read, "And without Him was not anything made that was made," and in Heb. 1:3, "Upholding all things by the word of His power." This is exactly in harmony with Col. 1:16,17, "For by Him [Christ] were all things created ... and by Him all things consist." In the Greek this reads "are held together."

Now shines forth a transcendent fact in Heb. 1:3, "Who being the brightness [effulgence] of His glory." Note, the brightness of the sun is the same essence of the sun. He is thus identified with the glory of God by being called the brightness of His glory. That is about the most convincing way of saying "He is God."

To erase forever the dim view Jehovah's Witnesses have of the glory of Jesus, by saying this is merely an outward manifestation of glory — like the glory reflected upon Moses' face when he came down from being with Jehovah — let us quote verse 3, "The express image of His person" (verse 3). In toto, not alone in outward appearance, is reproduced in Him the character of God. He is indeed Son of God — Father, Son and Holy Spirit — and not just a reflection of Him.

In Heb. 1:1-6, in ten strident facts, we have the Lord Jesus identified as (1) the Creator, (2) the Saviour God, (3) the glory of God, (4) the object of worship as God. Here then, is the *ultimo ratio* of proof that Jesus as the Son of God, is very God.

Another Impressive Fact — His Name

But there is more! In Heb. 1:8-12 we discover another impressive fact. Jesus is called by the three primary names of God used in the New Testament. If this is so, then we have conclusive proof that Jesus is God.

In verse 8, God the Father, speaking to God the Son [Messiah] calls Him God (Greek: *Theos*). This eighth verse is a quotation of Ps. 45:6 which reads, "Thy throne, O God [Hebrew: *Elohim*] is forever and ever."

Now let us look at Heb. 1:10. God the Father, who is still speaking about God the Son [Jesus] calls Him Lord (Greek: *Kurios*). This is a quotation from Ps. 102:25-27. Let us see how this passage is quoted in Heb. 1:10-12. "And, Thou, Lord (Greek: *Kurios*), in the beginning hast laid the foundations of the earth; and the heavens are the work of thine hands: They shall perish, but thou remainest: and they shall all wax old as doth a garment; And as a vesture shalt thou fold them, and they shall be changed; but thou art the same, and thy years shall not fail."

What is outstanding in these verses 10-12? Still, as in verse 8, the Father continues to speak to the Son. The Father actually says here that the Son is the Creator of the universe: "The heavens are the work of Thy hands" (verse 10). More than that, and all-conclusive, the Father says of the Son that He is eternal — unchangeable. The universe, as an old garment, will get old, but of the Son the Father says, "Thy years shall not fail" (verse 12).

This is overwhelming proof, you say? The Holy Spirit through Paul adds still more emphatic proof in verse 13: "But to which of the angels said He at any time, Sit on my right hand . . . ?" And one more, "Until I make thine enemies thy footstool." This assures Jesus, the Son of God, eternal victory, when 1 Cor. 15:28 becomes fulfilled and God — Father, Son and Holy Spirit — becomes "all in all."

Here is emphatic testimony from God the Father Himself, of the deity of Christ, as the Son of God and the Son of man. Fifteen statements of fact in Heb. 1:1-13, each more convincing than the other, reach the climax of victory fulfilled, "all in all."

What folly we shall now come across as we look into the

Jehovah's Witness textbook, *Make Sure of All Things!* Therein they actually deny the deity of Christ.

O, Jehovah's Witness, ignore this book of false doctrines called *Make Sure of All Things!* Come into the light of Christianity! Your future destiny, your salvation, depends on your accepting the deity of Christ.

Jesus says, "If you believe *not* that I am He [the Lord Jehovah], ye shall die in your sins" (John 8:24).

Chapter 13

DENIAL OF THE DEITY OF CHRIST BRANDS JEHOVAH'S WITNESSES AS UN-CHRISTIAN

An Ancient Query

"What think ye of Christ? Whose Son is He?" These were questions our Lord Jesus asked the Pharisees (Matt. 22:42). The proper response to these questions, outlined by the Lord Jesus in Matt. 22:43-45 so long ago, is still the touchstone of historic Christianity.

We often tolerate a sect with peculiar aberrations in Bible interpretation as being "Christian," only because they have a relatively correct view of Christ our Lord. This we do because we know that doctrine of God and Christ are the center of salvation. However, if a sect accepts a view of Jesus Christ which denies His deity, it cannot be considered Christian.

The predecessors of Jehovah's Witnesses were (1) The Millennial Dawnists, (2) then the nicknamed Russellites, (3) then the International Bible Students. The name changes were superficial. In all three instances they were and remained adherents and partisans of their founder, Chas. T. Russell. They believed his "say" on what is truth, and became and are to this day followers of a "hearsay" or "heresy" religion.

This is in contrast to historic Christianity which is a "revealed" religion. In other words, historic Christianity and its doctrines were revealed from heaven, and recorded in the Bible. The Watchtower religion of the Millennial Dawnists, Russellites and International Bible Students was based on hearsay of Chas. T. Russell, and can be labeled "Made in Brooklyn, N. Y., USA." This new doctrine among many other aberrations, denied the deity of our Lord Jesus Christ.

Modern Day Jehovah's Witnesses

Out of this Russellite background came the modern-day Jehovah's Witnesses. They are the partisans of the deceased Judge J. F. Rutherford. Failing to get the wholehearted support of the Millennial Dawnists, Russellites and International Bible Students to follow his pronouncements of truth in the Watchtower, Rutherford caused approximately 40,000 to be purged or disfellowshipped. He called his partisans "Jehovah's Witnesses."

Thus began a sect which follows the hearsay of Rutherford, rather than that of Russell. Since the Columbus, Ohio, convention of 1931, this sect is known as Jehovah's Witnesses. This sect certainly differs materially from Jehovah's witnesses of old (Isa. 43:10) who were Israel. It stole this name in 1931. In order to hide its recent beginnings it latched onto the long line of witnesses from Abel to John the Baptist.

In what way are the Russellites different from the sect known as the Jehovah's Witnesses? Largely it is that the former are adherents of Russell and are his partisans or followers, while the latter are the adherents and partisans of Rutherford and his Watchtower Society successors. They also differ in their interpretation of the Bible. However, both factions agree that our Lord Jesus Christ is not God. Thus they both deny the deity of Christ.

Doctrine Before They Became the Jehovah's Witness Sect

Let us look at the doctrines of the Jehovah's Witnesses. From their pre-sect beginning, when they were still followers of Chas. T. Russell, and to this day, they press a modern-day version of the Arian heresy. Russell stated his version of Unitarianism or heresy in his 1886 edition of *The Divine Plan of Ages,* pp. 173-184, early in this pre-sect history. The authorized doctrinal textbook of the Jehovah's Witnesses, *Make Sure of All Things,* which today is exclusively used by their Kingdom Publishers to argue their heresies in winning new converts and then to brainwash them into their "system of things," states the following on page 207, under the subheading "Jesus Christ."

"Jesus, the Christ, a created individual, is the second greatest personage of the Universe. Jehovah God and Jesus Christ together constitute the Superior Authorities (Rom. 13:1 NWT) toward all Creation. He was formed countless millenniums ago as the first and only direct creation of His Father, Jehovah, and because of his proved, faultless integrity, was appointed by Jehovah as His Vindicator and the Chief Agent of life toward mankind. Christ, one of his titles, means 'The Messiah.' 'The Anointed.' 'Jesus or Jeshua' is the shortened form of the Hebrew Jehoshua, meaning 'Jehovah is the Saviour.' "

The earlier version of this modern Arian heresy was contrived by Chas. T. Russell (see *Divine Plan of Ages*, ed. 1881, pp. 173-184). The gist of it is this:

Christ in His pre-existence was the archangel Michael, the first Creation of God, who was the Master Creator of all other creation. His coming to earth was not an incarnation. Because He was begotten of God, as a child, He became a perfect human, the equal of Adam before his fall. When Jesus died his human nature was annihilated as a sacrifice. His obedience unto death was rewarded by God in reviving Him in the spirit in divine nature. Thus throughout His entire existence Jesus was never co-equal with God. There was a time when He was not. Thus He is not eternal. On earth He was nothing more than a man, although a perfect man. The atoning effect of His death could never be more than that of one perfect man, for Adam another perfect man.

Thus from 1881 on, to this present time, they deny the deity of Our Lord Jesus Christ.

What Think Ye, Jehovah's Witnesses, of Christ? Whose Son Is He?

In the light of the above we ask the Jehovah's Witnesses the same questions our Lord Jesus asked their Jewish counterparts, "What think you of Christ? Whose son is he?" (Matt. 22:42).

Their textbook, *Make Sure of All Things,* and their New World Translation, give their answer to these questions. In doing so they arraign themselves as non-Christians.

In *Make Sure of All Things,* page 207, they appeal to thirty-eight Scriptures, all of which they have torn out of context, to prove their definition of Jesus Christ.

You have already read chapter 12. And as you read chapter 14 it will become very evident to you that in using thirty-eight Scriptures, they willfully neglect to take into account the many important passages which bear on the deity of Christ. That is bad enough. Worse still is their bold attempt to twist the clear meaning of the thirty-eight Scriptures they use to support their view on Christ under the subheading "Jesus Christ," on pages 207-210. I use their own quotations from the New World Translation on these passages. Through mistranslation they force these passages into forms which will support their Unitarian, Arian views.

We are astounded at the audacity of modern-day heresies. So hardened they have become that they actually put these aberrations into print! They spread these errors by word of mouth in going from door to door and by means of the printed page. In this way they have become a challenge to historic Christianity. They can only be defeated by the word of mouth of Christians going from door to door, witnessing to what Jesus has done for them (2 Cor. 3:1-6).

Now let us look at some of the Scriptures which the Jehovah's Witnesses list as proving that Jesus is a created being.

The Beginning of the Creation of God

First on the list is Rev. 3:14. "These are the things the Amen says, the faithful and true witness, the beginning of the creation of God" (New World Translation).

Obviously, this version of Rev. 3:14 is used to prove that Jesus was the beginning of God's creation. Yet in Heb. 7:3 we see Melchisedec compared to the Lord, the Son of God, as follows, "Without father, without mother, without descent, *having neither beginning of days, nor end of life; but made like unto the Son of God."*

The Son of God, our Lord Jesus, is here depicted as being without beginning of days. In fact, Rev. 3:14 says He is the beginning of the creation of God. God, the Creator, is always the "beginning" of creation. He begins or starts it. In Zech. 13:7 our Lord Jesus is called "God's fellow"; in John 10:30 He says, "I and my Father are one"; and Paul refers to Him as being "equal with God" in Phil. 2:6. He is the Creator. Thus He is the one who began to create, or is the beginning of creation.

The Firstborn of Creation

Watchtower men next cite Col. 1:15-17, quoting the text from their New World Translation, "He is the image of the invisible God, the firstborn of all creation...."

In Heb. 1:3 our Lord Jesus is called by God, the Son of God: "Who being the brightness of his [God's] glory, and the express image [impress] of his person." This denotes that he is one with Him in substance. The brightness of the sun is the very substance of the sun. The brightness of God's glory, is the same as God's glory Himself.

Then He is called the express image. This makes Him of the same essence of God's character, an exact impress of God's character. He is thus declared by the Father here to be of the same substance and of the same essence — of the nature of God.

The term "firstborn" in Hebrew usage means "heir." In time, Esau was born a few minutes ahead of Jacob. Yet eventually, Jacob was considered the firstborn. Why? This was because he became the heir. As a former Pharisee trained in all the lore of Jewry, Paul used this term in this sense elsewhere to denote that our Lord Jesus was the "heir." Since God, in the person of our Lord Jesus would die, and then be resurrected, he would become the "heir" of the whole creation of Adam which was thus becoming subject to Him by God, 1 Cor. 15:1-27. He would subsequently either lead them to salvation, saving them, or in judgment seal in eternal damnation those who abide in the wrath of God by refusing to accept Him. Then He would turn them all under subjection of his God: Father, Son and Holy Spirit (1 Cor. 15:28).

That He is God is proved by His becoming "heir" of God to the whole creation. This is supported by Heb. 1:2, "Hath in these last days spoken unto us by His Son, whom He hath appointed heir to all things."

Because He is heir of God He must have pre-eminence in all things. Look at the wealth of Scripture revealing this point. Compare Exod. 20:3 with Col. 1:18; compare Phil. 2:10 with Isa. 45:23 and you will see what I mean.

Coming now to Col. 1:16,17, quoting verbatim from the New World Translation:

"Because by means of him all (other) things were created in the heavens and upon the earth, the things visible and the things invisible, no matter whether they be thrones or lordships or governments or authorities. All (other) things have been created through him and for him. Also he is before all (other) things and by means of him all (other) things were made to exist."

I have quoted from the New World Translation because it is solely used in the publication, *Make Sure of All Things*. Adding to God's Word is a very serious offense. You can see that just by reading Dan. 4:2; 12:32 and Prov. 30:5,6 and Rev. 22:13. But the Watchtower men have added four times the word "other" in Col. 1:16,17, to make it read "all *other* things."

It is not in the Greek. The context does not require it. Why have they added it?

They try to justify its addition in the margin by referring to Luke 13:2-4. This is entirely arbitrary. The true parallel is not found in Luke 13, but in Heb. 2:10, where the reference is so distinctly to God, that the New World translators did not insert "other." In adding "other" to Col. 1:16,17, four times, the Jehovah's Witnesses deliberately attempt to place Jesus Christ on par with creation as though he were one of the created things of which there are others. This is blasphemy! It is accomplished by falsifying the Word of God.

To shock the Jehovah's Witnesses out of the above heresy, it is well to ask them, once you have read Col. 1:16,17 to them, "Do you agree that Jesus created 'all things'?" They will agree. Make them agree first. Only after they agree, take them to Heb. 3:4 and read, "For every house is builded by some man; but he that built *all* things is God." That should end the point.

Make another salient point here. Point out that not only did He create all things, but that He also created them for Himself, as it says in Col. 1:16. If He is not God how could He create all things for Himself? Compare this for them with Neh. 9:6.

Logos "A God"

The next Scripture they quote in *Make Sure of All Things* is John 1:1-2. We quote this text from their New World Translation:

"Originally the Word was, and the Word was with God, and the Word was a god. This one was originally with God. All things came into existence through him, and apart from him not even one thing came into existence."

The New World Translation creates here its own Greek grammar, suitable for John 1:1, to make it yield a rendering denying the deity of Christ. In a footnote which is added to the first word, "originally," they explain: "Literally in (at) a beginning." In thus conjuring up the indefinite article "an" they conveniently overlook the various reasons for which Greek grammar nouns may be definite, even though a Greek definite article is not there. For example: A prepositional phrase, as in Heb. 10:31, where the definite article is not expressed, can be quite definite in the Greek. Even the New World Translation had to accede to this, in its rendering of Heb. 10:31 which it makes read "unto *the* hands of *the* living God." Although not actually there, it expressed the definite article twice. John 1:1 is exactly in the same composition in the Greek. We see from this that *they do know* the rules, but deliberately twist them in John 1:1 to suit their purpose.

Even the lengthy appendix to support this mistranslation of John 1:1 cannot prove that the absence of the article in John 1:1 required that *theos* without "it," must be translated "a god." All thirty-five instances they use in support are parallel. In every single one of these thirty-five instances which they cite, the predicate nouns stand *after* the verb. Thus *they* properly have the article according to Caldwell's rule. Therefore, none of this conjured up evidence can be used against the usual translation of John 1:1. The Watchtower committee is just "beating the air" in order to distract attention from what it is trying to do with God's word in making it say that our Lord Jesus is just "*a god*." Do not let them do it. Remember, that is sleight of hand, or trickery (Eph. 4:14).

Example of a Technique

In fact, when the Jehovah's Witnesses present this kind of nonsense, do not argue Greek grammar with them. There are only a few Jehovah's Witnesses who understand some Greek, and these are usually of Greek descent, or just Greeks. Rather than argue this, make them come to you. This way:

You ask them, "Do you believe in one God?"

J.W.	"Yes," they will reply.
You	"All right, now let us see how you understand John 1:1. You say, 'In the beginning was the Word, and the Word was with the God.'"
J.W.	"Yes," they will reply.
You	"Who is the God?" you ask.
J.W.	They will reply, "He is Jehovah."
You	Continue, "Is he Almighty or Mighty?"
J.W.	"He is Almighty," they will reply.
You	"All right," you will continue, "and who is 'a god'?"
J.W.	"He is Jesus," they will reply.

You	"Is He Almighty?"
J.W.	"Oh no, He is the mighty one."
You	"Where did He come from?"
J.W.	"He was created by Jehovah."

Now you have their interpretation thinned out to where it becomes absurd. Make them see the absurdity of their Watchtower Society inspired interpretation.

Continue by saying, "Now you believe that Jehovah is Almighty, and that Jesus is a mighty God. You believe in a big God and a little God, and the big God created the little God."

You have made your point by showing the absurdity of their interpretation of John 1:1. Continue by summing it up with such words as, "But you said you believed in one God; but this makes two, a big one and a little one."

Now turn the tables on them by asking *them* to read Isaiah 43:10. Especially ask them to read the last clause of it, after you have first allowed them to read the first clause, "Before me there was no God formed, neither shall there be after me."

Then ask, "Does not this conclusively show that Jehovah never created another God? Where then did the Word, your so-called little God, come from?"

The Achilles Heel

In the third verse, even in their garbled version, we come upon the Achilles heel in their citation in *Make Sure of All Things*. For in using the first three, instead of two verses, to prove Jesus is not God, they prove too much.

They assert that Col. 1:15 proves Christ was the first and only direct creation of God. Here, it must be noted, that the adjective "first" refers not only to time, but most importantly, also to rank. Paul not only alludes to Christ's priority to all creation, but far more revealingly also to his sovereignty over all Creation. For in Col. 2:9, Paul declares, "It is in him [Jesus Christ] that all the fullness of the Godhead dwells bodily." This declaration is the quintessence of Col. 1:15.

More "cunning craftiness" (Eph. 4:14) of Watchtower men is evident in the statement they put into the mouths of Jehovah's Witnesses — that Col. 1:15-17 teaches that God created the Son. Nowhere in the New Testament does the verb "to create" appear in reference of the Son's relationship to the Father. It is here, right in this passage, he is spoken of as "the first begotten of all creation." Adam was created — his Son Abel was begotten. This is quite different. If Paul wanted to say that Jesus was created, he could have used the proper Greek word for "first created." It was available. Actually, Paul passes by this word and uses the Greek word meaning "first begotten."

When you create you produce something different from yourself. When you beget, you beget something like yourself. A man begets human beings; a fox begets foxes. But when you make, you make something of a kind different from yourself. Therefore what God begets is God. What God creates is not God; it is creation.

In connection with Col. 1:15-17, John 1:1-3 and Rev. 3:14, let me say emphatically that they have reference not to the time when Jesus was born on earth as a man, when He was born the son of a virgin. These Scriptures have nothing to do with the virgin birth. Christ was begotten before all creation began, or before worlds came forth.

It is in a bold twisting maneuver of John 1:1-3, Col. 1:15-17 and Rev. 3:14, that the Jehovah's Witnesses make Christ say of Himself that he "is the beginning of the creation of God." No matter how they twist this in English, the Greek stops them. The Greek verse does not say Christ was created *by* God. The genitive case means *of* God, not *by* God. The word "beginning" signifies that Christ is the origin, the first cause of God's creation. Even the mistranslation of John 1:3 of the New World Translation, the way they have put it, proves that. Compare John 1:3, "Apart from him not even one thing came into existence." This means that *He* created all, *He* began and completed all existing things.

That is why we stated that in adding verse 3, they proved too much for their own purpose. They themselves prove their rendering of verses 1-2 grossly erroneous, for they show He was not created, but begotten. As John 1:18 says, "No man hath seen God at any time; the only begotten Son, which is in the bosom of the Father, hath declared him." Then we continue in this context to John 1:23, where we read, "He said, I am the voice of one crying in the wilderness, Make straight the way of the Lord, as said the prophet Elias."

Whom does John the Baptist announce here? It is the Lord Jesus. Of whom does Isaiah speak in 40:3, from which John 1:23

quotes: "The voice of him that crieth in the wilderness, Prepare ye the way of the Lord, *Make straight in the desert a highway for our God*"? All of Isaiah 40, including verse 3, speaks of Jehovah. John the Baptist announces the Lord Jesus, who is God.

The Five Favorites

There are five favorite texts the Jehovah's Witnesses like to use to contend that our Lord Jesus was *created*. It is no surprise to me to find these five texts in a 1, 2, 3, 4, 5 order on page 207 in *Make Sure of All Things,* under the subheading "Jesus Christ."

The Wisdom of God

We have already dealt with three of these five texts. Now we come to the fourth one. It is Prov. 8:22, 27-30. Again we will use the quotation from the New World Translation omitting the important verses 23-25, which the Watchtower men obviously want to hide. We will go along with their game of hide and seek, and then spring 23-25 on them at the right moment. Here is how it reads in New World Translation interpretation:

"Jehovah formed me as the beginning of his way, the first of his works of old. When he established the heavens, I was there: when he set a circle upon the face of the deep, When he made the firm skies above, when the fountains of the deep became strong, when he gave to the sea its bound, that the waters should not transgress his commandment, when he marked out the foundations of the earth: then I was with him as a master workman."

The Jehovah's Witnesses in their Hebrew version translate the verb "to create." One of the most eminent Semitic scholars, F. C. Burney, renders it, "The Lord begat me as the beginning of his way" (*Christ as the APXH of Creation,* 1926).

Now, let us look at verses 23-25 which they have bypassed. What do we find? Note the growth of the embryo, as in verse 23, and the birth of Wisdom, as in 24-25. Because the context of verse 22, and verses 23-25, prove the verb of verse 22 to be "got" or "begot," instead of "to create" or "made me," those who compiled *Make Sure of All Things* have taken great pains to hide it. So they only quote verse 22, omitting 23-26, and then again quote verses 27-30. What does this prove? Again it shows that reading the whole context is the surest way to expose and disprove Jehovah's Witnesses errors, and for Christians to make *sure* of all things.

Turning the Tables on Them

Again the Jehovah's Witnesses attempt to prove more than they should, and in so doing lay themselves open to having the tables turned on them.

What does Prov. 8:22-30 prove? Compare it with John 1:1-2. It proves the pre-existence of Jesus Christ, the Messiah — no more, no less. To say it proves more is to lay oneself open to be asked, "If Christ is the Wisdom of Prov. 8:22-30, and was created by God, then there must have been a time when he was not?"

The Jehovah's Witnesses are now forced to answer, "Yes, there was a time when our Lord Jesus was not."

Then you ask, "Then there was a time when God was without wisdom?"

That is both ridiculous and absurd. In proving too much, the Jehovah's Witnesses lay themselves open to this. Just make them think it through.

Then in verses 27-30 we see them get into even greater difficulty. Jehovah is here depicted in their New World Translation as the Creator of Jesus and of all phases of heaven and earth.

If so, which is what the Jehovah's Witnesses want to prove, then how can they apply Heb. 1:2, "Hath in these last days spoken unto us by His Son, whom He hath appointed heir to all things, by whom he made the worlds"; and in quoting Ps. 102:25 concerning the Son, Heb. 1:10 says, "And thou, Lord (Greek: *Kurios*), in the beginning hast laid the foundation of the earth; and the heavens are the works of Thine hands." In Ps. 102:25 from which this is quoted, Ps. 102:16,19,21,22-25, reference is definitely made to *Jehovah*.

Thus Jehovah created the world. Jesus created the world. The Holy Spirit created the world as we read in Ps. 102:15,19,21, 22-25; Heb. 1:10; Job 33:4; Gen. 1:2. What is the conclusion? It is God who created the worlds, the God of the Bible: Father, Son and Holy Spirit! That obvious answer escapes the Jehovah's Witnesses because they deny the Trinity of God.

Equal With God

Let us now turn to Phil. 2:5-8, the fifth text with which in cunning craftiness the Jehovah's Witnesses "lie in wait to deceive" (Eph. 4:14) in *Make Sure of All Things.*

Again I quote this text, Phil. 2:5-8, from their New World Translation:

"Christ Jesus, who, although he was existing in God's form, gave no consideration to a seizure (scorned a thing to be seized), namely, that he should be equal to God. No, but he emptied himself and took a slave's form and came to be in the likeness of men. More than that, when he formed himself in fashion as a man, he humbled himself and became obedient as far as death, yes death on a torture stake."

Why do the Jehovah's Witnesses give Phil. 2:5-8 such a unique twist? Under deep doctrinal impulsion, inherited from both Russell and Rutherford, they cannot allow this exalted description of the pre-existence of Christ to stand. You see, their immediate predecessors, already eighty years ago departed from the faith, when Chas. T. Russell, in his book *The Divine Plan of the Ages,* pp. 173-184, ca. 1886, adopted a view of Christ held by the heretic errorists.

Russell based his doctrine on the heresy of Arius. He said Christ was an archangel in his pre-existence. Then he became a man, and now he is a spirit. The constant looking upon this three-stage existence of Christ has given them triple-vision seeing things in threes, with everything out of focus. This has totally blinded their minds so that they cannot believe the light of the glorious gospel of Christ, who is the image of God, (which) should shine unto them (2 Cor. 4:4). Who does this blinding? The devil blinded Arius, and again was able to blind Chas. T. Russell, and now finds it easy to blind the leaders of the New World Society, and their followers who walk in their footsteps as in a hypnotic trance.

Wherein does the blindness, discussed in 2 Cor. 4:4, occur? It results in denying "the light of the glorious gospel of Christ, who is the image of God." Christ is the center of the gospel. If He is a mere creature, then He cannot save at all.

Their blindness thus came about when they allowed the devil, the God of this world, to lead them to attack the deity of Christ. When the central idea of the deity of Christ had been destroyed in their minds, they did what Paul accused the pagans of doing. They "changed the glory of the incorruptible God into an image made like to corruptible man, and birds, and four-footed beasts and creeping things" (Rom. 1:23). Instead of Christ being the image of God, or as Heb. 1:3 says, the express image of the person of God, he becomes to them a creation of God, an angel, then a man, then a spirit. Thus the light of the gospel, who is Christ, and of whom Heb. 1:3 says "is the brightness of God's glory" cannot shine unto them; and so they remain in darkness.

This should not surprise us about the Jehovah's Witnesses! How can they think highly of Christ, as the image of God, when they have for so long been thinking so little of themselves, that they declare themselves to be on par with birds, beasts and creeping things, going to the same place, having the same destiny? (cf. Rom. 1:23).

But these men, who today promote the teaching, tone and gospel of the New World Society are to be pitied. I know! I am of the same age as most of the leaders in the organization. We, all of us, who came into the Watchtower movement when Russellism still held sway, and then became partisans of Rutherford, became thoroughly trained by Rutherford, directly or indirectly. We became thoroughly brainwashed. We believed these heresies whole-heartedly. They were seared into our conscience.

We fought hard to get rid of the Russellite faction, then fought hard to get all followers to believe and accept this constantly changing light. We forced the Theocracy across the lives of all Jehovah's Witnesses from 1938 on. All of this gradually created a deep backdrop of heresy in our minds because we fought so hard for it — because it cost us so much.

It cost all of us the major portion of our adult lives. Can you understand this? Paul being a Jew, could understand the reason for the Jew's blindness to Christ! So long had the Jews told themselves and fought for the hope, that they believed they were the people of God just because they were the Jews! *They were* the people!

These present Watchtower leaders are like that. They have fought and bled for the New World Society and its false doctrines. So today this background conditions their thinking. Only the power of the gospel of Christ can save them from it. I know it. From my own life comes the prayer that Christ our shepherd, will cause His voice to penetrate their hearts. If it ever does, what a witness for Him they will be — with their superb training in the New Testament way of preaching! Lord Jesus, come into their hearts!

Apart from being blind, or blinded, these leaders of the New World Society are also very stubborn. Their heresy lies particularly in their denial of the deity of Christ in His pre-existence. This denial came to them in the days of their youth, as it did to me, who was one of them. In everything we were taught and in our continual warfare from door to door in restating and arguing for this heresy, it was indelibly impressed on our own sub-consciousness. It became seared into our conscience by a thousand battles. All of us, by the time we were thirty years old were veterans in this sort of thing. I know. By 1950 I had put in twenty-one years of full-time service. This is typical of all present-day leaders of the New World Society.

What did we proclaim? We proclaimed Christ to have been created — and thus failed to see the glory of God. We succumbed to gnosticism and made Christ out to be the Logos, and at one time to have been in company with Lucifer. Using Isa. 14 and Ezek. 28 we blamed Lucifer to have defected because he had a desire to be God. He wanted to seize God's throne. But the Logos, so we explained, never wanted to seize God's throne. On the contrary, He humbled Himself by emptying Himself of the form of God to the form of a slave. This confused kind of thinking permeated our minds. We repeated it over and over. It filled and controlled our hearts.

Bear their background and resultant condition in mind when the Jehovah's Witnesses present their twisted description of Christ's pre-existence (Phil. 2:6).

Blindness has come to those Watchtower men. Do not argue with them; pray for them. Like Paul prayed for his beloved Israel, pray that the light of the glorious gospel may shine into their hearts.

Their version is at best a misunderstanding of the Greek. This is evident from the Greek lexicon of the New Testament by T. H. Thayer, page 418, col. b: "(Christ Jesus) who, although he bore the form [in which he appeared to the inhabitants of heaven] of God, yet did not think that his equality with God was to be eagerly clung to or retained."

J. B. Phillips' translation renders it, "For He, who had always been God by nature, did not cling to His prerogatives as God: Equal, but stripped Himself of all privilege by consenting to be a slave by nature and being born of mortal man."

If, according to the New World Translation of Jehovah's

Witnesses, Christ was a mere spirit creature, and was thus not of the nature of God, and the equal of God, how then can they cope with the following Scriptures?

(1) How can all the fullness of the Godhead bodily dwell in him? (Col. 2:9)

(2) Why must Christ have pre-eminence in all things? (Exod. 20:3 with Col. 1:18; Phil. 2:10 with Isa. 45:23)

(3) Why is He the Creator? (Col. 1:16 and John 1:3; compare these with Neh. 9:6 and Isa. 45:23)

(4) How could He create all things for Himself? (Col. 1:16)

(5) Why will He subdue all things unto Himself? (Phil. 3:21)

(6) Why does He draw all men unto Himself, and the Father draw men unto the Son? (John 12:32; 6:43,44)

(7) Why will He present His purchased unto Himself? (Eph. 5:27)

(8) How can believers be complete (made full) in Him? (Col. 2:10)

(9) Why the command to believers to grow in grace and in knowledge of our Lord and Saviour Jesus Christ? (2 Peter 3:18)

(10) How can He be everywhere — know everything — foretell the future — have all authority? (Matt. 18:20; 1 Peter 1:11; John 16:30; 14:29; Matt. 28:18; Rev. 2:23)

(11) How can believers count all things as loss for the excellency of the knowledge of Christ Jesus the Lord? (Phil. 3:8)

(12) How could His riches be unsearchable? (Eph. 3:8)

(13) How could His be a love that surpasseth knowledge? (Eph. 3:19)

(14) How can God and Christ jointly receive the same honor, glory and praise? (Rev. 5:12,13; with Isa. 42:8; John 5:23)

(15) How could the Son's person be equal to the Father's? (John 14:9,23; Matt. 11:27)

(16) How could He baptize believers with the Holy Spirit? (Matt. 3:11)

(17) How could He have power to forgive sins? (Mark 2:10)

(18) How would He have the right to be worshipped? (Matt. 2:11; 8:2; 9:18; 14:33)

(19) How would He have power to do miracles? (Mark 2:11,12; 3:5; 3:10,11)

(20) How could He have a sinless character? (Heb. 7:26; 1 John 3:5 compare with Luke 18:19, where our Lord taught, indirectly, that none should call him good unless they admit that He is God, for there is none good but God. All they would do was call Him Master. That is all Jehovah's Witnesses do today either.)

(21) How could He give these promises: Matt. 11:28,29; John 14:23?

(22) Why should men trust Him even as they do the Father? (John 14:1-3)

(23) Why would we read of Him in Luke 1:68, "Blessed be the Lord God of Israel: for he hath visited and redeemed His people"?

(24) Why would we read of Him as deity in Romans 9:5; John 20:28; 1 Cor. 2:8; 1 Tim. 6:14-16; Titus 2:13; Heb. 1:2?

In order to support their errant contention that in His pre-existence Jesus was a creature, the Jehovah's Witnesses can find to list in *Make Sure of All Things,* only thirty-eight Scriptures in the Bible which lend themselves to be twisted to agree with their Unitarianism that Jesus is not equal with God. In fact, it is their claim that He scorned such equality. Against the brilliant light which shines in Christ Jesus, illuminating His person in the brightness of God's glory, the Jehovah's Witnesses have great difficulty with their adopted view of Christ.

Christian Doctrine More Excellent

But look how much more excellent is the historic doctrine of Christ revealed in the Bible and believed in by Christianity! Christ is and always was equal with God, of the nature of God! In mystic union of two natures, divine and human, He lived on earth; He died on the cross; He was resurrected and became the heir of all things and He now proceeds to subject every knee in heaven, earth and under the earth to bow in subjection. All are subject to Him in one way or the other. Eternal salvation is the gift of God to all who receive Him in faith and find forgiveness. Theirs is a new life in Him and salvation at once. They are free to the uttermost. Condemnation remains on those who fail to accept Him. Their destiny is sealed in the day of judgment. God in Christ has done all! Will you receive this boon? Will you accept it? In any case, you are the one to decide! Will you choose the gospel of the spirit of love, and of the spirit of power — a gospel that makes for a sound mind? (2 Tim. 1:1-14) ; or "another gospel," in which Christ is but a creature, which comes into the heart by a spirit of fear?

Once the deity of Christ in His pre-existence is seen, then the Biblical concept of the fusion of the divine nature with the human nature of Jesus becomes the soul-satisfying, doubt-destroying, complete assurance that our Saviour-God can save to the uttermost. Then all fear is forever cast away. This is good news for all of us — to all lost souls. Do you see this? Have you experienced it? Yes? If so, you will be so full of it, that you will want to tell others of the Lord Jesus, our Saviour God. And wonder of wonders, the more you tell this to lost ones, the sweeter and surer will the Lord Jesus become to you. He thus lives in you — and talks with you — and His image grows within you until He fills you. When He does, you will have so much more to tell about Him to lost souls. Look to Jesus the author and finisher of our salvation. Believe in Him; follow Him in unselfish sharing with all mankind!

Christ Our All, Who Humbled Himself as a Man

As Christ Jesus looms thus large — over all — in our hearts, we will appreciate Isa. 9:6, "For unto us a child is born, unto us a son is given...." Born as a child, our Lord Jesus grows to manhood and from the cradle to the cross plays the man. This is why He said in John 14:28, "My Father is greater than I"; in Acts 1:7, "It is not for you to know times and seasons, which the Father had put in His own power"; and in another crucial moment of His life as son of man, "If it is thy will, Father, let this cup pass" (Matt. 26:39) ; and finally, as He was dying, "My God, my God, why hast thou forsaken me?" (Mark. 15:34) . As partaker of flesh and blood, because of us, the children even of that nature, he was made lower than the angels. But at the same time He was the Son — whose divine nature was inextricably interwoven with His human nature. How wonderfully this is described for us in Heb. 2:9, "But we see Jesus, who was made a little lower than the angels for the suffering of death, crowned with glory and honor; that he by the grace of God should taste death for every man."

Why He? Note, His divine nature now was the reason for this, "For it became Him, for whom are all things, and by whom are all things, in bringing many sons unto glory, to make the captain of their salvation perfect through suffering" (Heb. 2:10).

Here the secret of Phil. 2:6-8 is out in the open! The Lord Himself said, "I have power to lay down my life, and I have power to take it up again" (John 10:18). Still, He endured to the end on the cross the life of a man. He played the man, failed to call on His superior power as God, refused to call it quits. In all things, He was found a man. Because He fully subjected Himself in the form of servant, is why in that low position He said, "My Father is greater than I" (John 14:28). It is why He made all those statements which Arians have liked to use to imply His inferiority and inequality with God! What a subjection! What a humiliation! How blind have become eyes when beholding this strength of the Son of God, they see in it a display of humility, a sign that He is not God. Only as God, could He have endured that ordeal, could He have died freeing us from our sins, could He have been resurrected, could He have become our High Priest!

Indeed, He spoke truth when He said, "I and the Father are one" (John 10:30), and so did Paul when he jubilantly says, "In Him dwelleth all the fulness of the Godhead bodily" (Col. 2:9).

What do Phil. 2:5-8, Col. 2:9 and Isa. 9:6 so lifelike portray? Here we learn this great truth: that Christ was equal to the Father as touching His Godhead and inferior to the Father as touching His manhood. If you come to see this wonderful truth, and believe, you have everlasting life! You will then know, "This is life eternal, that they might know thee the only true God, and Jesus Christ, whom thou has sent" (John 17:3).

The Lord Jesus had become the glory of God on earth and now His task was soon over. What does He say to the Father? Read on in John 17:4,5, "I have glorified thee on the earth: I have finished the work which thou gavest me to do. And now, O Father, glorify thou me with *thine own self* with the glory which I had with thee before the world was."

With this ringing testimony of the Lord that He is God come to earth to do His Father's will, returning to become again what He had been before the world began, *clothed with God's own self,* is it any wonder that believing on Him and the Father, brings everlasting life?

Chapter 14

THE SECOND MAN IS THE LORD
FROM HEAVEN

Creation of the First Man

"Let us make man in our image; after our likeness" (Gen. 1:26). This presaged the creation of the first man.

This body of the earth, or the flesh, was formed "out of the dust of the ground" (Gen. 2:7a), and God "breathed into his nostrils the breath of life; and man became a living soul" (Gen. 2:7b). Thus man became the earthly vessel of the image and likeness of God or the quintessence of all His Creation in a capsule (Heb. 2:7,8).

The execution of this fiat of creation is elsewhere wonderfully described: "Even everyone that is called by my name: for I have created him for my glory, I have formed him; yes, I have made him" (Isa. 43:7).

In the Image of God

Man was to keep his body alive by "eating thou shalt eat" (Gen. 2:16). The Hebrew text shows this to be a continuous process. The spiritual man's God-consciousness was to grow in similar fashion, by constantly meditating upon, and associating with His Maker, which activity was climaxed at the end of each day in the cool of the evening, when God came down to converse with man. The hallmark of God's image and likeness in man then, was the complete harmony of both body and soul, making for one harmonious whole: man.

Thus man held within his body of flesh the essence of all material creation on earth (Gen. 2:15-20), and within his spirit the possibility of being and remaining a son of God, who is "the Father of spirits" (Heb. 12:9).

Man so constituted would not live by "bread alone," with which to sustain his body; but by every word coming out of the mouth of His Father, the Father of spirits, would he *live* (Heb. 12:9).

Death or Separation

If man was thus created in the image and likeness of God, could he die? Was he mortal, or immortal?

This question is emphatically answered for us in Gen. 2:17, where the possibility of death is mentioned.

If to *live* means to live unto the Father of Spirits, then to die, which is the opposite, would mean to die unto the Father of spirits. "Eating thou shalt eat" then is the *modus operandus* of living, both for the body and the spirit (or soul). How then, in the light of this, could man die?

The answer comes to us clear in the projected punishment upon Adam if he should become disobedient: "For in the day that thou eatest thereof thou shalt surely die."

Did Adam die the day he ate of that tree? If so, how? Before the day ended in which Adam transgressed God's commandment, did he die as a soul? But, you say, he lived on for almost a thousand years?

The Hebrew text for Gen. 2:17 gives us the clue. It says, "Dying thou shalt die." It would be a continuing death of torment and torture, as decay came step by step. How long would this take? It would continue until the body and soul would be separated. For separate they must. We read in Eccl. 12:7, "Then shall the dust return to the earth as it was: and the spirit shall return unto God who gave it."

But also at the very moment man sinned came the most devastating blow: *spiritual death*: which is man's separation from God because of sin (Gen. 3:17,18).

If *life* for man is living unto the *Father of spirits,* death then is an end of living unto *the Father of spirits.*

Death Is Separation

Eternal life means thus "eternal fellowship with God." Those who cared for this fellowship of the spirit, or *living* with God, commended their spirit to God. Acts 5:59,60; Gen. 35:17,18; Luke 23:46; 2 Cor. 5:1-8; Phil. 1:21-23. *Eternal death* means to be bereft of all ability ever "to fellowship with God." Of such a one who lived only to the flesh, and not to the spirit, the Psalmist in Ps. 146:4 says, "His breath goeth forth, he returneth to his earth; in that very day his thoughts perish."

Eternal death, or eternal separation of the soul from fellowship with God, comes to the soul in the day of Judgment. Such a soul can never again receive a body of glory (as do the souls of just men made perfect, Heb. 12:22-24), as will Abraham (Luke 16:19-31), as will the tribulation saints (Rev. 6:9-11), but is not annihilated. A man's body being of the earth, may be destroyed. A man's property may be destroyed. But a man's spirit cannot be destroyed; it returns to God who made it, and God is eternal. Eternal death then means to be eternally banished from fellowship with God (Jude 12, 13; Matt. 10:28; Rev. 20:10-15).

Can Man Be Saved?

"Dying thou shalt die," the sentence of death upon man, is a sentence of separation of the soul and body, as well as man's separation from fellowship with God. Could man, since God had withdrawn from him, follow God into His heaven? The Lord Jesus shows the impossibility of this when He said, "And no man hath ascended up to heaven, but he that came from heaven, even the Son of man which is in heaven" (John 3:13).

This was man's dilemma and God's opportunity. Was man's fate to become sealed as eternal separation from God? Or would God reclaim man who had lost "the image and likeness" of God in which he had been created?

If man was created in "the image and likeness of God" and had lost it, then obviously only God Himself could restore the image and likeness.

As Jesus so revealingly states in John 3:13, only the Son of Man which is in heaven could do it, and to become the Son of Man, he had to come as "Lord from heaven" (1 Cor. 15:47).

How Can Man Be Saved?

The Psalmist says, "But God will redeem my soul from the power of the grave; for he shall receive me" (Ps. 49:15).

Since man was created by God, he can be saved only by God. Such salvation would have to come as *new creation*. This is completely tied in with our Lord Jesus Christ. It is wonderfully described for us by the inspired apostle in 1 Cor. 15:45-47, "the first Adam was made a living soul; the last Adam was made a quickening spirit. Howbeit that was not first which is spiritual, but that which is natural; and afterwards that which is spiritual.

The first man is of the earth, earthy; the second man is the Lord from heaven."

How was this salvation to be implemented? "For God so loved the world, that he gave his only begotten Son, that whosoever believeth in him should not perish, but have everlasting life" (John 3:16). It is the coming of the *Lord from heaven* which ushered in everlasting life, and "brought life and immortality to light."

The weakest link of Adam, created in the beginning, was his body, which could return to earth. It came first in order. But now, with the second Adam who is a quickening spirit, the Spirit comes first in order, and since it is immortal, it, if saved, will become the seed for immortality in the body, in the day of resurrection. Such is the glorious argument of 1 Cor. 15:50.

The Hidden God

The day Adam sinned, that day he also died. On that day, God left man and disfellowshipped him. God hid from man, for man had become like a beast, living unto the flesh.

God then revealed to man the need for atonement through blood. Men began to look for "the seed of the woman" who would destroy the "seed of the serpent." Man's gathering around altars sacrificing the blood of animals was no mere rite, or empty dream. It was based upon the prophecy of the Lord to Eve in Gen. 3:15. From Abel on men began to put blood between them and their God, as a propitiation. When Noah came out of the Ark, into a new world, he put the blood of his sacrifice between that wicked world and himself, indicating how this evil would be taken from man.

Is it any wonder then that when God came down to man He appeared behind the blood of sacrifices?

God became the personal God of men who sought him. Such men were Abraham, Jacob and Isaac. God was known as God the Almighty, as Abraham's God, as Isaac's God, as Jacob's God.

Coming nigh to man, God appeared to Moses in a fiery bush. He appeared as fire, the symbol of His presence, the Shekinah! He had not come to torture man. God had another purpose. His purpose was to save the offspring of Abraham, Isaac and Jacob. He revealed Himself as their God. Their plight excited His love. He came down, and He revealed Himself by a new name, His personal name *Jehovah*.

With a mighty hand He saved a whole people in one night.

He brought this people into a desert. There He caused them to build a tabernacle. In the Most Holy of this tabernacle, in the shabby surroundings of fleshly works, in the *shekinah* on the Ark of the Covenant, there dwelled Jehovah visibly! In the most humble circumstances of a people addicted to wandering over the earth He dwelled with His people as their God, as a voice, in a light.

Deliverer or Saviour?

When God revealed Himself as Jehovah unto Israel, was He come to be the promised Saviour? No; He came to be their deliverer from Egyptian slavery, and to set them apart for the time when He would come as their *Saviour*. That Jehovah had not yet come as their Saviour is evidenced in the fact that they were commanded to continue to sacrifice the blood of animals, to celebrate the *Passover* continually, until the true Sacrifice would appear. How beautifully that is pictured for us in Gen. 22:1-18, revealing in verses 16-18 His coming purpose as *Saviour!*

More Than One Jehovah?

Is there then more than one Jehovah? If the Jehovah revealing Himself to Israel and conducting them into the desert was not the promised Saviour, then who is?

Always remember, that man cannot pursue God into heaven in order to re-establish the broken fellowship with God. God had to come to man (John 3:13).

Jehovah of the "thorn-bush" and of the "Shekinah" established the way in which men were to come to him — by sacrificing in obedience to His commandments, the blood of animals, and living under the law. Man had to learn that he was a sinner, separated from God, and on the road toward eternal separation from God. Then he had to learn that he could not save himself, that he needed a *Saviour-God.*

If Jehovah appearing to Moses in the fiery bush was not the *Saviour-God,* then who was He? He was the King of Israel, come from heaven to save them from fleshly slavery unto another nation, so that within their new national and spiritual entity, over which he was King, he could keep them from scattering all over the earth, to remain together, for

His Coming Appearance as Jehovah the Saviour

In Isa. 44:6 we read, "Thus saith the Lord [Jehovah] the King of Israel, *and* his Redeemer the Lord of hosts [Jehovah of

Hosts]; I am the first, and I am the last; and besides me there is no God." There are two aspects of Jehovah here. Which one is the first? It is as Jehovah who appeared unto Israel as their King and delivered them from Egyptian bondage.

In Isa. 48:12-15 we read, "Hearken unto me, O Jacob and Israel, my called; I am he, I am the first, I also am the last. Mine hand also hath laid the foundation of the earth, and my right hand hath spanned the heavens: when I call unto them, they stand up together. All ye, assemble yourselves, and hear; which among them hath declared these things? The Lord hath loved him: he will do his pleasure on Babylon, and his arm shall be on the Chaldeans. I, even I, have spoken; yea. I have called him: I have brought him and he shall make his way prosperous."

Let us pause here for a moment. Notice, up to now, the work of Jehovah is described in bringing out Israel, in defending it against its earthly enemies; the Babylonians, the Chaldeans, etc.

But now prophetically we have described for us the work of the coming Jehovah Redeemer, to whom Jehovah actually speaks. "Come ye near unto me, hear ye this; I have not spoken in secret from the beginning; from the time that it was, there am I: and now the Lord God and His Spirit hath sent me" (Isa. 48:16).

Check this passage closely. It is necessary to do thus, for Jesus says it could only be discerned with the spirit, not with the flesh, for there still are many today, as then in Isaiah's day, and later in the Lord's day, who have eyes but do not observe, have ears but do not hear the voice of the Lord.

Well, see and observe, hear and listen, as I quote Isa. 48:17, "Thus saith the Lord, thy Redeemer and the Holy One of Israel...." Here Jehovah appears in His role of Redeemer.

In the opening verses of the 6th chapter of Isaiah we are given by Holy Spirit a vision of how God is worshipped in heaven. A description of the throne is afforded unto us, and then verse 3 reveals the act of worship. "And one cried unto another, and said, Holy, holy, holy is the Lord of Hosts: the whole earth is full of his glory."

Who is the Lord of Hosts? He is Jehovah of Hosts. Another vision of such worship in heaven is given us in Rev. 4, and there we read in the 8th verse, "And the four beasts had each of them six wings about him; and they were full of eyes within; and they rest not day and night, saying, Holy, holy, holy, Lord God Almighty, which was, and is, and is to come."

The Lord of Hosts, or *Jehovah,* is the triune God. "Who was," when in His moves to save man He was present as Jehovah in the fiery bush and was the King of Israel. "Who is," when He came as Jesus the Saviour, the same "yesterday, today and forever." "Who is to come," as we read in 1 Thess. 4:13-18, "them also which sleep in Jesus will God bring with him," and the "dead in Christ shall rise first" and the living at His coming.

The last book of the Bible, speaking as it does of the consummation of all things, describes Jehovah as the first and the last, thusly, "John to the seven churches which are in Asia: Grace be unto you, and peace, from Him which is and which was, and which is to come; and from the seven Spirits which are before his throne; and from Jesus Christ who is the faithful witness, the first begotten of the dead, and the prince of the kings of the earth. Unto him that loved us, and washed us from our sins in his own blood" (Rev. 1:4,5).

First we have a description of the triune God here. The "is" phase of Jehovah is focused upon Jesus Christ: "Because He washed us from our sins in His own blood."

But not only has He saved us, but He comes again: "Behold he cometh with clouds; and every eye shall see him, and they also which pierced him: and all kindreds of the earth shall wail because of him. Even so, Amen" (Rev. 1:7).

Who is described here in all three phases of His appearance on earth? Who is it who is described in His "presence" with Israel in the Shekinah, His "appearance in the flesh of man" and His apocalypse in His Second Coming? Read and learn: "I am Alpha and Omega, the beginning and the ending, saith the Lord, which is, which was, and which is to come, *the Almighty*" (Rev. 1:8). The appearance and revelation of God in three aspects affects the salvation of man's soul.

Jesus Is Jehovah!

In Isa. 6 a discussion of God's purpose ensues. "Whom shall I send and who will go for *us.*" The pronoun here, observe, again is plural. Who uttered this statement? To whom was it addressed?

The Holy Spirit leads us to John 12:36-41 where we read, "While ye have light, believe in the light, that ye may be the children of light. These things spake Jesus, and departed, and did hide himself from them."

Why did the Lord do that? "That the saying of Esaias the prophet might be fulfilled, which he spake, Lord, who hath believed our report? and to whom hath the arm of the Lord been revealed?" (Isa. 53:1). Therefore they could not believe, because that Esaias said again, "He hath blinded their eyes, and hardened their heart; that they should not *see* [observe] with their eyes, nor understand with their hearts, and be converted, and I should heal them" (John 12:40).

Thus John 12:36-41 identifies Jesus as the God set forth in Isaiah 6, as God, high and lofty in the heavens.

How Revealed?

"In the beginning was the Word, and the Word was with God, and the Word was God" (John 1:1) — so begins the revelation of the *appearance* (or Epiphania) in human form of *Jehovah Saviour*.

Jehovah had been present in the shekinah and in the temple. Now Jehovah came down in the flesh, hiding in a body of man. He is described as the very essence of God, for He is said to be the Wisdom of God, the Word, or Logos.

As His eternal antecedents are related we come with startling clarity upon the 14th verse, "And the Word was made flesh, and dwelt among us, (and we beheld his glory, the glory as of the only begotten of the Father,) full of grace and truth."

How different was His appearance on earth from the announcement of the *presence* of Jehovah in the fiery thornbush.

Jehovah announced His presence to Israel in one of the most terrifying sights ever seen. Six full days there was pitch darkness, a howling wind, shrill blasts from God's trumpet, and the alarming voice of the Lord. Three million Israelites were sick with fear (Ex. 19:16-19). Paul said centuries later of Moses saying, "I exceedingly fear and quake" (Heb. 12:21). Only one nation of all the world, Israel, ever heard the voice of Jehovah. Why? "So that ye might know that the Lord He is God, there is none else beside Him" (Deut. 4).

The fire of the shekinah, in which *Jehovah* dwelt amidst Israel, revealed His presence in an awesome way. The Syrians heard a great noise (2 Kings 7:1-16). The walls of Jericho fell

flat (Josh. 6:14-20). The sundial turned back ten degrees
(2 Kings 20:11). The sun stood still (Josh. 10:12,13). Hail fell
from heaven (Josh. 10:11). Egypt was destroyed by hail (Exod.
9:19-26). Twenty-four thousand Israelites were beheaded (Num.
25:1-9). Thousands died, whose death was caused by the Ark of
the Covenant (1 Sam. 5), 5070 Israelites were struck dead
(1 Sam. 6:19), 14,700 died in a plague (Numbers), 185,000
were slain by the Angel of Death (2 Kings 19:35). Hundreds
died in Egypt in one night (Exod. 12:21-30). The shekinah
fire, which is not a natural fire, but the fire of the Lord, in
which *Jehovah* announced His presence to Moses in the fiery
thornbush, is mentioned seven hundred times in connection
with Jehovah's presence.

The fire of the Lord, or the shekinah in which He was
present, cast a cloud over Israel for forty years. It slew Nadab
and Abihu (Lev. 10:1-5). It burned up and actually consumed
rebels (Num. 16:35). One hundred two of the King's men were
consumed by this fire (2 Kings 1:1-12). The Sodomites were
destroyed by this fire (Gen. 19:1-16).

But Jesus, the *Saviour-Jehovah,* was announced as follows,
"John bare witness unto him, and crying, saying, this was he of
whom I spake, He that cometh after me is preferred before me:
for he was before me" (John 1:15).

Why was the Lord announced in this manner? He had
come to save, not to destroy. When Moses saw Jehovah he
quaked. From that day on men knew they could not see God
and live. That pointed up their great disability of separation.
Only by seeing God, and having direct fellowship with Him,
can man ever hope to *live.* This was indeed a great disability!

Now note how God, in His *appearance,* or epiphania, overcame this dilemma. "No man hath seen God at any time; the
only begotten Son, which is in the bosom of the Father, he
hath declared him." First let us note, that the Son *is* in the
bosom of the Father. He still *is.* Then notice that the Son declares the Father. He is *Jehovah the Saviour.*

How is that proved? Let us go down to the 23rd verse and
read, "He said, I am the voice of one crying in the wilderness,
Make straight the way of the Lord, as said the prophet Isaiah."

What did the prophet Isaiah say about this? John gets his
very words from Isa. 40:3, "The voice of him that crieth in the
wilderness, Prepare ye the way of the Lord, make straight in
the desert a highway for *our* God."

Jesus then, our Lord God, came to dwell with us in the flesh, so that we could feel him, touch him, handle him. He came as the beginner of a New Creation, to restore His image and likeness in man.

In John 12:41 we read that Isaiah saw the glory of Jehovah, which in John 12 is described as the glory of Jesus. Israel tempted Jehovah in the desert (Exod. 17:2,7; Num. 21:5-7) and died for it. Paul warns Christians not to do the same ". . . for they drank of that Spiritual Rock that followed them: and that rock was Christ"; and again, "Neither let us tempt Christ, as some of them also tempted, and were destroyed by serpents" (1 Cor. 10:4,9). Here Paul shows Christ to be Jehovah.

Jehovah laid the foundations of the earth, says Ps. 102:25. In Heb. 1:8-12, it is shown that the one who laid the foundations of the earth is Jesus Christ, which is further emphasized in John 1:3, Heb. 1:10 and Col. 1:17.

Turning the Tables on the Unitarianism of Jehovah's Witnesses

The Jehovah's Witnesses translate the title Lord by the name of Jehovah some two hundred thirty-seven times in their New World Translation. As you look up Matt. 3:3 in this version and you read "Prepare ye the way of Jehovah, make his roads straight," you are aware that this is a direct quotation from Isa. 40:3, and more importantly that it is applied to Jesus Christ by all four Evangelists. Unmistakenly, the Jehovah of the prophecy of Isaiah is the Jesus Christ in the Gospel (Matt. 3:3; Mark 1:3-8; Luke 3:2-17; John 1:6-8, 15-29; 3:26-31). The full equivalent of Jehovah is accorded by the Evangelists to the title LORD.

The Jehovah of Joel 3:32 is perfectly blended with the Lord of Romans 10. That becomes even more clear in the New World Translation of the Jehovah's Witnesses where we read, "For if you publicly declare that word in your mouth, that Jesus Christ is Lord, and exercise faith in your heart that God raised him up from the dead, you will be saved. . . ." The *kurios* translated "Jehovah" in the Septuagint Book of Joel, is the *kurios* given in Romans 10, and shows the identity and oneness of Jehovah-Jesus.

The Jehovah's Witnesses say there is only one Jehovah. The name allows no limitations. The name is I AM, and is from the Hebrew root word Jehovah. Yet, we read in John 8:58 Jesus saying, "Before Abraham was, I am." That points back to the same I AM of Exod. 3:14. The Jews full well understood it, and were ready to stone the Lord for blasphemy. This is capped off in Rev. 1:17,18, where Jesus says, "I am he that liveth, and was dead; and, behold I AM alive for evermore"

In their definition of the 144,000 which alone are to be saved to heaven, and the Great Multitude of Jehovah's Witnesses to be saved now on earth, the Jehovah's Witnesses like to use John 10. The remarkable statement of John 10:16, "There shall be one fold and one shepherd," is totally overlooked.

Who is this one Shepherd? It is Jesus Himself. Ezek. 34:23 and Ps. 23 show Jehovah to be this one shepherd. This shepherd will be the Lord God who will come to feed His flock (Isa. 40:11) and which is applied by Peter to Jesus (1 Peter 2:21,25). Jehovah-Jesus is the one shepherd.

Effecting Salvation

Because Jesus was *the Saviour*, His death is to us of paramount importance.

The image and likeness of God was upon Adam who bore it in an earthly tabernacle. Of him it was said, "What is man, that thou art mindful of him? and the son of man that thou visitest him? For thou hast made him a little lower than the angels; and hast crowned him with glory and honor. Thou madest him to have dominion over the works of thy hands; thou hast put all things under his feet..." (Ps. 8:4-6).

Yes, because man was thus made, and then sinned, and became separated from God, and became lost, God in His love sent Jesus Christ, who *is* in the bosom of God. And what do we see? "But we see Jesus, who was made a little lower than the angels for the suffering of death, crowned with glory and honor; that he by the grace of God should taste death for every man" (Heb. 2:9).

Those who dishonor Jesus Christ by denying His deity, cannot truly appreciate the magnitude of man's need of salvation. Unless we rightly understand our condition of sin and death, and the absolute separation these brought about in our hopes of living in fellowship with God, we will not appreciate that Jesus is Jehovah-Saviour, who has appeared in these last days. "How shall we escape, if we neglect so great a salvation...?" (Heb. 2).

The Lord from heaven came into the flesh. The reason is stated: "Forasmuch, then, as the children are partakers of flesh and blood, he also himself likewise took part of the same; that through death he might destroy him that had the power of death, that is, the devil" (Heb. 2:14).

Thus again we read the drama depicted in 1 Cor. 15:45-50, "And so it is written, The first man Adam was made a living soul; the last Adam was made a quickening spirit. Howbeit that was not first which is spiritual, but that which is natural; and afterward that which is spiritual. The first man is of the earth, earthy; the second man is *the Lord from heaven.* As is the earthy, such are they also that are earthy; and as is the heavenly, such are they also that are heavenly.... Now this I say, brethren, that flesh and blood cannot inherit the Kingdom of God; neither doth corruption inherit incorruption."

Jesus, the God-man, died for us (cf. Phil. 2:6-11; Eph. 4:8-10). He not only died for us, and shed his blood for us (Acts 20:28), which God calls "his own blood," but He also arose the third day, and ascended to heaven forty days later. At Pentecost he sent the earnest, the Holy Spirit, to his disciples as a token of the *new life* in the Spirit, into which they had entered. A *new creation* was in the making, once again, *in the image and likeness of God,* one which would put on immortality in the place of mortality, when the Lord would come with their spirits from heaven in His apocalypse, and the resurrection would begin (1 Thess. 4:13-18).

For this Lord from Heaven, Jesus Christ, has the same power as has the Father. "For as the Father raiseth up the dead, and quickeneth them; even so the Son quickeneth whom he will" (John 5:21).

Jehovah gave bread from heaven to keep the bodies of his select nation alive in the desert. Yet they died because of disobedience. But this Lord from Heaven, Jehovah-Saviour, says of Himself in John 6:33, "For the bread of God is he which cometh down from heaven, and giveth life unto the world." Only God can give life to the world, for he has taken it.

The Lord from Heaven Is the Image of God and the Likeness of God in Us

Because man sinned, and the image and likeness of God was destroyed in him, it required a creative act of God to restore that image and likeness. How was it done?

It is said of our Lord Jesus by the Apostle Paul in Heb. 1:3 that He is the express image of God. Our Lord said of Himself,

"He who has seen me has seen the Father" (John 14:9). He, Jesus Christ, is *the image and likeness of God.* Coming down and partaking of our flesh and blood condition, and bearing our image of the earth, He has identified Himself with us. But much more, He restores the *image and likeness of God* in man, as we in faith identify ourselves with Him. Thus if we bear the image of the earthy, which He bore for us, we shall also bear the image of the heavenly, to where He has gone. If we accept Him crucified, and die with Him, He shall become the magnet to draw us up to Him, to sit with Him in Heavenly places.

Chapter 15

CHRISTIANITY OR CULTS: WHICH?

Christianity Is a Heavenly Society

How blessed is the lot of Christianity. Coming home to the Lord, as it were, as a prodigal Son, I have been led into her midst and find her filled with pleasant places.

Like our Father's house, which has many mansions, Christianity has many wonderful facets. She has diversity of "mansions" or denominations enabling even the most unique of humans to find a suitable place for worship and fellowship. Cognizant of the diversities of nations, kindreds and tongues, the Lord graciously allowed her to develop in a manner, which makes for a free evolvement of structures on earth, which at the same time remains fluid and stable. Think of the "seven Churches of Asia."

Indeed, Christianity has diversity of gifts. The cults attack her for having this diversity. They wish to create a platform of unity of structure, to be ruled rigidly, top down, from some earthly headquarters.

How I rejoice that Christianity is not so constructed! Its head is in heaven, and its saved ones all sit in heavenly places. From the unsaved ones of Noah's day (cf. 1 Peter 3:19) to Abraham who is in heaven (Luke 16:19-23), to Moses and Elijah (Matt. 17:1-3) who appeared long after their death, to "the spirits of just men made perfect" (Heb. 12:22-24), across the whole age of salvation and up to the tribulation "where the spirits of martyrs cry out for vengeance," Christianity's places or mansions are filled with "the spirits of just men made perfect." Soon, in great triumph, will her Saviour-God appear in the clouds and he will bring with him the spirits of all these saved ones, and will give them a resurrection body. That will be the hour of triumph for Christianity!

Blessed is Christianity's lot, and thrice blessed are we to sit in her heavenly places.

Enemies Behind Clouds of Darkness Attack Christianity

As the twentieth century dawned, historic Christianity began to face its darkest period. Major cults emerged from the 19th century rebellion of laymen (Rev. 6). These appeared in the garb of righteousness, "conquering and to conquer." In their wake "the sun became black with sackcloth" (their organizational sackcloth cover blotting out personal salvation coming alone from the true sun of righteousness, Jesus Christ.) As time wore on, "the moon became as blood" (as they turned the word of truth into the lie of Armageddon wrath) and "the stars of heaven fell unto the earth" (as they once again projected salvation at Armageddon to be wrought in the flesh on earth, and not in heavenly places).

They began to come in a "march of the millions" across the earth. These major cults were followed by an endless train of lesser ones. A veritable "Babel of confusion" began, and "every unclean spirit and thing" is now in evidence in the Babylon of the cults. They "are performing great signs and wonders." As they parade in their "march of the millions" over the earth, back and forth, they bid fair to raise so big a cloud as to blot out our Saviour God Jesus Christ and His great salvation, and to turn to blood (or destruction) the spiritual promises of the word of God. In the hearts of many these enemies are wreaking a bloody carnage in our midst, Christian brethren! Who are they? Why are they so successful?

Why Cults?

For more than thirty years, all of my mature life, I lived the Watchtower way. I was truly a modern Gnostic. I was a Russellite, became a Kingdom Publisher, then as a partisan of Rutherford called myself a Jehovah's Witness, and finally became a "theocratic slave" of the New World Society.

For years I studied the structure of the major cults in order to devise methods of combat. From this long experience I know that of the four major cults plaguing Christianity today, along with the long line of cultlets, that the Watchtower movement of Jehovah's Witnesses is the most effective way of error today.

It has enshrouded itself self-righteously as "the clean organization," and banks for salvation on its own works. It has created for itself an organization, which the Watchtower magazine calls "a beast of burden." This horse, or organization, it says is pure white. Upon this White Horse it aims to go forth and establish a New World Society.

Jehovah's Witnesses are the leading organization of modern cults, and set the tone and pattern for attack against historic Christianity. Their way is not the way of Jesus who said: I am the way, the truth and the life. Their way is the way of the Watchtower.

Ancient Gnosticism

Looking at Jehovah's Witnesses in a retrospective way, from within the precincts of historic Christianity, I can see how completely the Watchtower Society has succeeded in weaving the threads of all former heresies and cults into the make-up for a New World Society. In my coming book, *The New World Society of Jehovah's Witnesses,* I will trace for you the all-comprehensiveness of this coming great subversion.

The promoters of the New World Society are confident that it will last a thousand years. Yet, ancient Gnosticism lasted but a generation, or at the most, two. Arianism lasted a bit longer. Montanists, Manicheans and many others followed one another.

What is and was Gnosticism? It was the result of soul-washing. That was its strength, and also its weakness. Because of the soul-washing aspect, Gnosticism did not have "the faith once delivered to the saints," for it had washed these out of the thinking of its adherents.

While this made for departure "from the faith," it also made for a scattering of its thrust. Its way of propagation was to tell it by word of mouth. No longer having "the form of sound words" to go by, soon fantastic "old wives tales" emerged, until a heresy sank into absurdity by its many versions extant. That was its weakness.

The strong point of Gnosticism was its misuse of the New Testament way of preaching. Its damage to historic Christianity was in no longer bringing the gospel of Jesus Christ, and its failure to declare "the faith once delivered to the saints."

This weakness of Gnosticism, its Babel-like confusion of preaching, made for its early demise. It was blotted out by the Roman Catholic Church in a public sense, and submerged in a private way by the force of a total organization.

Modern Gnostics Appear

Held by authoritarianism, like horses on a bit, the cults

remained inarticulate and immobile. With the Reformation the shackles of this authoritarianism were broken.

Wonderful things came to view. A new atmosphere ozonized by the doctrine of free grace, was created. The true pattern of the two aspects of historic Christianity emerged. They crystallized on the one side the position of pastors, teachers and evangelists and the doctrine "once delivered to the saints." On the other side was "the sitting in heavenly places" of all Christians in a personal relationship with Jesus Christ and the duty and privilege to personally share so great a salvation, by preaching it to lost ones. While the Holy Spirit worked a work within each individual, He also worked for doctrinal unity and preaching in the pastors, teachers and evangelists.

As Christianity emerged again into full view in this two-fold aspect, the Gnostics of old also were once more released from their restraint. Again they levelled their attack against the fountainhead of Christianity and against "the form of sound words," and vilified the position of pastors, teachers and evangelists of historic Christianity. The coming of the light of Christianity obviously was accompanied with the emergence of error and darkness and the enemies of historic Christianity.

The Fatal Move

In Martin Luther's times, historic Christianity had once more come into free play. The Word of God was being unshackled, as translations of it occurred into modern languages. So vital for personal study, and for the new birth of a Christian, the Word of God was again being read and studied daily. It was becoming once again "the living word of God" in the hearts and lives of many.

Unless study of the word of God leads to drawing unto Jesus Christ, a conviction of sin, a repentance, a new birth in the spirit, thus becoming the living word, such study may be "a savour of death unto death" (2 Cor. 2:16). This negative result produces "ministers of the letter, not the spirit" (2 Cor. 3:6) — great arguers of Scripture passages, deft jugglers of citations. There were many such failures to allow the word of God to transform them from the flesh into the spirit.

Everywhere in Germany and in Central Europe, as if coming out of the dark caves of the past, there suddenly appeared a lot of queer looking itinerants. These were dressed in drab gray. They perambulated all over the country. They did not labor.

They obeyed no authority. They were against the political powers of the earth. They refused to fulfill their obligations towards these, claiming that these were of Satan.

How did they work? They appeared from house to house. They shied away from the public and accredited ministry of the pastors, teachers and evangelists of historic Christianity. They proceeded to cause division by creating sects and cults, drawing personal followers after themselves.

In sly, underhanded ways, they proceeded to draw Christians into new ways of thinking — their ways. They believed only in those portions of the Bible which they could juggle into position to support their peculiar aberrations. They would say "we preach by an inner light" through which the "Lord teaches us what to say." They still lacked the printed word coming from a Watchtower Society in Brooklyn.

Their appearance resulted in a great tragedy to historic Christianity. Having just come out from under authoritarianism, leaders did not wish a condition to again obtain which made suppression of light necessary. These neo-Gnostics of Reformation time made great inroads upon Christianity and often caused Roman Catholics caustically to say, "See what happens to you when you leave the authority of the church behind?" In fact, it is rumored in the corridors of history that these Gnostics were largely responsible for the Peasant Revolt which ravaged Europe in the 16th century.

Finally the Reformation suppressed preaching by itinerant laymen in order to stop Gnosticism and schisms. That was a fatal blunder. For years, the Ark of the Covenant had been held in captivity by the Philistines. It brought plague upon plague on them. Finally, the Philistines thrust it out of their midst and it came into Judea. The Spirit of the Lord guided the whole situation. Later in transport, it appeared it would fall. Those wanting to prevent it from falling were killed.

Such examples were left for us in the word of God, so we may appreciate that the Lord takes care of His own. The mere prevention of cultists and heretics from making inroads on Christianity is no valid way of coming to the rescue of Christianity. If it is of God, He will allow its way to emerge as the more excellent way, "the way of life." By the suppression of witnessing by laymen, and frowning upon this New Testament way, in order to prevent the rise of sects and cults, historic Christianity committed a fatal error. In so doing they blurred one of the major aspects of historic Christianity, namely the "sitting in heavenly places" of every single Christian, and the performance of his duty to go out and disciple the nations for Christ by sharing "so great a salvation" with them. The Lord's blessing did not rest upon this move.

Abrogation of Personal Witnessing Leads to Disaster

Gnosticism has many outcroppings today. These have fed upon the failure of the Christian church to promulgate personal witnessing of its laymen. If Martin Luther and other Reformers had found Gnosticism in its misuse of the New Testament way of preaching a great nuisance with harmful effects to Christian freedom, it has become today a thundering avalanche of mass bodies. The Reformers back there were misled to wrong conclusions.

The frowning upon and the discouraging of laymen witnessing has created a condition which led to the tragic loss of the New Testament way of preaching in all major Protestant Churches, as well as in the Catholic Church. It is proving a tragic loss to historic Christianity, and a great boon to the cults.

Woe Is Me If I Do Not Preach

Paul stated he could not exist if he did not confess what the Lord had done for him. More so, he said it would be woeful to him.

Millions of laymen now began to settle in an atmosphere of subjection of expression about their salvation, limited to fellowship in their churches, in charitable works, and in catechizing their beliefs. Things went from bad to worse in this manner as new church bodies kept tight reign upon schismatics, gnostics and others within their midst. Gradually, the need for study of the Bible became perfunctory, the knowing of the creed was enough. Since laymen no longer gave an account of the faith that was within them, they soon no longer needed a complete knowledge of Scripture, to "rightly divide the word of truth."

Within the church many laymen chafed at the bit. The uncaring lulled themselves into a false peace. The evidence of "being born again" faded with the abstinence from confessing it unto others; and soon many began to play with "strange fire." All sorts of isms, pet doctrines, began to occupy the minds of many. Playing with strange fire, in the place of allowing the Holy Spirit to work a work in them to bring forth the "image and likeness of Christ" in them, such found themselves completely burned out, with only their clothes, or outward profession remaining. They were buried as members of a Church.

Let me give you one pertinent example: "And Nadab and Abihu, the sons of Aaron, took either of them his censor, and put fire therein, and put incense thereon, and offered *strange fire* before the Lord which he commanded them not. And there went fire out from the Lord, and devoured them, and they died before the Lord. Then Moses said unto Aaron, This is that the Lord spake, saying, I will be *sanctified in them* that come nigh unto me, and before all the people I will be glorified. And Aaron held his peace. And Moses called Mishael and Elzaphan, the sons of Uzziel the uncle of Aaron, and said unto them, Come near, carry your brethren from before the sanctuary out of the camp. So they went near, and carried *them in their coats* out of the camp; as Moses had said" (Lev. 10:1-5).

This is a striking simile. Nadab and Abihu were burned to death inside their clothes, and these were left intact. How tragically true that has become of many, who having a confession of salvation to make, to the glory of the Lord, fail to do so. Subsequently they are led to play with "strange fire" and soon, nothing of their former faith remains but the coat.

Having come "into the light of Christianity" in a wonderful way, as you have read in the opening chapters of my story, I am blessed beyond measure. I have great freedom not only to confess what the Lord has done for me, but to call out to historic Christianity, Let us once again embrace the New Testament way of preaching. We have the faith, we have the doctrines, we have the pastors, teachers and evangelists. We have the testimony of what the Lord has done for us.